THE SHELL BOOK
OF COUNTRY CRAFTS

The Parlour at The Black Lion, Bishop's Castle.
Many country homes are living folk museums.

The Shell Book
of Country Crafts

Text and Drawings by
JAMES ARNOLD

*with twelve colour and sixty-four monochrome
plates, and fifty-three line drawings*

JOHN BAKER
5 Royal Opera Arcade, Pall Mall
London S.W.1

This book is for
JEANNE
who gave me
inspiration

Contents

List of Illustrations

The Colour Plates

The Monochrome Plates

The Drawings

ACKNOWLEDGEMENTS

The information contained in this book has been obtained from many sources, over many years, and is the result of an intensive study of the various crafts and aspects of craftsmanship all of which has been collected in the course of thousands of miles of easy wandering. To Raphael Salaman, of Harpenden, and to Andrew Jewell, B.Sc., and John Anstee, of the Museum of English Rural Life, Reading University, for scrutinizing the manuscript and offering comments and advice and placing so much material at my disposal, I have an especial debt. To all the craftsmen and people listed below, my appreciation for giving so much of their working time to explain the finer points of their crafts. To the owners of the photographs for their permission to use their pictures.

1. The Abbey Horn Works, Kendal, Westmorland.
2. The Alltcafan Mill, Pentre Cort, Card. Weavers.
3. John Beedie and Son, Dundee. Wood-carvers.
4. Brakes, Skelton and Tyzack Ltd, Oldbury, Birmingham.
5. James Davies, Abercych, Pemb. Wood-turner.
6. N. E. Davies, Much Wenlock. Saddler.
7. A Deans, Bridgnorth, Salop. Basket-maker.
8. J. Fielder, Cranleigh, Surrey. Hurdle-maker.
9. The Fownhope Pottery, Fromes Hill, Herefords.
10. R. Gillanders, Forfar, Angus. Bagpipe-maker.
11. The late H. E. Goodchild, Naphill, Bucks. Chairmaker.
12. Robert Hardy, Henley-on-Thames, Oxon. Bowyer.
13. T. Heatherwick, Auchterader, Perths. Woodcarver.
14. Heathfield and Sons, Ashford, Kent. Wheelwrights.
15. J. Jennings and Co., Ledbury, Herefords. Saddlers.
16. F. T. King, Barley, Herts. Blacksmith.
17. Mrs M. Lambeth, Fulbourn, Cambs. Dolly-maker.

18. The late Ethel Mairet, Ditchling, Sussex. Weaver.
19. Robin Nance, St Ives, Cornwall, Furniture-maker.
20. L. W. Philips, Flore, Northants. Wheelwright.
21. R. Rees, Carmarthen. Coracle-maker.
22. A. F. Rich and Co., East Hoathly, Sussex. Trug-makers.
23. D. Riley, Cullen, Banffshire. Wood-carver.
24. W. Savoury, Notgrove, Glos. Cotswold waller.
25. E. Sims, Pamber End, Hants. Rake-maker.
26. C. Watson, Cuddington, Bucks. Thatcher.
27. H. Watson and Co., Wattisfield, Suffolk. Potter.
28. A. F. West, Tadley, Hants. Besom-maker.
29. E. W. Wilks, Cilgerran, Pemb. Coracles.
30. R. W. Young, Hereford. Cooper.

1

Preface

This book, in its treatment of the various crafts, makes no distinction between those which are thriving, those which are no longer practised, and those which have been revived. It is concerned with people's ability to make things by hand, out of the materials which are suitable. Nor is there an implied 'social' distinction between, say, weaving and pottery on the one hand and hedge-laying and hurdle-making on the other. The weaver and the hedge-layer could, in fact, talk together in mutual comprehension just as a Welsh and a Japanese blacksmith would become so engrossed as to become oblivious of their language barrier.

Some crafts are naturally more primitive, or less complicated in procedure, while others may require a greater background knowledge and have more involved techniques. That is all; though there may be individual craftsmen and craftswoman who like to surround their activities with an aura. Those who have left their imprint on the history of craftsmanship have been too busy or preoccupied to bother about auras. Were most of our craftsmen not perversely dedicated, some might have given up, in the face of the dual obstructions of bureaucratic 'short supply' and of public bad taste. The strongest of them are slowly creating an enlightened and discerning market. The gift shop is also changing its image, to the advantage of everyone.

It is not enough to dismiss this or that craft as one no

longer practised, or knowledge of that craft would become lost in oblivion. It is thus the more important that such a craft be written about and not by one writer alone but by a couple of dozen, so that each might stress an aspect of that craft. It may be written about by one of its practising craftsmen, or it may be a regional approach, or again, the study may be set in relation to other relevant crafts. These studies may therefore be practical, scientific, cultural, or aesthetic. Taken collectively, all these approaches make a comprehensive picture of craftsmanship.

To treat exhaustively all the crafts in one work would require the dimensions of both volumes of the 'Shorter Oxford'. Within the still generous dimensions of this present book an endeavour has been made to leave the reader well informed on a considerable cross-section of crafts, which cover most of the working and leisure hours of this country. Not only the crafts, but their origins and evolutions, with some reference to the tools and materials. The book may be read from cover to cover, or be delved into for individual crafts. In the bibliography, information has been given to enable the reader to follow up an especial interest. Where practicable, the reader has been given information where to find these crafts and where to see historical examples in museums, many of which contain some very fine collections of 'bygones' together with the tools and impedimenta of past and present industries.

The term 'primitives', in reference to certain crafts, occurs a number of times in this book, and in consideration of possible misinterpretation it must be explained. It has been applied, in a collective sense, to those crafts whose origins lie far back in our social history; to those crafts in which all or nearly all the work has been done in the coppice or the field, with a very small range of tools. These tools are quite simple and have barely changed, if at all, since their inception. Very often they have been made 'on the spot' from material ready to hand. Such things cannot be pur-

Huens

chased. The whole science of such crafts is therefore un-
complicated, and it is interesting to realize that such crafts
have been the least affected by cultural or industrial changes.
For the guidance of readers who may like to see 'how it's
done', the Council for Small Industries in Rural Areas
(CoSIRA) has prepared a *Visitor's Guide to Country Workshops in Britain*. In most cases the craftsmen may be called
on without preliminary arrangement, but in many others it is
necessary to make an appointment. The Booklet covers
England, Wales, Scotland and Northern Ireland and is
obtainable free from, 35 Camp Road, Wimbledon Common,
London S.W.19. The Council also issues a *Select List of
Books and Information Sources on Trades, Crafts, and Small
Industries in Rural Areas* (price 5s 6d). Other useful
addresses are: CoSIRA office, The Plas, Machynlleth,
Montgomeryshire; Scottish Country Indus tries Develop-
ment Trust, 27 Walker St., Edinburgh 3; Scottish Crafts
Centre, Acheson House, Canongate, Edinburgh, 8.

2

Introduction

DISTANT BEGINNINGS

The first industries in the British Isles, those of weaving, pottery, and agriculture, cannot be thought of in their primitive state, as crafts in our modern terminology. Man was looking for something 'handy', to do what his hands alone could not accomplish. He picked up a stone, but found it too large, so he tried another, which proved the wrong shape or too heavy. He broke the first into two pieces and found that one of them served him better, and noticed, incidentally, that the other had a good cutting edge. Held in the hand, either piece still had its limitations, but if he secured them to a stick he could greatly increase their power and improve his own dexterity. Necessity and curiosity were to lead far beyond his present capacity and comprehension.

Craftsmanship, the skill of making things by one's own hands, has evolved and developed from these far-off simple origins, among many centres of civilization, among peoples who, however illiterate they may have been, were none the less able to exercise themselves in the original industries of weaving and pottery. Out of these distant beginnings, through all the cultures, their migrations, conquests, and influences, there has spread to every region and country a considerable range and diversity of skills, each consistent with the standards of the various ages in which they developed. From their elementary origins some of these crafts have become more complicated through the centuries, attaining higher and higher standards, as techniques and aesthetics have advanced through various stages. Other crafts have changed very little, if at all, since they began, not for want of creative ability, but simply because the peak of development was reached quite soon. Considered all together, the history of these crafts is the story of peoples' efforts to do better every time, and thus to go further along the path than previously, benefiting all the time from experience.

The first crafts were the staple ones that originated with the discovery that certain kinds of soil could be cultivated and several kinds of animal could be tamed and domesticated. Tools were needed for various tasks, and a piece of stone, in the natural shape in which it was picked up, was not satisfactory for these tasks. So their shapes had to be altered by some means, and the first manner of doing this was to break these stones or flints up, and then by flaking to produce the right kind of edge. The shank of this new tool was made by further flaking.

The wool from the backs of their sheep was found to be capable of being twisted into a continuous thread. This, being spun, could be woven into a cloth by interlacing two sets of thread, at right-angles to each other, being so retained as a permanent fabric. These first weaves, of untreated fibres, were quite coarse in texture, but were a great improvement as clothing over the former skins of animals.

Containers for water were now required, and it was found that some earths, those having a heavy clay content, became very plastic in a wet state, but dried hard when subjected to the heat of fire. Various ways of shaping this clay were resorted to, but these early efforts, though pointing to a future solution, were anything but permanent in their results; they were, in fact, extremely fragile and their shapes were crude. The finished pots, though permeable in the clay body, nevertheless served their purpose.

These three crafts, of tool-making, weaving, and pottery, were the first stepping-stones, and once men had stepped inquiringly across them, there was to be no turning back, whatever difficulties, failures, and successes might be experienced.

The earliest tool-heads were of flint and stone, with their cutting or striking edges produced by chipping and flaking. This process must have incurred many failures before a satisfactory tool was made. Initially these tool-heads were bound to their handles by thongs—a method which has been used among many peoples right through history to the present time; some tribes have brought this method to a very fine standard. A great improvement was effected when the heads were inserted into holes made in the enlarged ends of the handles, but men were still dissatisfied with this arrangement—partly because it required a clumsy end to the handle and because the head tended to work loose. This we gather because very soon the position of the hole was reversed by putting the hole in the tool-head, and inserting the handle into it. Later still, the end of the handle was made with a very slight taper, so that it could be wedged firmly into position. Still later, the tapered end was made with a very thin notch into which a wedge was tapped. The reversal of the hole made a much more efficient tool. At the same time men must have found that ash was the most suitable of woods for the handles—wood, in any case, was an improvement on any bone. Because ash was the most resistant to shock from blows, it was therefore the least liable to fracture and the most comfortable to hold, because it transmitted the least shock. These two principles, the handle or haft, of ash, inserted in the hole in the tool-head have been followed right to our own age.

A further step was made when it was found that the old tool-heads of flint, with flaked cutting edges, had become inadequate for the work being done and that a better edge must be arrived at. Now, by grinding and polishing the edges, it became possible to produce much finer edges, with smooth, even faces to the new axes and other tools. With such tools men could hew and cleave the timber and, indeed, work to a greater precision. It also became possible to fell much larger timber than before.

The principle of the saw became understood when a serrated edge was made in pieces of flint, but not only were such pieces of short length, but the minimum possible thickness of flint prevented such primitive saws from entering sufficiently into the material to be sawn.

Stone, by its virtue of responding to flaking, also had the defect of being susceptible to fracture. This liability increased as the tool was used more effectively and with greater force. So men had yet to find the most suitable material for their tools.

The earliest pottery found in some degree of preservation was that of the Nile Valley. Later work, attributed to the civilizations of the Euphrates, reached a high technical and aesthetic degree. This pottery was a terracotta, thrown on the wheel, the principle of which appears to have been discovered by a number of races, independently of each other, but which did not reach this country until many centuries later. We may note incidentally that whereas the ceramics of Babylonia, Persia, and Egypt were covered with a heavy glaze, the Greeks, in pursuit of their ideal of form, gave their work either a fine lustre or a thin 'slip' glaze, which did not interfere with the decoration, but rather enhanced it.

Wheel pottery was a tremendous step forward on the previous methods, which began by winding the clay in continuous coils in order to build up the crudely shaped pot. The potters realized the fragile nature of such pots, however, and their next attempt to remedy this defect was first to make a willow basket, woven to the required shape, and to impress the clay in to that, so making a kind of reinforced clay. There is no essential difference between this and the reinforced concrete of several millenniums later.

Later improvements came when experiments were made by the addition of certain minerals to the clay to render it much harder after it had been 'fired'. It was the invention of the potter's wheel, operated by foot action, which enabled potters to produce a true spherical or cylindrical form and to manufacture not only better and finer shapes of pot and vessel but further more to turn them more quickly and much less laboriously.

The weaving of linen was well understood, technically, by the Egyptians some 2,000 years before the advent of the Christian era, and likewise the Chinese were well practised in silk during the same age. Rather later, about 800 B.C., the Indian weavers were competent in the making of cotton weaves. In Britain wool has been the dominant fibre from the earliest origins. The climate of Britain within its comparative fluctuations, together with wide variety of breeds of sheep, has resulted in fibres quite superior to those of any other country.

The earliest weaves were made on an inclined frame, lying on the ground, for it was on the ground that every activity was then performed. Some thousands of years elapsed before the invention of the first looms. Looms, in the plural, because they appear attributable to a number of peoples in various parts of the Mediterranean and Asia. We may note with interest, that all the researches made by qualified scholars have pointed to the conclusion that the primary inventions, such as the loom, the wheel, the potter's wheel, and spinning and weaving, all occurred among a number of peoples in different parts of the civilized world, not necessarily during the same eras. None was the result of one people's activity.

In weaving, the principle of warp and weft had been established on the primitive looms, so that the later fixed, upright loom permitted considerable advance in weaving. By the time the Romans had arrived the Celtic peoples were exploiting the early possibilities.

The megalith builders were a hill-dwelling people, preferring the open hills to the lowland forests. They understood the early forms of cultivation and tended their flocks and herds, which they pastured on the high grass lands. They relied upon stone and flint as heads for their tools. Their sheep provided the wool for their woven cloth, but they were limited to the spindle and frame for spinning the fibres into thread and then weaving it. They had the advantage of a comparatively war-free life which they were able to pursue in a climate more equable than ours. The great stone circles of Wiltshire, though doubtless of some ritual significance, were the focal centres of their agricultural way of life. A people capable of the quarrying of stone, weighing in some instances as much as a hundred tons, were obviously equipped with the necessary tools, ropes, and appliances, however simple they may have been. The largest blocks, the sarsens, were obtained from the capping of a tertiary sandstone which once covered the whole area. These sarsens, or grey wethers, are present for all to see today and are especially numerous about Marlborough. To obtain and transport these was therefore relatively easy procedure. Far more difficult, and today considered impossible, were the 'blue' stones which are known to have come from as far away as the Prescelly Mountain, in Pembrokeshire. It entailed transport either by an all-land route across South Wales, over the Severn and so across country to the heart of of what is now Wessex or the alternative was a sea route from the Pembroke coast around Cornwall with its dangerous tides and so up the Channel and the Hampshire Avon. The land route was the shorter in distance, but either journey presented difficulties, the one laborious and the other perilous. But the builders wanted those 'blue stones' for their own very good reason; they were undaunted and had time on their side. To all agricultural people of those distant times, Midsummer's Day would establish their calendar and enable them to determine the dates for the various farming activities. Whatever their beliefs, this day would obviously be an occasion for festival, as it is even to this day in Scandinavia. The design motifs which one finds on their work was quite simple and undeveloped and they appear to be symbolic of their culture and beliefs.

These remarkable people came to the islands and mainlands of Britain, settling in a large colony all over Ireland, in the western parts of Wales, in the north of Scotland and Shetland, all over what are now known as the Cotswolds and the vast area of Wessex. They built their houses with a form of wattle and daub, clustered in small communities, which were sited all over the areas mentioned, wherever conditions were suitable. All these centres were linked with communicating routes, some of which must have been much more than paths, to facilitate the movement of their megaliths. The various types of house were usually thatched with straw or heather.

One may conjecture on the origins of many of the remains of that culture, but in these matters we must await further conclusions by qualified people. At only two points in all the radiating fingers of their homeland hills is the 1,000 foot contour exceeded. Along the Ridgeway, perhaps, more than anywhere else, one can sense a proximity in time with those Hill-Folk. That strange animal they call the White Horse, may be no horse, but simply a guardian symbol.

BRONZE AND IRON

The development of the arts and skills received a considerable impetus when the minerals copper, tin, iron, gold, and silver were discovered. The original sources of the ores of these various metals were found at comparatively shallow levels, and were obtained in quantities sufficient for those times until, in one area or another, the sources became exhausted. This entailed further and deeper extraction.

It had long been known that copper, used alone, was too soft a metal for making tools and weapons, but that when fused with tin produced an effective and extremely useful alloy. These ingenious people were the first to mine ores and to forge and cast in metal. Henceforth bronze became the material for their tool-heads and weapons. In a molten state from a furnace, it could be cast in moulds of a predetermined shape required for a particular implement. Even more important to these people, this tool or weapon, when carefully ground and polished, acquired a much more accurate and sharper edge than had been possible with stone or flint. In addition, bronze was infinitely more durable and less susceptible to damage. When worn out beyond resharpening, bronze axes and weapons could be recast to begin a fresh lease of life.

It now became possible for axes, implements, and weapons to be improved by design, instead of being arrived at by chance. They were no longer the clumsy affairs of limited and brief use that they were previously, but could be improved from time to time by experiment and trial. Some were altered considerably according to the uses to which they were put. As time went on men were using the wood from bigger trees, which could only be thrown by a felling-axe, whose edge was quite broad and the handle long enough to be held in both hands and swung in a part-circle. For reducing the felled timber either a short cleaving-axe or a froe was evolved; the axe being used with one hand in a chopping motion; the froe being 'started' with something heavy, like a mallet and then pushed as a lever to follow the split along the grain.

This use of bronze and later iron enabled men to forge metal saws which for the first time would go right through wood. This increased the scope of this tool, but until they produced saws with teeth set alternately 'left and right', it was difficult to clear the kerf and so there was continuous trouble with the resultant friction.

With all this major development in tools and technology, it was but a short step to be taken when iron was brought into the industrial usage of this country by a people who had arrived from central Europe. When iron was reduced in a furnace of oak-wood, it could, in its plastic condition, be used and treated much as bronze had been. Although, by comparison with the ferrous metals of our own time, it was softer in its natural state, it was none the less much harder than bronze. Indeed, it was so hard that the customary method of sharpening by sand-abrasion was of no avail. Now the iron-makers must use a stone, and this, in turn, necessitated experiment with various types of stone until one of the right texture and hardness had been found.

A kind of steel was produced during the late part of the Celtic time, by placing wrought-iron, at red heat, in contact with carbonaceous material. The carbon was absorbed by the iron in this condition. A form of tempering was obtained by immersing the hot metal in water. This, however, rendered the metal brittle and further heat treatment was necessary to counteract this tendency. The earliest saws cut both ways, but raking of the teeth in the backward direction was now made so that the relatively soft metal saw could be worked on the *pull*-stroke.

The greatest of a number of advantages with iron was that when rendered red-hot it became extremely malleable. It could be heated and forged and reheated and reforged until the desired shape of the tool or weapon had been accomplished. Gradually, the smiths were learning the minimum heat necessary for the forging. This was the advent of a new craft, to become one of the primary ones, together with that of the carpenter, for whom the smith was able to make and supply all the tools he required.

In developing this craft, the blacksmith, having become adept at elementary work, found that he needed something extremely hard on which to strike the red-hot metal; something so shaped that it would facilitate the process. The

hardest of woods available to him proved quite unsatis-
factory. But a block of iron pointed the way to a solution of
this problem. From this rudimentary block there came the
anvil of the Saxon and medieval times, which, in turn later
acquired the familiar and distinctive 'beak'.

Equipped with a forge, a hearth fired with charcoal or
other suitable fuel, an anvil and hammer and tongs, the blacksmith was able to make continuous improvements, making
all manner of things for agricultural work, for domestic life
and, of course, for war, all increasing in their range and
numbers as the smiths experimented and explored possibilities. These Celtic peoples, the Welsh, the Gaels, the
Irish, and the Cornish, had too frequently to defend themselves, first against one foe then another. For the 'arts'
of war all the weapons and the armour came from the blacksmith's forge.

In between these skirmishes they pursued a more advanced form of agriculture. They had put iron tips to the
wooden shares of their ploughs, each of which was hauled by
a pair of oxen. In some parts these Celtic farmers increased
the areas of their arable land by excavating some of the hillsides and making terraces or 'lynchet', thus forming level
strips which followed the contours. These lynchets were
sown with corn. Their widths varied according to the slope
of the hill. Their lengths varied also; while some were fairly
short, others were in some cases as much as half a mile. On
Fyfield Downs, near Marlborough, where the slopes are
moderate, they are shown by aerial photographs to be all
proportions of a rectangle, but at Mere, near Wincanton,
where the slope is quite steep, the lynchets are literally
terraces, one above the other in giant steps up the hill. Thus
in an area where the hilly nature of the country imposed
restrictions, especially where there was less level ground,
it was well worth the time and labour required to create
these terraces.

The Celts were settled farmers, having their arable and

grazing fields properly defined and bounded. Their cattle, though small to our eyes, were bred for stock and provided the food. When killed, their hides were tanned to make leather for a variety of purposes; they had found that the bark from felled oaks was not so much waste but contained tannin. From the beginnings of the far-away Neolithic times, the new farmers were evolving strains of cattle and types of corn. Some of their cattle were becoming milk producers for dairy products. Their sheep were growing longer, finer hair and the shearing of this wool was being done at a regular time of the year. Some of these sheep became the forebears of the Down breeds.

Within the homesteads the women pursued the art of weaving. They wove not only with various fibres of native wool, but also with linen, which had been introduced from Egypt. Not the least of the cultural crafts were those in gold and silver, in which metals some fine ornamental work was produced. The ores of both metals were to be found in the hills of Wales and Cornwall.

These people left considerable evidence of their arts and a language which is now the oldest in Europe. It is not without interest that nearly every one of our rivers, if not all, are known by their Celtic names. The Iron Age was an un-settled time, so the people had perforce to create earthworks of a defensive nature, generally sited upon some eminence that afforded a military advantage. Just as the Neolithic and Bronze peoples left us their vast circles and barrows, so the earliest of the Celts left their hill-forts and lynchets. Successive eras of Roman, Saxon, Medieval, and modern life have not entirely obliterated these astonishing works. Not by their hands alone did those people create Avebury and Mai-dun. The works which remain for us today are not to be seen by the full, discerning light of high noon, but in the fine evening, when the low sun casts long shadows and they appear in relief.

Potters had progressed a great deal in their craft, from the original 'coil pottery', through the succeeding phase of 'basket pottery', in which the clay had been impressed into a previously woven willow basket. The techniques were considerably advanced during the second wave of Celtic life, the La Tène. The early pots had been shaped on a platform which had to be turned from time to time as work progressed. The advent of the wheel made it possible to produce truly circular pots. These early wheels had no kind of crank, but a flywheel which was literally 'kicked'—the crank motion was a much later introduction.

The Romans developed a remarkable way of making moulded pots. Moulds were made beforehand, each in two vertical halves, incorporating any embossed design motif in reverse or 'negative'. These moulds, once fired, would permanently retain their size and shape. The clay body of the intended pot was moulded around the interior of the moulds, and when fired the body of the pot shrank within the mould. So it became possible for the first time in the history of the craft to produce identical pots in number.

We find the potters of that time firing their work in properly controlled kilns. They finished off their work by burnishing and adding a surface-lustre which they had a long time previously acquired from the Greeks. With the employment of an improved kick-wheel for 'throwing', they were able to make tremendous advances from the former hand-moulded work. Once these two appliances, the wheel and the lathe, were established in general use there appears to have been no further material advance until the advent and application of mechanical power. Even today, the modern hand-potter continues to use a kick-wheel, not from any fetish, but because the larger pots can be rotated at lower speeds than possible on the electric-wheel. It would be a digression to discuss here the relative merits of two systems in relation to a craft so individualist as that of pottery.

The introduction of clay bricks and tiles enabled the Romano-Celtic builders to employ methods hither to unknown in Britain, and to use bricks in addition to stone, where clay was available in quantity, or to build solely in brick where stone was not readily to be had. We may see these bricks, today, incorporated in the Norman tower of St Alban's Cathedral, looking like wafers among the later material. Again, tiles were used in the little chapel of St Peter, which was built by St Cedd, hard by the sea-wall near Bradwell, in Essex. In both cases, there was an intermixture of material. At St Peter's they say the remaining foundations of the Roman town may be discerned, not quite engulfed by the alluvial mud of all the tides that have since ebbed and flowed.

For the villas, which in some cases were the houses of the larger farms, some fine tessellated pavings were laid. Beneath them, lay a remarkable system of central heating, for which the potters made sets of perfectly fitting pipes to form the hypocausts.

Decoration was somewhat restricted in the range of motifs and subject and was of short duration in a country populated principally by farmers. It did not outlive the Roman occupation. The tutors, however, were accomplished far above their contemporaries in the mechanics of their crafts and they were ingenious in the solution of the many problems they encountered, and however coldly formal and lacking in self-expression they were in their aesthetics, the proportions of their work were literally golden, if lacking in the vitality of their host.

The Romans and Celts together continued the working of gold, silver, copper, tin, and iron for the variety of purposes we have noted. In weaving, the loom was developed to produce cloths not only of the old, coarse fibres of this country, but the newer and finer ones from the Mediterranean, cotton, and silk, from China. Larger houses, very much on the arrangement of the villa, continued to be built; all centrally heated against a climate which had become colder since the time of the megalithic cultures. Where

Roman roads met new centres of civic and urban life came into being, with the resultant increase and grouping of cultural activities. For the first time since people had lived in Britain the lowland country of England was being developed and penetrated with new communicating roads that followed a predetermined course for mile after mile without deviation. The Romans, for all their conquests, seemed essentially a lowland people, and the straightness of their roads suggests that they considered our own comparatively gentle hills 'just weren't there'. In some places those roads did have to make detours about some insurmountable obstacle, or to alter course a few points, but these were the exceptions that proved the rule.

In pursuit of their business with the various parts of their Empire, they used their own coinage, which was Latin in origin and system. Amid this social and economic complex, the wealthier Britons imitated their overlords by living in as Roman a manner as the climate would permit and even adopted the Roman forms of their Celtic names. Here was a way of life far superior to the past, and provided one had the resources one could 'keep up with the Joneses' for the duration of the Pax-Romana. The many craftsmen working in the base metals and the precious ones, masons and brick and tile-makers, weavers and potters, wheelwrights, saddlers and shoemakers, were all in demand. It is the considered opinion, as has been already stated, that the advances made in all these crafts were in the technological field rather than the aesthetic; in the methods of manufacture rather than in their beauty.

The later Celts and the Romans improved their saws by setting the teeth alternately left and right, so that the action produced a kerf wider than the thickness of the saws. And it is to these same people that we look for the invention of the plane in its principal types. Unlike the saw, the plane has ever since been a 'forward'-working tool; i.e. it cuts when pushed away from the user.

Since the pattern of the arts was a formal one, based on the classic orders, it was consequently a colonial one, so different in idea and origin that it left no impact on the Celtic mind. The tide came and went as a long interlude between the Iron and the Saxon ages. In short there was no amalgamation between the Mediterranean and the Atlantic thinking. We have no standing monuments, only vestigial walls and extensive foundations, by which we can judge the Romans and all that they contributed.

With the collapse of the Roman Empire and the consequent complete withdrawal from Britain, the Celtic population made no real recovery. They later fought their rearguard actions against new, invading hosts, the Saxons, who centuries later, found themselves doing the same thing, first against the Danes with an eventual compromise, and then against the Conqueror, who succeeded in maintaining his reputation.

THE NEW FARMERS

While the Saxons were establishing a revolutionary system of farming over the southern half of England the Celts retreated to their mountain fastnesses, only venturing periodically to make sorties into the borderlands. The new system of agriculture was based on the manor estates of open fields, all centred on the village. These fields were divided into long strips, each of which was allocated to a different farmer, who held a number of these strips dispersed over the manor. Good land and less so were thus equally shared. All the fields were thus uniformly distributed and worked as part of a two- or three-field rotation, which was an essential feature of this system. Grass meadows were worked in a similar manner. The open fields were very large by comparison with the fields of the present day. From their establishment they increased in area through generations of acquisition from the surrounding undeveloped land, reaching their limits at the end of the thirteenth century. Two or three of these fields lay on either side of, or about a village or hamlet. Whilst one field, or two, were being worked, the remaining field was left fallow.

This type of agriculture served adequately the needs of the manorial community and continued until its eventual demise. That was a long-drawn-out process brought about by a variety of causes. Together with its material advantages over any previous system, it engendered a communal way of thinking and was sound enough, economically, as long as each farmer was producing food for the manor and his own family. It also created a close relationship between farmers and craftsmen, who consequently had an immediate appreciation of what was required of them. It was due to increasing need during the early Plantagenet era to supply the national needs that there arose the necessity for a change.

Side by side with this system of cultivation was the breeding of sheep. This department of farming was growing very much in scale and was to increase still further. A new architecture, having nothing in common with either the structural principles or the plan which were peculiar to the Classic, came into being with the advent of the Christian religion, in Northumberland and Ireland. The churches which were built were executed in a style which was simple, robust, and often austere, but the masons were feeling their way. Notably, they designed their roofs with a steeper pitch than was characteristic of the Roman.

With the departure of the Romans there followed a period in which the use and condition of the roads declined considerably. The peace of the previous era was gone and in its place there followed a very disturbed one, of intermittent conflict between the new English and the invading Danes and Norsemen, casting avaricious eyes on a country of increasing wealth, which was assailable along many points of its coastline. To minimize the effects of any surprise attack, villages and towns founded by the Saxons were established away from the old arterial roads, accessibility being maintained by lesser routes.

The need for ancillary industries in this manorial life increased to provide much work for craftsmen in the wood industries: the carpenters who, in collaboration with the blacksmiths were inventing a new range of tools; the woodcarvers who were to produce some of the finest work in Europe, and the wheelwrights who served the farmers. From the eighth century millwrights were constructing mills driven by water-power for grinding corn. There were many more in both the staple and the cultural arts. Master-masons were directing the work on the larger churches, while many village craftsmen were working together to build the smaller churches which have survived the course of history to become 'minor' gems. The scribes and illuminators were to contribute their very ample share toward this great flowering, the first in the cultural history of Britain. In the Book of Kells we have perhaps the finest record of their work.

This pace accelerated greatly in the centuries immediately following the Conquest. It was an era of church-building. Cathedrals and abbeys were begun in one style, to be finished many generations of masons later in another style. The Normans had brought their own masons and sculptors with them, but the English proved ready pupils and very soon were to vie with their masters and eventually to surpass them.

Although this or that cathedral is habitually attributed to the senior of that church, it was, in fact, the anonymous master-mason to whom we should give the credit. Under his direction, the art of stone-dressing improved every decade. The method of working the faces of the blocks with chisels produced the perfect rectangles or necessary curves, and also left a very pleasing 'texture' to the outer surfaces, which we have come to associate with the medieval work. The Victorian restorers 'knew better', and expressed their arrogance in an immaculate geometric finish and gloss on the stone. Vandalism takes many forms and derives from several causes. The Victorians meant well, but were out of their element, succeeding better in other spheres.

The Normans also brought back the arch, which had been lost to us after the departure of the Romans. By means of the transition in which the arches were overlapped, the masons arrived at the pointed arch, which became the dominant and identifying feature of the ensuing styles. It enabled the masons to build more vertically than was possible by any previous method.

During this time the three-field system of farming had evolved. During the fifteenth century and onward enormous sheep and cattle pastures were created. These were among the first of the enclosures which followed the fourteenth century. These large pastures were quickly found uneconomic and were divided by hedging into smaller ones. It was not until the late eighteenth century that this process reached its maximum. Till then it had been a mutual agreement between the owners concerned. During that time many villages were 'lost' by demolition, so that the only clue now is an extremely uneven field or the name of a farm. When the Enclosure Acts were passed the scale was so great that thousands of erstwhile peasant farmers and the smaller yeomen were rendered landless. On the other hand it paved the way to more advanced methods of farming, by making it practicable to implement the theories of the new four-course rotation. In its wake there followed other changes affecting craftsmen; better ploughs from the blacksmiths, improved carts from the wheelwright.

The richer soils of the southern counties were suitable for division by means of permanent hedges of thorn, which the soil could support, and which could be maintained and cared for during the winter, in accordance with the farming year. The thinner soils and the more acid lands, and also those of the wet hills of the Pennines and Wales, were divided by walls made of irregular blocks of local stone and slates. On the Cotswolds, the most northern of the gentler hill ranges of the south, and the most southern of the higher, rougher hills of the north, the farmers put up walls made of rectangular blocks of the natural stone, the material for which came from locally worked quarries, which also produced the building stone for farms and villages. These Cotswold walls were all constructed according to a 'dry-stone' principle, by which we mean that no kind of cementing was was used, the builders relying upon the regular shape of the stones for the stability of the walls. This was an advantage to the farmers, in that construction, maintenance, and repairs could be relatively quickly made and that alterations to field divisions could be made where necessary. These forms of division, the hedge and the wall, greatly changed the visual pattern of the countryside from a literally open one, unbroken except by the natural woodland and forest, to the eventual chequered pattern of neat definition which has become so familiar to our generations.

MEDIEVAL HIGHWATER

Whatever language might be spoken at the Court, no matter how the Church conversed, Chaucer was writing in a dialect which was to pave the way for Caxton a century later. The mason's science and artistry was to flower in a vernacular of its own, in the forest of tracery and the soaring splendour of the Perpendicular. It was acquiring an Englishness which was not to be found on the Continent. The same Church was likewise fostering the art of the illuminated manuscript, which once before had flowered in the Kells Manuscript and was to equal this glory in the Luttrell Psalter. Such illuminations were not surpassed by the best in Europe.

The art of the stained-glass window reached its glory during the three hundred years up to the commencement of the sixteenth century. The details which were distinctive to each century were in the symbolic forms of the earlier

Norman Font at Curdworth, Warwickshire

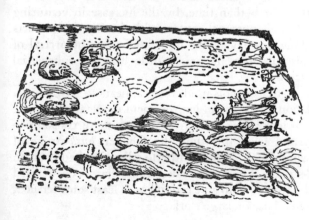

Romanesque relief at Chichester Cathedral.

windows, which gradually changed to more realistic work, especially in the positions of the figures and the arrangement of draperies. The sizes of the component pieces of glass increased with a corresponding decrease in their numbers. The dominant colours likewise underwent a change, generally becoming lighter in overall tone. We may note that the peculiar 'richness' of the thirteenth-century windows was due not so much to the intention of the craftsmen as to the current method of glass-making, which caused unequal thicknesses and uneven staining. With little loss of quality, there was some improvement during the succeeding two centuries. The glory, however, was little dimmed until the change in technique employed by later craftsmen.

Complementary to these arts were those of the goldsmiths, the carvers of wood and stone, and the embroiderers, all together working to such standards as to evoke comment in other countries. The reformation of the religious services and the curbing of former ritual put some brake on the patronage of the Church, and amid all the ensuing conflict much of the physical splendour was destroyed.

During this phase, there slowly emerged the early evidence of a new patron. This was the wealthy merchant, whose patronage gained much impetus and crystallized during the Elizabethan time, by the increase in venturing and travel. This personal contact with the Continental arts and thinking was laying the foundations for the arrival of the Renaissance in England, a little late but substantial nevertheless.

In the matter of tools used, there appears to have been a consolidation, but with an improvement in metals it became possible to make saws which were much more resistant to bending, and from this time the familiar *push*-stroke of hand-sawing may be dated. Hitherto, all action had been on the *pull*-stroke. The frame saw, which has been devised during the Iron Age, to give rigidity or at least some tension, was in general use on large work.

Wrought-iron work had evolved from a staple industry to make an important cultural contribution and the smiths were also called upon to make the mechanism and frames of the clocks, which were designed to strike the 'canonical hours'. Both in this country and on the Continent, where the mechanics of clocks were far more advanced, there was much to be done in the invention of controlling devices and striking mechanisms. It was not until the seventeenth century that the craft of clock-making came into being as the work of specialists. The early clocks made for the churches had been the work of blacksmiths, but the new pieces were the work in many cases of the best locksmiths on the Continent, especially in France, Germany, and Italy, and it was a Dutch astronomer and mathematician who succeeded in applying Galileo's pendulum to control the mechanism. In the face of this continental domination of the craft, the London makers established themselves, and went ahead to so develop clocks that it became possible to design time-keepers that could keep time for weeks and even months.

In the woollen industry new standards were being set for anyone who attempted to follow or imitate. Concurrently, there were changes taking place in the matter of wool exports. Sheep had for a long time been the wealth of the nation; they dominated the pastoral scene and many of the flocks were very large and some of the monasteries at that time were the largest owners; in fact, much of the wealth and prosperity of the Church was staked in wool. By the breeds of the sheep of East Anglia and the Cotswold and elsewhere, we were able to produce the finest and softest wool in Europe. With these breeds and others we were able to suppy not only the whole of the requirements of the weavers at home, but, in addition, to export to Flanders and other countries a quality of wool not to be obtained elsewhere.

Until the middle of the fourteenth century all of this export had been through Calais, with the wool in its raw, staple condition. From this time, however, there was an increasing trend toward the export of the finished woven cloth, which indicated a declining power of the Wool Staplers, and a growing influence of the Merchants. Thus there accrued not only a profit on the fibre, but also on the cloth. Towns on the trading routes were growing richer in consequence of this change. It is of interest that the actual spinning and weaving processes were essentially rural industries, not carried out at any kind of mill but in the cottages and villages.

While the women spun as they had always done, the men were the websters, weaving a coarse cloth for the peasantry. It was in this period that common speech acquired so many metaphors from the manufacture of cloth and craft as a term was acquiring its first industrial connotation. Ever since the thirteenth century there had been a migration of these two processes from the main centres out to the villages, and this decentralization continued and was maintained until the industrial revolution and the invention of a number of machines which enabled production to be carried out on a mass scale. When that happened the migration ceased abruptly.

During the period of rural production a complex system was operated whereby the wool thread was woven by the village craftsmen, all working on their own looms. The woven cloth was passed to the town mills for the finishing processes, after which the finished product was placed on the market. The town guilds resorted to some restrictive practices, but their obstruction was ineffective.

The East Anglian village weavers flourished exceedingly, as did those of the Cotswolds. The merchants were living in an age when learning and appreciation of the arts was not exclusive to the connoisseur or the practitioner and they exercised their wealth by enriching their villages. They built exquisitely and lived graciously. It is the coeval tradition that has been perpetrated throughout the Cotswolds, to

grace these hills with what one may without contention regard as the finest homes in stone. No less charming in their
vernacular are the houses of East Anglia. The best churches
are equally to be judged in Chipping Campden and Laven-
ham.

The furniture-makers and the glass-makers, in fact every
craftsman, made their contribution to this astonishingly
beautiful era. That excellent workmanship and a high
sensitivity abounded on every hand, we have evidence
enough.

By the time of Elizabeth I there had been increases in the
use of metals and more lead, tin, and iron were needed. Some
of the mines of that time were quite small, often being
worked by no more than several men. In the Forest of Dean,
of course, they had been mining for iron for nearly 2,000
years, and in the Weald of Sussex the drop-hammer had
forged iron since the fourteenth century for a hundred and
one uses, on through the years until the beginning of the
Industrial Revolution. The mills have decayed now and only
water-fowl disturb the silence of the hammer-ponds. The
open fireplaces of many homes are now enhanced by 'Sussex
Fire-backs'; the most common form of decoration was the
royal arms of the reign in which the backs were cast. Also,
in the Weald, as in other parts, a coarse glass had been
blown since the fourteenth century. In those days the best
glass had come from abroad, but now drinking glass and
window glass in imitation of continental wares was being
made under the aegis of French craftsmen. At the tables of
the larger houses plates and ware of pewter were coming
into fashion, to displace the former treen and other ware of
turned and carved wood. In the cottage homes and especially
in the remote hill-regions of Wales, the West and the North,
the art of the bowl-turner was to remain in demand right
into the nineteenth century.

The age of church building was past and the new merchants were building in the new material of brick. It was a

time of the growth of country estates and holdings, large and small. The wealthier families of the yeoman class were finding their medieval houses inadequate for their rising standards. Very many of these old houses were extensively rebuilt; old, large, high-ceilinged rooms were subdivided and given lower ceilings with additional rooms above. Modern fireplaces were installed. The term yeoman did indeed embrace a broad cross-section of the farming population, not all of whom were able to participate in this wave of building.

Out of this varied stock there has flowed the love of rural living and pursuit which is inherent in so many English. The merchants had this vein as richly as the yeomen and to the country life they returned after their lives of service. They provided an educated stimulus to those industries and crafts which were followed in the country; although rural industries for the most part were then still too remote to be much affected by the first influences of the Renaissance. The main impact of which fell upon London. This individuality was especially true of such a region as the Cotswolds, which, over the medieval centuries, had developed a very high standard in every craft, without any historical breaks in this continuity.

In agriculture there were a great many enclosures of the dwindling open fields, and the ox, which from the earliest use of draught animals had been almost unchallenged was now meeting a rival at last. As early as the thirteenth century the first use of the horse in draught had been made, necessitating the complete redesigning of the harness to suit the horse. The wooden yoke was quite satisfactory for the ox, but the anatomy of the horse required a harness quite different from that used with war chariots. For road transport, of goods, coal and minerals, the pack-horse was universal and continued so until the seventeenth century, when four-wheeled road carriers were designed for heavier transport during the summer months. In 1560 a Flemish coach-builder had designed and constructed a coach for the use of Queen Elizabeth I, but the woman who addressed all her sons at Tilbury was perhaps not the kind to lower her dignity from the back of a horse to this lurching, ill-sprung contraption. Roads were poor and springing was in its infancy.

Coastal waters were still the main routes over long distances for the transit of merchandise and coal. At this time, the first use of coal as a domestic fuel was made in London. It was brought by sea from Durham, and at the same time there came the use of tiles, from Flanders, for the better houses, in place of thatch. The walls of such houses continued to be built of timber and wattle. At the mouths of the bigger rivers the transfer to river craft was made, for during this age there was an extensive use made of the navigable rivers, some of which were improved by partial canalization.

In the ensuing century there was an increasing use of road carrier services. This affected considerably the craft of the wheelwright. Hitherto vehicles had changed little, but now these new carriers were of a shape and design showing a clear ancestry to the farm-wagon. These carriers were operated in a manner similar to the new stage-coaches which were also appearing. They were hauled by teams of eight horses, under the charge of a wagoner at their head. The wagons carried both goods and passengers in stages of about twenty miles per day. The craft of the wheelwright became of corresponding importance, and from this time, just after the middle of the seventeenth century, the evolution of this vehicle may be said to have begun.

Each wagoner became familiar with his stage of the overall journey and likewise acquired a familiarity with the rural scene. It was generally one composed of field and wood, demarcated with untrimmed thorn hedges or by walling or earth banks where the soil was too thin to support thorn hedges. In addition to the older farmsteads lying in close proximity to the villages there were the new, scattered farm-steads which were a characteristic of the enclosures.

The Puritan brake which was applied to ritual had the curious and unexpected effect of affording the now hard-pressed English craftsmen of the towns a respite from an excess of Renaissance craftsmen from the Continent. Those patrons who had not fled the country were dissuaded from indulging their assets in a manner unseemly to the time. The quieter, traditional 'Englishness' of the design of furnishing and wares derived some benefit. A type of pottery which in its style and technique was unmistakably English and, to our contemporary eye, refreshingly provincial, was slip-ware. It is without comparison outside this country and, in its Staffordshire home, attained a peak at this time.

THE AGE OF PRECISION

During the eighteenth century the ox and the horse were, over the country as a whole, about equally divided in use for draught-work in agriculture and horse harness had more or less reached its present arrangement of collar, pads, and straps. Wagons were essentially of the many county designs that remained to the end of the nineteenth century, the changes which were made being in the matter of weight-reduction and wheel dimensions.

The cloth-weaving industry was increasingly a divided one—a 'blowing in the wind' of the revolution to come. In the valleys of Wales, however, there continued the tradition whereby all the processes were undertaken in one mill. This supervision was conducive to a personal interest and resulted in a very high individual standard in the finished article, a tradition perpetuated to the present day. The mills were sited where good water was abundant and dependable in supply.

For transport the use of the roads had been divided be-tween the pack-horse in winter and the early designs of

carriers during the summer, but after a great deal of ineffective legislation the system of turnpikes was established
and there was some improvement in roads. It became
practicable for wheelwrights to build with narrower wheels.

The rural, agricultural economy and way of life was little
affected by the Renaissance, and it followed that those crafts
and industries which expressly served farming continued
along their own course, only changing to conform as the
pattern of farming changed.

The enclosures were now about to make their greatest
impact, enabling such men as Weston and Townshend to
introduce new crops in a four-course rotation. Jethro Tull,
of Shalbourne, in Berkshire, demonstrated the sowing of
seeds by means of a horse-drawn 'drill', a machine of his
invention. Ever since the Neolithic times seeds had been
sown 'broadcast', rhythmically by hand. Now, with Tull's
drill, there was no longer 'one for the crow'. The drill sowed
in equidistant, regular rows, which it automatically covered,
in its progression up and down the field. Together with the
drill, cultivators were used before and after sowing, all to
ensure a better and fuller crop, which in the harvest-time
was cut and threshed with new machines. While the larger
farm-lands and the more progressive farmers were coming
round to these remarkable pieces of equipment, the majority
of farmers, for want of capital and because the size of their
land made these things uneconomical, continued to broadcast, by hand or with fiddle, and to scythe and flail in the
time of the year.

Until the Fenland had been drained, during the seventeenth century, this area had remained as Hereward knew it,
a vast area of water and reed, the *Phragmites communis*,
which the hardy, resourceful inhabitants had long used for
thatching their homes. Out of this use of the common reed
there was growing a very long tradition of thatching in the
Norfolk style. It has proved the best and longest-living type,
albeit more costly than straw, whether threshed or in the

'Devon' manner, that is unthreshed. Here, too, and else-where, on Sedgemoor, there were willow and alder in suffi-cient quantity and quality to enable the basket-maker to produce every kind of woven container for agricultural, industrial and domestic use. In the district of Furness they were making a different style of basket, in which thin leaves of willow were woven on a hazel frame. The traditional potato-skip is very well representative of Furness basket-work.

Timber was the original material for houses, founded on the cruck and roof-tree, and construction developed from this through the centuries. The oaks for these houses, all through the medieval era, had been felled, split, hewn, and adzed to the required dimensions. Pegged in place they grew hard as iron as only oak can. Whilst the earliest houses had been constructed from timber felled for the purpose, many of the later ones were constructed from ships' timbers. When the road carriers brought the farmers' produce up to London, instead of 'returning empty' they were laden with old timber from the dockyards. So we find today many old houses with odd cuts and corners in the frame-work having no connection with the present use. For all these features and their great age, they are quite suitable to present-day habitation. They are likely to outlive by a substantial margin some of our contemporary accommodation units.

It may be said of the Renaissance that everything in regard to building was worked out by mathematics from the architect's inherited knowledge of the building sciences, whereas the medieval master mason must have resorted to a great deal of experiment and trial and error. We find old churches with leaning walls and cathedrals with buttressing and shoring additional to the original intention, such as the inverted arch at the crossing of Wells Cathedral.

The Renaissance not only brought new learning into the arts, but brought a dramatic change in the status of crafts-men and the relationship between craftsman and employer.

The Vault, Herefordshire.

The master mason gave place to the architect. The master mason, who had been responsible for the overall conception of the building, continued with that work as a mason, but senior to everyone else. For the most part he remained anonymous and the credit went to some high-ranking officer of the Church. The artisan ceded to the artist and the workshop became a studio. With the new thinking the tasks of the cultural crafts became subdivided and there were born, too, the roots of a new social division.

In the home pewter-ware, which in Elizabeth's time had displaced treen, was now giving pride of place to the best ceramics. The medieval faience, together with the later majolica, was being displaced by a fine earthenware, and during the eighteenth century china clay, from Cornwall, was being used as a constituent in the manufacture of fine pottery.

Some fundamental changes in the structure and layout of the larger houses was taking place. The high, raftered hall, the centre of life in the Saxon days, and right up to the Tudor period, all rendered in heavy stone and timber, was giving way to a division whereby this hall lost its status and became subordinate to a number of one-storey rooms, each for various purposes of the day and the night. Dining-rooms, drawing-rooms, and bedrooms grew larger and came to be accepted parts of the new houses. In place of stone, many were built in brick alone, while the half-timbered ones were often reconstructed internally or had new wings added. It resulted in the characteristic loose, 'accidental' arrangement which contrasted with the newer homes built in some conformity with the designs of Palladio and others.

In the new rooms and the new houses the craftsmen of the day applied their skill. For the new grand staircases and landings, the best carpenters and wood-carvers were employed. The wrought-iron workers were likewise contributing their wealth of ability. In this matter of house interiors, a new class of specialists were establishing themselves as

designers of room decoration. Some were already architects or craftsmen ascending the social staircase. Such men were usually directors of the whole operation, delegating the various tasks for furniture, soft-furnishing, wood-carving for the large mirrors which had become fashionable, and the new plaster-work ceilings. In collaboration with these designers, they were responsible for the arrangement and disposition.

This period, the eighteenth century, was notable for the increase of small-scale manufacturers and craftsmen located in country districts. While wealthy people often went to London or other big cities for their special requirements in furniture, wares, and clothing, the 'country' people went to the nearest small town or village. Cottage furniture, Windsor chairs, Suffolk rush chairs, Welsh dressers, York-shire settles, and many of the long-case clocks—those not made in London or Liverpool—all came from these quiet little sources. These pieces were all made in the cottage or the village, with the nearest big town as the distributor, for the towns lived as much by commerce as by manufacture.

If the eighteenth century was the 'age of reason', it was also the age of precision and of considerable progress in technology, fine workmanship, and overall skill. Among these crafts was that of wrought-iron work, which, after a long phase of fine work in the medieval tradition, was receiving a new life-blood from the work of some French smiths, whose pattern-books were circulating very widely at this time. The mechanisms of various types of clock and watch were being invented and in the field of marine chronometers. England easily led in the production of accurate and simple mechanisms. English names were becoming known, whereas formerly continental craftsmen had held a molopoly. The striker of the canonical hours had become part of history.

This precision in manufacture demanded a great variety of tools. Tools for the silversmith and glass-maker, and a lot of small tools for the watch-maker. Tools for the cabinet-maker, who was making much use of exotic woods, such as mahogany, as well as the native kinds. And in consequence there came into use in every craft a wide range of tools for special and limited use, but without which the new work could not be produced.

The subdivision of labour had become an integral part of the craft of clock- and watch-makers. Whereas in the seventeenth century it had been 'one man one watch' the increasing complexity of mechanisms and decreasing sizes were requiring a greater precision. It produced men who were specialists at each stage of manufacture. Often it happened that the 'watch-maker' did no more than inscribe his name on the case. There undoubtedly was craftsmanship, but the identity of the individual with the completed product was becoming lost in an intricate network. The merit of the system was that it enabled the industry to meet a greatly increasing demand and to lay the foundations for modern precision watch-making.

Furniture was going through a transition from the former heavily built kinds which were acceptable until Jacobean times to the new pieces which were lighter and constructed with great ingenuity and skill. Foreign woods were often employed and the surface decoration underwent a radical change. In this craft, as with clock-making, there was a transfer from one craftsman to another. The carpenter and the wood-carver, skilfully incorporating the vine-motif and the linen-fold, gave place to the cabinet-maker by whose name this new furniture became known to posterity. In this craft, as in watch- and clock-making, a division of work responsibility was taking place, and the man who designed a chair or a cabinet was not the maker, at least among the leading names. The designer employed a number of artisans, each a craftsman in his own right. Taken as a group, they were moving towards specialization, each man performing his own task in the making of a piece of furniture. It was precisely in these crafts that the Renaissance produced its finest flowering and by which we now recognize this period for its worth.

The consistent features of medieval work had been spontaneity, exuberance and freshness and not a little daring in the construction—a portent of things to come six centuries later. The abiding splendour of church construction may be symbolized for sheer daring by the Octagon at Ely. Whence came those eight bulks of oak, each 63 ft. in length? The innumerable capital ornamentals, and one may compare the angel playing a lutina in the choir of Gloucester with a Corinthian capital. The sculptors imparted life into the one and cold formality into the other.

Quite incidental to the subject of crafts, the growth of hunting as a sport, and its especial place in that part we know collectively as the Shires, was calling upon something to be done about 'those hedges' which, in their untrimmed, unruly state were a serious impediment. In Leicestershire there grew the art of pleaching, or 'laying-back' the hedge so that it did not outgrow its strength and go all awry. Hunting, being a pursuit followed in the winter months benefited greatly from this new practice, which skilled farmhands carried out during January and February. The practice of pleaching eventually spread all over the Shires, and in fact, to nearly every country where hawthorns hedges were to be found.

FROM SUSSEX TO THE NORTH VIA COALBROOKDALE

The iron industry and its relevant crafts which had begun some centuries before the Romans, in such places as the Forest of Dean, became well developed in the Weald and was now migrating northwards by way of Coalbrookdale and the Severn into Shropshire. One man among the ironmasters realized his ambition of spanning the Severn with a bridge of cast iron. He accomplished this in 1777, to set the pace for further advances. The best bridges and viaducts served to enhance the composition of the landscape. Iron-bridge achieved this with an astonishing grace. Close by they made clay pipes for smokers and prided themselves particularly on the churchwardens which came into fashion then and indeed continued to be made up to and including the first quarter of the present century. But these interesting pipes properly belonged to a more leisurely age. At Coalport they produced fine pieces of china decorated with a motif quite unusual for its floral arrangements. Coalbrookdale, like the Forest of Dean, is a rare place for studying the span of industries both for their remarkable variety within a comparatively small area and for the time through which men have been actively making things.

They had been smelting and casting iron in the Weald of Sussex ever since the fourteenth century and the fuel for these processes may have seemed inexhaustible to the early iron-masters. But by the seventeenth century coal, from various recently discovered seams, was being mined and used increasingly. The Wealdan wood sources were, however, seriously diminishing by this time and the long-established industry began to decline. In its great days it had cast firebacks and andirons and in the reign of Henry VIII it had also cast cannons; formerly these weapons had always been of bronze. It was in Coalbrookdale that the change in character of the industry came about thus to found the coming revolution in industry.

During the first half of the eighteenth century many rivers had their courses improved by deepening and by installing locks or by cutting off certain loops. By the second half of that century the new industries of the Midlands and the North were in need of improved communication with the sea and the big industrial centres. The new canals, surveyed by Brindley, were being constructed and, with those surveyed by Telford, a vast network of inland waterways was in use during the turn of the century until their eventual demise, brought about by the railways. These canals were used to transport every kind of fuel, mineral, and manufacture. The increased use of slates and tiles for homes resulted and coal as a domestic fuel increased tremendously. Brindley in surveying the routes had largely followed the contours, locking and tunnelling only where necessary. Telford, on the other hand, drove his canals through hills and across valleys. One can but marvel at the sheer daring of such works, as the aqueduct at Pontcysyllte; the tunnel at Stand-edge, near Huddersfield, over three miles in length; and the 'staircase' of locks at Devizes.

From the Trent to the Tyne, on the east and west sides of the Pennines, new towns were growing—the manufacturing towns—and for the first time in our history there came about a cleavage between 'town' and 'country'. Many country craftsmen, whose business had always been derived from their regions, were losing this source to the new industrial centres. Tailors, boot-makers, and the makers of clocks, wares, and furniture were to suffer dwindling occupations. This change in the location of manufacture was accelerated by the improvement in road-making begun by Macadam and sealed by the advent of the railways. Weavers were affected by the invention of different kinds of machine which were to revolutionize the manufacture of textiles by large-scale processes.

The majority of villages, by the middle of the nineteenth century, were left with only a few craftsmen—such as the carpenter, to whom everyone still came for the hundred and one odd jobs, the blacksmith who was still required to shoe horses, and the wheelwright who, surprisingly, was soon to produce the ultimate in his craft.

The canals and the railways, without which this industrial change could not possibly have been made, involved in the lock equipment, the canal-boats, and the locomotives and carriages, a new art, in which craftsmanship excelled splendidly. In an environment where the exhibitionist

Victorian arrogance took the place of standards of beauty inherent in the medieval and Renaissance eras, the art of the canal and the railway was epitomized in the theme of 'Roses and Castles' and the resplendent liveries of such railways as the Great Western and the London and North Western.

People have conjectured on the origins of the narrow-boat theme, but from whatever source it came we now compare the 'riot' of colours, all placed together in such a happy juxtaposition, at its best in the Barlow boats from Tamworth, with the self-conscious 'aesthetic' of British Waterways. A scheme which could not possibly have been devised by anyone at Stoke Bruern.

Of the railway liveries, it was much to the credit of the Great Western that its green and gold engines and the 'chocolate and cream' coaches were only obliterated by a dictat from British Rail. We remember, too, the more sober and no less stately dignity of the North Western—blackberry black for the engines and the deepest of sepia browns and 'off white' for the carriages. The Victorians may have been overbearing, but their engineers inherited from some source, possibly the Renaissance, a fine sense of dignity. Even in the turmoil of their age they had time—or made it— where we today have no time to stand and stare, for fear of what the other person may say. In the face of destruction of craftsmanship in nearly every field, the shipwrights, who had built tall ships, were to build them still taller and faster. In the fields, the farm-wagon, basically still utilitarian in design, flowered in its final splendour before succumbing to the internal combustion engine.

This was an age, from the late eighteenth century onward, of a rapid increase in machine production and of a transfer of manufacture from country and small town. The use of machinery increased the quantity but not the quality of the product. It was an era during which there were two movements in conflict, the principles of good designs and workmanship sustained by most of the potters, of whom the inevitable name of Wedgwood comes out. Incidentally Wedgwood was also a sponsor of canals, whereby his wares could be transported without damage. In architecture he was followed by the Regency builders who carried the Renaissance to its most English climax, as the Perpendicular did for the Medieval. Wedgwood was typical of the best of the machine potters. Whilst some were equalling the finest work of the Continent, Wedgwood was equating superlative design and technique with cheap production. He was a practical visionary. So pewter, which in Elizabeth I's time had displaced treen, was in turn giving pride of place to the best ceramics. Such men, not only in pottery but in glass and silver, exercised their most advanced techniques and employed the best craftsmen. It is to be noted that among the pottery manufacturers of this time there was not one 'movement' or trend, but a diversity, some classic, others romantic, and a considerable number excelling in the 'provincial' which graced many a Welsh dresser and, together with many other art forms of this twilight period, have become very much sought after. Some of our present-day small potters went through a mistaken phase of production, a present-day version of the 'provincial', but happily have left this phase to devote themselves to creating a sincere style expressive of contemporary thinking.

The second movement was derived from the new master —the machine, before which all the principles of good design went to the wall. The machine proved itself to be in the wrong hands, and in those hands it produced quantity at the expense of design, and wealth for a few at the price of poverty for the many. The inherent sense of beauty acquired by the Grand Tour gave place to the new dicta. The country which produced Regency Bath and Brighton was responsible for the limitless sea of back to backs, sprawling under a pall of smoke and grime. The cultural values, the worth of human beings, the standards and techniques of many crafts went down before the scythe of the Revolution. In this environment, the design of domestic wares took a downward plunge into a sea of bad taste, all to be displayed at the Great Exhibition. It was a curious irony that it was housed in a building which was designed and erected within the space of nine months. Paston, being a sincere and honest man, simply sat down and put pencil to paper, and the result was an enormous greenhouse, which satisfied everyone except Colonel Sibthorpe.

Rural crafts, themselves, did not immediately suffer, but the drift of labour from the country to the towns, consequent upon the rise of the colonial wheat industry after 1870 and the revolution in methods of farming which took place during the ensuing years, whereby agriculture became increasingly mechanized, were factors, which had their impact upon the crafts of the wheelwright, of farriery and of the making of saddlery and harness-work and other ancillary activities.

THE PRACTICAL VISIONARY

As a young man William Morris is said to have visited the Great Exhibition—and to have rebelled. Later he resolved to do something about it. He made it his life's work to remedy this situation by every means in his power. He was fortunate enough in being already a wealthy man, so that there were never any circumstances such as too often forced others less fortunate to debase their art. In all the confusion and diversionary movements, Morris saw as clearly as was possible in those cloud-obscuring years. It was his great merit to master a dozen highly skilled crafts and to produce work of an exemplary order in printing and typography, bookbinding, tapestry, wallpaper, furniture and stained glass. By his writing we realize that he was instrumental in stemming the tide and infusing designers and craftsmen with the original conception of the importance of craftsmanship, but it was a long uphill task in the face of the forces of mass-production.

When printing and typography were well set on the descent to abysmal disorder, Morris gave us the Kelmscott Chaucer to lay by the side of the Luttnell Psalter and the Book of Kells. By example, he sought to revive pride in the job, fitness for purpose, excellent workmanship, and above all honesty in design. Morris and a few men were maintaining a fine standard in design and technique. Not every head of industry had lost his senses. Sanderson still uses Morris' blocks for hand-printed wallpapers.

There is ample evidence that the teachings of Morris were to be a long time in taking effect, so long that even today there is a false image of the craftsman. The lesson was not quite lost, with craftsmen in furniture, such as Gimson and Barnsley, who turned over a clean sheet to adopt, not the medieval or even the Renaissance, but to think in terms of contemporary requirement. But these men, and a few more in other crafts were only islands in a sea.

With all the changes in the methods of agriculture and the population drift there were corresponding changes in the demands for craftsmen. There was no future for the work of the wheelwright and examples of their wagons can rarely be seen now, except in museums. Whilst some black-smiths have retreated before the storm, being content to modify their profession, to master the equipment of oxyacet-ylene welding and become 'automobile engineers', others, having especial accomplishments and not a little dedication, have turned their attention to the very great potentialities of wrought-iron work. Only modern economy stands in the way of a revival of the aesthetics of the past masters. Fire-dogs, and andirons, screens, lamps, and gates can, in the best forges, become products embodying the highest ideals in design and workmanship.

With continued improvements in the design of tractors, the horse was ceding its place on the farm. It is said that the tractor is more efficient, but one may be excused a little sentiment in feeling that something rather fine has gone out of farming. A tractor cannot induce pride in the job, and the very harness repaid all the work entailed in cleaning and polishing. However, farriery, saddlery, and harnesswork have in recent years experienced a considerable boost, consequent upon pony-trekking and the custom for very young ladies to ride at week-ends.

Through all the vicissitudes in history, a number of crafts have remained unaffected and virtually unchanged. In spite of the competition with plastics, baskets of willow continued to be woven in essentially the same manner that they always have been. In most regions where hedges have been laid or pleached, this continues to the great advantage of those farmers who are clearer-sighted than some. In the matter of thatching, many craftsmen have had difficulty in obtaining young apprentices. The dwindling number of thatchers are finding sufficient work to keep them fully occupied and many of them are accustomed to travelling long distances, in execution of their orders. This is especially the case with Norfolk men who specialize in the reed-thatching.

The business of the coopers, mostly employed by the brewers, is contesting its long-established ground with the makers of the new metal casks. Some people consider that the craft of walling in dry-stone is going out, but notwithstanding this it appears to be still practised among a number of the Cotswold men.

Hand pottery, having suffered a near extinction in the repercussions of the machine, though to a lesser extent than hand-weaving, has revived enormously, is able to supply a now-discerning market. The potters of today have availed themselves of new appliances. It is customary for them to use both the traditional kick-wheel and the electric. Some kilns are fired by solid fuel, some by gas, and others by electricity; much depends on the situation of the pottery.

At the turn of the present century there were no more than half a dozen hand weavers at work in England; but here again there has occurred a healthy revival. What Leach and others have been to English pottery, Ethel Mairet was to hand-loom weaving. This remarkable lady, a disciple of William Morris, acquired a mastery of all the processes of the craft and set a standard by which her work came to be highly esteemed in several continents. In these two crafts we may note a change once more in their relationship with the big machine potters, Hitherto, there had been competition. This has been replaced by a complementary relationship in which the machine pottery is producing in quantity, while the hand pottery supplies the quality market.

Both the hand potter and the hand weaver are also able to carry out many experiments in design and technique which would be impracticable in the highly organized quantity-production machine processes

There is most fortunately a growing new conception and appraisal of the place and relationship between hand and machine manufacture, in which new standards appropriate to new methods of production are being established. This enlightenment is vital to a healthy future for handcrafts, whether they are old established or new and whether they are carried on by traditional methods or modern.

3

Craftsmanship

DEFINITIONS

What is a craftsman? He or she who, broadly speaking, makes things individually by hand, using only such tools and appliances which are manipulated. With a few exceptions, these tools are quite simple in themselves and in many cases are little more than perfections of the original tool of centuries ago. A craftsman is usually the designer of the thing he is making, but in some practices there may be a mutual division of operations, though not to the extent that one person is isolated from the other or is not concerned with what the other is doing. In fact, an important feature *is* the close co-operation.

A craftsman may be an individual working alone, such as a hedge-layer, or he may be one of a team or a unit, such as a wheelwright. Where design and execution do happen to be divided between two or more persons, there must be the closest co-operation. The situation whereby the designer and the executant are strangers and do not meet is unknown.

A craftsman makes things by hand, one at a time, and can therefore impart an individuality in each product according to his or her own will. In fact, with certain exceptions, one may fairly say that 'no two are alike'. The industrial operator, having set up the machines to produce what is required of them, sets the machine or machines in motion for quantity production, during which process he, or she, maintains an expert supervision, which is not without its own kind of skill. Once the machines have been set in motion, no change in design or quality can be made. Each article produced is one of thousands, all of which are identical. A craftsman, having made one thing, can, at will, change the design. This is especially true of the potter, whose day's output may consist of a number of 'pots', all different. Provided they have the same 'body' and are to be fired by the same process, they may be placed in one kiln.

Some craftsmen produce work in which design or pattern is quite elementary or even absent and the essence of their skill is different. A hedge-layer, working along a hedge in winter, is hardly concerned with aesthetics, though he is none the less entitled to 'stand back' and admire his own handiwork. As he progresses he makes decisions and solves problems as they arise. At a distance the laid-hedge appears uniform, but at close hand variations all along are noticeable.

IDEA AND EXECUTION

The Renaissance produced the first real systematic division of operations in this country, but in this division the successful outcome has depended upon a sympathy and comprehension between two or more persons. It is probable that the essentially formal character of classic design was an advantage to this end. A medieval design or theme or indeed a whole work could not have been carried out unless each craftsman had produced his own idea in co-operation with the rest.

Generally, the medieval masters and artisans knew what could be done with the materials of their crafts. Their ornamentation was primarily a vehicle for telling a story and the treatment was often light-hearted and humorous. Yet they were adventurous in the mechanics of their work or they could not have accomplished such breathless daring.

Toward the end of the Middle Ages it is likely that what we now accept as the glorious climax might have burnt itself out in excesses of design, 'turning in on themselves'.

Once the Renaissance had established itself and had become Anglicized, craftsmen settled down to a prodigious output. In everything to which they put their hands there were features which distinguish this work from the medieval. No longer is it the expression of an idea or the telling of a story. The new work, whether in base metals or precious, in wood, glass, ceramics or textiles, showed a preoccupation with Golden Rules, proportion, precision and mathematics. The tremendous increase in the use of window and mirror-glass caused an admission of light hitherto unknown; a light that necessitated attention to details that had dwelt in comparative obscurity.

William Morris set up not only in opposition to the worst consequences of the Industrial Revolution—bad design and debased conception, but to the 'Romantic Movement', which was superficial and not fundamental in its approach, that is, it was a sentimental reversion to the current image of medieval England. It did mothing to examine the under-tone. In one sense, Morris was almost too soon, in so far as he was faced with a solid opposition of ignorance. His was a voice in the wilderness. At the same time, had he not 'arrived', to apply some kind of brake, the decline would have continued.

He applied himself so thoroughly and insisted on such a high standard in design and workmanship in all his en-deavours that he now has his place among the great names in British design. At the time, and for years and even de-cades after, this country was still too blind mentally to see either the wood for the trees or the trees for the wood, so that instead of learning his philosophy, manufacturers could do no better than imitate the surface effects of his design motifs. And the 'Arts and Crafts' movement was likewise sterile. The result was a body with an anatomy but without life—the opposite of Morris's teachings. The lesson of Morris was to be learnt later. Even Morris was not infallible, as one may judge on entering his Room at the Victoria and Albert Museum.

A craftsman, by the nature of the work, produces in small quantity work of high quality, both in choice of materials and in the design and finish. All operations, from commencement until completion, are under direct and personal supervision. Some craftsmen work, not in competition with the machine or as an alternative to it, but simply because no alternative machine method has been devised. An industrial craftsman is actually not a craftsman in the strict sense, but a skilled operator, fully qualified to give expert supervision to machine processes, or production in quantity. Designers in industry must possess a great knowledge of materials and machines, and processes past and present and an appreciation of scope and limitation.

SATISFACTION

The question is sometimes asked: Can a craftsman be an artist? Properly, the question should be: Can a craftsman *not* be an artist? In the narrow sense, an artist is one who paints or draws pictures, but, in the broad sense, he or she is one who is imbued with an acute sense of what constitutes beauty and can impart beauty into the work. We must blame the Renaissance for the confusion, for the term ARTIST is indefinite and inconclusive. The medieval artisan was elevated from the workshop to the studio. It is a useful digression to point out that the primary cause of bad cooking is a lack of artistry, so unless a person *is* an artist in the broad sense, he or she cannot succeed as a craftsman, since all the physically skilful manipulation of a tool is rendered lifeless in the hands of an insensitive person.

A craftsman will, from time to time, stand back from the work, to judge, to criticize, or merely to admire—a permis-

1 BRONZE AGE SHIELD, FOUND AT BATTERSEA

British Museum

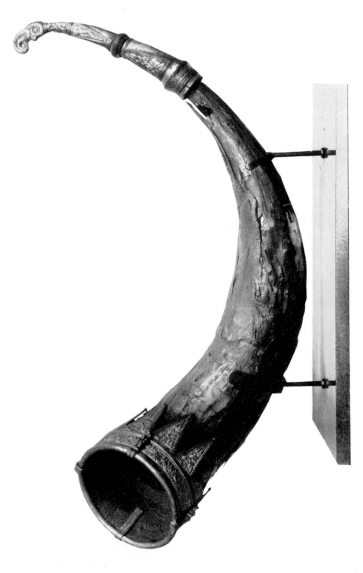

2 SAXON DRINKING HORN

3 SAXON BROOCH   *British Museum*

4 FROM THE LINDISFARNE GOSPEL   *British Museum*

sible conceit since it is also a characteristic of craftsmanship that satisfaction is to be derived from a good job well done. It is a satisfaction which is additional to the monetary return and sometimes that satisfaction is the greater of the two. There are some people who believe it to be sufficient in itself.

A further distinction is to be found in the presumption, by the maker, that a thing once made will give service, satisfaction, and pleasure for a very long time. That is why it was common enough for a farm-wagon to last a hundred years—or more; why a pair of shoes, properly craft-made, can be expected to last ten years and more; why comparatively wealthy people take an infuriating delight in wearing a really old suit, one that the less affluent would cast aside for something in the 'latest fashion' and correspondingly badly made.

A craftsman is neither a curio for idle-gazers nor an anachronism in the social order—or disorder. He need not trouble himself with trying to cater for people who do not know the difference between the excellent and the indifferent, or between the genuine and the spurious. Individual crafts may be moribund or thriving, surviving or reviving, but craftsmanship will continue as long as it is natural for intelligent people to want 'to do something with their hands and to derive pleasure from it'. In fact, such people are unhappy or ill at ease when they are 'empty-handed'. Hand creation, furthermore, is not only theraputic but antidotal to the increasing mechanization of our daily lives.

One may safely say that this satisfaction is the reason why so many people attain a splendid seniority. A man of 70 is a young man with ten or twenty years of activity before him, whatever the high priests of technology may say. Take away his occupation and you will take away his life-blood. A man of 85 may, or may not, be a trifle slower than one of 20, but he has the incomparable asset of a lifetime of experience. Such people do not know how to do a job indifferently, let alone badly, and they will refuse to work with materials of inferior quality. We should not expect it of them.

A craftsman may have to effect a compromise between his ideals and the situation at the time, in terms of the cost of materials and their availability, but open and shut the drawers and cupboards which he has made and we find that in spite of everything his work is not 'all front and no back'. The drawers slide like oil, in a dead fit, and they never catch'. The doors create their own 'air-buffer' as they close to. Despite daily usage over a considerable period, it will be found that no deterioration has taken place.

Wattle hurdles will not stand up to ordinary usage if the rods are cut off at each end instead of being turned round in a continuous weave. Potters who have received a thorough grounding in design and manufacture will eschew trivialities which might 'get by' with an undiscerning purchaser, but which will be immediately rejected by the informed one. The best thatchers will make a roof which will last the full estimated span according to the material. They could tell us why a badly thatched roof will show signs of disintegration within a year or two of completion.

HAND AND MACHINE

There is yet another characteristic which distinguishes the best and most able craftsmen. Between the mind, in which the idea lies, and the end product there is an unbroken line of communication, by way of the hands, the tools, and materials. There is a total harmony in the tools which, with their handles, through long and accustomed use fall easily to the hands and without any kind of hindrance carry out what their users are thinking. This is especially true of tools which have been locally made to the user's own requirements, and it is likely that the same tool, in the hands of another and no less competent person, would not perform the task required of it. In this way a brand-new tool will take a little while before it has become acclimatized in the hands of its user.

Tools, as we understand them, are intended for manipulation, and are a necessary equipment in the processes involved in handcrafts. Machines, as we understand them, are power-driven appliances which so far displace the hands that they require only qualified supervision. Machines have a number of merits. They can perform repetitive work, producing in quantity, and can also make things which a person alone, using hand tools, could not produce. They can perform tasks which do not entail manual work at all. Conversely, a craftsman can make things not required in large quantity, but which must be of the highest quality, and which can only be attained by individual attention. He, or she, can make things impossible, or impracticable, by machine, and can give an intrinsic value by the infusion of 'personality' into the work. To identify the machine-made product, and certainly the mass-produced one, it is usually necessary to look for some form of 'branding'; but the majority of hand-made products usually have an 'appearance' by which we identify them with their makers. But there are obviously many exceptions to this.

No machine can reproduce the astonishing flexibility, manipulation, sensitivity, and response of the human arm, wrist, and hand. This one unit can pick up a trunk or a feather, it can dig a trench or conduct an orchestra, it can write a letter and manipulate tools, it can navigate a ship and perform a surgical operation, caress another human being or feel its way in the dark. All these actions are controlled and determined by the brain, which in turn responds to messages from the five senses. When someone has devised an electronic brain and a mechanism which will be universally able to do all these things, then all that will be left for man will be to 'programme' the contraption. Until that happy day arrives people will go on responding to an inner compulsion to make something.

QUALIFICATIONS

In consideration of the demand of our time, and of modern techniques and materials, a craftsman must possess the following qualifications:

1. An appreciation of what can and cannot be done with the materials of a craft.
2. An appreciation and knowledge of the qualities and the possibilities of the materials.
3. A knowledge of the processes involved.
4. A knowledge of the processes involved in the work of any related crafts.
5. A knowledge of what can and cannot be done with the tools of the craft.
6. An ability to visualize the finished article, during the draft stage and at all subsequent stages.
7. Some crafts, such as weaving and pottery, demand a high technology and a historical and cultural background.

One or more of the foregoing is called upon in every craft.

LOCATION

The craftsmen of this country may now be considered according to the place at which the work is done.

1. Those who work at their own shop, in a village or town. This group includes all the cultural craftsmen; such as weavers, potters, and wood-carvers. It also includes coopers, chairmakers, basket-makers, turners, besom- and rake-makers (though the last two may be found in the vicinity of woodlands), coracle-makers, sawyers, and saddlers.
2. Those who work at the source of their material supply. This group includes quarrymen, chair-bodgers, hurdle-makers, sawyers, and charcoal-burners, and most of the woodland crafts. All of this group must 'move on'

as each source is exhausted. In the cases of the woodland industries this amounts to a rotation from one plantation to the next, and so eventually back to the first.

3. Those who travel from one place to another in order to execute their work 'on the site'. This includes millwrights, masons, thatchers, sawyers, drystonewallers and pargetters.

The first group works in workshops, some of which may have a retail department or at least some form of display. Bowl-turners, exceptionally, also 'took their wares' to market. Both the boat-builder and the coracle-maker will have their 'shop' or yard adjacent to or in the vicinity of a river. The coracle-maker is usually a fisherman who makes his own craft. This group includes all those who sell their wares in the open market.

The second group includes those who produce things required by another industry, such as quarrymen for masons and chair-bodgers for chair-making.

The third group are the 'travellers' who contribute their part to some kind of structure.

It will be noted that sawyers fall within all three groups. They may work at a timber-yard, where there is a permanent and substantially constructed saw-pit. In this, they are usually employees. Again, either as employees or as 'temporaries' they may work in team with other woodmen in forestry. Finally, they may, in between, the above activities, move about from one merchant or carpenter or wheelwright to another. They, too may be 'travellers'. It is this last kind to which George Sturt makes reference in *The Wheelwrights' Shop*.

ADAPTATION AND TRANSITION

In the course of the centuries every craft has been passing through various kinds of transition and adaptation. It may simply be one of style in design, or it may run more deeply, brought about by changes in industry as a whole, or in the requirements of agriculture or the 'consumer market'.

The cultural crafts supply principally the requirements of leisure, even though the article made may have a purpose of utility. Such crafts may either set a trend or follow one and their work is usually recognizable as belonging to a period, e.g. Medieval, Renaissance, Victorian, Contemporary as the changes from one to the next occur, so craftsmen must recognize them.

The staple crafts, most of which are ancillary to agriculture or forestry, become subject to change only in conformity with the requirements of those industries. If at any point in the history of those industries there occurs a major change, the crafts will echo that change, either by disappearing or by radically changing their nature. Such crafts as those of the draught-harness maker, the wheelwright, the millwright, and the sawyer may be said to have succumbed, while others, by a drastic adjustment, have maintained their place. Of these, the crafts of bridlery and saddlery and wrought-ironwork may be mentioned.

Some crafts have changed very little, if at all, since their inception, either because the product has continued to be in demand or because no alternative method of manufacture has been devised or can be devised. Among such crafts we may note basketry, hedge-laying, and dry-stone walling. Older than nearly every other craft is that of coracle-making, not because boat-building techniques have not improved, which, of course, they have, but because the coracle is perfectly satisfactory for the rivers on which it is still used.

Certain craftsmen, such as thatchers, have been passing through a different kind of transition. This was caused, initially, by a transient prejudice against thatched roofs adversely affecting the number of thatchers. In the revival, men have had to travel a great deal more than formerly. Where a kind or a style of thatching was peculiar to a region, it is now common to find men working very far from their native heath. This position was at one time aggravated by the difficulty in persuading young men to take up the craft.

'PEASANT' ART

Essentially, rural crafts or industries are those serving rural, agricultural economy. By their nature, practice in them is acquired by apprenticeship or by heredity, father, son, and grandson being in the business. These crafts have tended to be traditional in their employment of design-motifs and in techniques of construction, simply because the need for changes have occurred at comparatively long intervals in history.

We now have no 'peasant' culture, but in many countries, irrespective of their overall standards of living, from Scandinavia to Portugal and from Holland to the Balkans, there are such cultures, alive and flourishing. In Scandinavia, for example, the design of the equipment of a living-room reflects very strongly a peasant origin. And it shows itself in any of those countries in pottery, weaving, lace-making, furniture, and turnery. In this country the class of people upon whom it was founded disappeared for ever in the mêlée of the eighteenth and nineteenth centuries.

The arts and skills of the peasantry have always been particularly lively and exhilarating to the senses, and they still provide a colourful foreground to the scenes and the scenery of those countries which are graced with this form of art. Returning to this country, we may turn to much of our provincial pottery, particularly the slip-ware which was unequalled outside this country, and then to the astonishing vitality of decoration upon the canal narrow-boats, especially the 'number ones' in private ownership.

This theme may be followed further. Folk music has a rough, primitive quality, often enhanced by being rendered on instruments which never evolved much beyond their original form. This music is of the village green and the cross-roads on the heath. It has always been performed without scored music, by people playing by heredity or from 'ear to ear'. Classical music, in all its subdivisions, is always sophisticated, whether played in the concert hall, the theatre, or the chamber, and depends upon the interpretation of scored music by disciplined players. It is subject to a considerable degree of convention. Farm-wagons, folk music, and Welsh dressers have a feature in common, that their creators have worked by inheritance and without 'pattern-books'.

If all these craftsmen have a philosophy, it comes not from Parnassus, but from the fields and the woods. Their demeanours and their hands will reflect their faith. Their fingers, though some be rough and gnarled will conceal a fine sensitivity. Their apparently slow movements will bely an apptitude for thorough workmanship, in which no movement is a waste of time and energy.

Some writers consider that it is a characteristic of British craftsmanship that the workmanship, the execution, the quality of manufacture, is often better than the design, and that components could be improved with more thought beforehand. While this criticism is very well true of the products of heavy and light factory industry, concerned as it is with mass-production, it can hardly be made of handcrafts. Tradition can be misinterpreted. While some products might benefit from a detail change or an application of new techniques, many things have become 'traditionally' made a particular way, especially in the more 'primitive' crafts, simply because finality in design and manufacture have been long arrived at. There has been a disinclination to make changes in the essentially rural industries, because practices in usage have been altered but gradually during their respective histories.

The spirit of craftsmanship will continue as long as there is a strong enough creative impulse and an intelligent satis-

faction with the results of creation. Creative people who derive a full life from their activities are notably given to a
healthy and active longevity.

We may look back over the centuries and ages and notice
the manner in which various crafts came into being; how
they thrived and flourished and how the products of these
crafts have served society, either industrially or domestic-
ally; how these products have been in harmony with the
materials of which they were made, and how the structures
and shapes were designed to meet the conditions of their
use. In the subtle curves of the snaith of the English scythe
we have something so perfect, yet so incredibly simple that
the experienced user could put in a day's work in the hay-
field without unusual fatigue. The shapes of the hulls of
various types of coastal and inland water-craft, each
expressly designed to ride the kind of water of coast or
waterway it will sail on. The Teifi coracle is as primitive now
as in the days when it was designed, simply because the Teifi
has not changed, because salmon still leap and sheep have
to be dipped.

Machine- and mass-production, together, have had a
tremendous impact not only on hand-crafts but on the mind
of the population. Our sense of beauty and what is right
have been subjected to something like a total war, and the
consequences have been to eliminate some crafts altogether,
to divert others and to stimulate a profound opposition by
the stalwarts. Many of what were 'everyday things' in times
past must be sought among the 'bygones' in the museums
and in the literature of historians and scholars. The present
attitude regarding hand-craft and machine-manufacture is a
healthy and logical one; it is not a 'machine-breaker', but
one which fully understands that the hand and the machine,
properly exercised, can co-operate in a rational manner.

A constituent of this lies in the encouragement of
'amateur' crafts. Given the right direction and the best
guidance, we may follow the example of tutors in various

crafts. People have said to me, 'I wish I could draw' and my answer has been 'Why don't you?' In the early stages you will make every mistake, but this is important because you cannot *learn* without mistakes. Good or bad, you have the satisfaction that the product is *yours* alone and no one else's. Once you've started you will go on, on, in answer to the creative impulse. If a thing is worth doing at all, it is worth doing well.

4

Sociology

An interesting aspect of craftsmanship has been the changing status 'in society' of the craftsman. When the nomadic 'culture' slowly gave way before the advance of the more settled life of agriculture the resultant civilization gave more time and created a new demand for things. It was then the practice to make things for immediate use of the tribe or the clan, domestic and agricultural. When the stone and flint techniques were augmented by those of bronze and iron, and later of tin, lead, gold, and silver, there evolved special crafts for the making of things from these metals. It is doubtful if people working in these metals enjoyed any sort of recognition, nor for that matter did those who worked in clay and textiles.

It was not very long before the leaders of other civilizations in Europe and about the Mediterranean came to know of these metals. Some had such things as rich textiles, in fibres other than wool and flax, to offer in exchange, though there were some who later sought to obtain them by less orthodox methods. So it was that the Celts, in between thwarting the attentions of marauders, began to export metals, either in ore or the finished condition, to such as the Phoenicians, who in return brought textiles. Thus, by barter, there grew a considerable export and import activity, doubtless without an accruing adverse balance either way. Even the unwanted attentions and the skirmishes may have had their benefit in advancing craft techniques.

Through all the succeeding phases of history the crafts increased and craftsmen acquired new skills, attaining their first great flowering during the Christian era in Ireland and Northumberland. Much of this work came from the scribes and early masons of the churches. The craftsman, as such, continued in anonymity and without recognition.

The first step in the establishment of crafts came with the medieval guilds, which managed the affairs of masters, apprentices, and journeymen, who were all of one social class, poor men by modern standards, but proud of their skill. A noticeable change during the fourteenth century was in the relationship between the master and his employees. The master was becoming less a brother-craftsman, however senior and increasingly the entrepreneur, who gave increasing time to organization and selling, with a consequent rise in his status and the acquisition of power. The opposition to this voiced itself in the 'yeomen guilds', which looked to the interests of not only the employees but the 'small' masters. The big masters were ceasing to be craftsmen.

The 'markets' which were supplied by this time were regional, national, and foreign, and mostly centred around the cloth industries. This kind of trade continued and developed to the present time, but it was not until the vogue of the medicinal spa and the later, eighteenth-century 'discovery' of the seaside, that an entirely new kind of trade came into being. It is in the present century, that the full potentiality of tourism and the holiday resort have been exploited.

Whereas in all the previous forms of trade the craftsman's place had been essentially a utility one in which he or she knew no status but that of employee, this new tourist trade had from the outset a leisure character, in the one, people bought things from material necessity; even the great churches were a necessity no less material for all the spiritual expression which they contained. In the new business, people bought to satisfy leisure and pleasure, for they were in 'holiday' mood, even though the article they bought may have been put to a daily use. One might go to the Saturday market to buy half a dozen plates, but to the craft potter to buy a salad-bowl. In all this new market a new kind of craftsman was appearing, working on a basis of self-employment, often selling his own wares. It may be noted that the bowl-turners of Wales at one time took all their weeks' work for sale on their own stalls at the weekly market 'in town'. And wherever a potter may be situated it will be unusual if he or she has no shop attached where the pots can be sold direct.

It does not follow that the utility market lacks discernment or that it is supplied with inferior wares. Nor that the tourist market is discerning and supplied with well-designed and well-made wares. Many a 'cottage' home quite unconsciously may contain exquisite pottery, though the wallpaper may be atrocious. In too many shops one will find good and bad manufactures cheek by jowl.

It is the long-term business of the craftsman to produce the very best that circumstances will permit, a process which may not show an early return capable of measurement. The customer must be persuaded to discriminate between the genuine and the spurious, and to realize that in the long run of a lifetime of usage the well-designed article, made of good materials, will score hands down over the inferior and probably outlive several such articles. Too many manufacturers, with a pretence of having 'their fingers on the pulse', profess to know what the public wants, when they mean 'This is what we want the public to buy'. Too frequently, the buyer gives in to the sledge-hammer which goes with this catering.

In the face of this, the best of craftsmen have pursued a course full of risks and pitfalls. William Morris made it a life-dedication in a dozen crafts, paralleled with a great deal of writing. Ethel Mairet travelled widely, spun, wove, wrote, and taught. 'Jack' Goodchild quietly produced his gems of chairs that are now so much sought after.

From 1563, it was enacted that every would-be craftsman must learn his trade for seven years, under a master craftsman, who must accept responsibility for him. On completion of his apprenticeship he could, at the age of twenty-four, become a journeyman, marry, or set up in his own business (pp. 191–2, Trevelyan's *English Social History*.) The success of the system appears to have hinged on the relationship between master and apprentices, among whom there were, as ever, good, bad, and indifferent.

To the parent industries of agriculture and weaving, all the remaining hundred-and-one crafts of rural life were ancillary and therefore closely integrated. In weaving, there were a multiplicity of activities: carding, spinning, dyeing, weaving, fulling, and finishing, each undertaken as separate activities, and many centuries passed before the comprehensive manufacture within mills was established, as in Wales and later Yorkshire.

When the apprentices had completed their indentures they became journeymen and sooner or later rose to become masters. The status of master mason or master weaver finally disappeared with the Renaissance gulf between designer and craftsman. Right down to Hanoverian times it had been customary for the sons of the squires and above to be apprenticed to a trade. It was not only good for their discipline, it interwove them into a society which even in Elizabethan times was not greatly aware of arbitrary divisions. The distaste for soiling the hands with trade was born during the eighteenth century and grew to ludicrous proportions during the nineteenth, quite regardless of the fact that the 'family prosperity' had been founded on the pursuit of trade. The men and women of gentle birth would have been scandalized to learn what they already knew, that the ancestors gazing splendidly from the walls of the big house were not only citizens but mercers.

In medieval England weaving was second only to agriculture and in the fourteenth century, the expansion of trade was such that marketing, hitherto in the hands of the guilds, passed to the new figure, the merchant, whose place was in the specialized marketing in foreign countries, which looked to us for the finest wollen products. The merchant was thus distinct from the master craftsman, whose responsibility remained with production. Where wool had passed in staple to the Continent it now went as finished cloth, through the Merchant Venturers. The wealth of the Cotswolds was founded on the staplers and that of East Anglia on the merchants. Grevel House, at Chipping Campden and Pay-cockes, at Coggeshall, became the architectural symbols of the two systems.

Until the establishment of fulling-mills, during the eighteenth century, nearly all work in weaving was on a domestic basis. The websters and the spinners worked in their own homes. The eighteenth century proved to be a high-water mark in most if not all of the crafts. In the rural industries the division of labour did not run so deep as to separate master and employee. This division was to be found in the work of architects and interior decorators, where the designer was to become distant from the craftsman. There was a great deal of enlightened patronage.

One of the aftermaths of the Napoleonic Wars was a rural pauperisation on a large scale, which created a 'drift from country to town, and remained a feature throughout the nineteenth century. It followed, therefore, that those crafts which were situated in the country and were ancillary to rural life were adversely affected. During this long phase some crafts, such as tailoring, boot-making and clock-making, were ceasing to be a part of the village. So people had increasingly to shop in a distant town to buy things which, incidentally, were not designed for 'country use'. Beneath the thin crust of national prosperity there was a growing unrest and even periodic rebellion. The wonder is that any remnants could survive.

Such craftsmanship as did thrive was not of the country-side at all, but was contained within the new civil and mechanical engineering, and Tyneside was its principal cradle. There were many brilliant minds: Telford, the Stephensons, father and son, the Brunels, also father and son; all men who were not afraid or convention-bound. Their visions and plans involved accuracy and skill in building the new bridges, in driving tunnels, in surveying the railways and providing the motive-power and rolling-stock. In all this vast output there were failures, of course, but the successes were glorious.

In the rural economy the long-established cottage industries, weaving, spinning, lace-making, and quilting, were steadily declining. The final blow came in the 1870s, when agriculture, riding on a crest, plunged suddenly into a trough without precedent, a trough compounded of a succession of poor harvests and the import of wheat from the prairies of North America. To add insult to mortal injury, the winter of 1879–80 saw the country rigid in a four-month frost, during which every farm was immobilized.

The rural industries, declining before the onslaught of the new industries, reflected all this in the staple crafts of the blacksmith, the wheelwright and the thatcher. Then in the first decade of the present century the petrol engine made its first knock on the door and the blacksmith knew he would be shoeing fewer and fewer horses.

In 1885 the agricultural labourer became enfranchised and the general election of that year caused unease for the immemorial squirearchy. In 1888 the patriarchy of squire-cum-justice of the peace gave way to the administration of the county councils. But it came too long after the big drift had begun.

In the midst of it all Morris had preached, raved, and practised, and if his vision of a happier England was a little misty, his accomplishments in the crafts were none the less brilliant for their time. The Education Act of 1870 had yet

to bear its first frail fruits, and since most of the harvests of corn, fruit, and potatoes, etc., depended largely on child labour and many children had part-employment in village industry, such as lace-making, all in all the Act was difficult to enforce. (Even today, country children are absent from school for many weeks for harvesting and there are some people who openly advocate this on the ground that children learn more in the field than in the school.)

The life-cycle of the rural worker had too often terminated in the unquiet grave of destitution, but this was being changed for the happy prospect of the institution, where husband and wife were torn apart and cast into the opposite ends. What other prospect when the women painters of Coalport china, in return for a consummate skill, could earn as much as 12s. a week, while the man who built wagon wheels could make as much as 24s. a week. The sense of 'security' which such people enjoyed depended on the integrity of their employers. It was possible, at the end of the nineteenth century, for a fully skilled craftsman to pass through his adult life in this way, because his employer, often little better off, was a human being with a mutual dedication.

If the manufacture of pillow-lace necessitated the employment of girls from the age of five or six for 10 hours daily in 'lace-schools', then obviously we would have been better off without lace. Even the physiotherapy of the Poor Law establishments could not disguise the evil from the eyes of thinking people. In 1862, for example, a child of six could earn no less than 4d. a week, from which 2d. was deducted for 'schooling'. At the beginning of the century conditions had actually been better, when a child of ten might earn 2s. a week and an adult as much as 6s. The hidden cost of lace-making was deprivation of normal education, permanent injury to health, malnutrition and social degradation. In an era when Christian virtues were cultivated with the aid of physical punishment and sadistic torture, it may have occasioned less notice, but to us it makes harrowing reading.

It is very much a tradition that in many crafts there is a father to son continuity which may last from several generations to several centuries. This is often miraculous, because children do not necessarily inherit the traits and tastes of their parents, often to the regret of those parents. In itself, this inheritance is neither a good nor a bad thing (I did not inherit my father's inclinations, therefore I am not a retail tobacconist). Many famous people acquired their fame by making a radical break with a family line. Where all the conditions are favourable, however, environment will produce a continuity. This was so in the great days of steam on the railways, where son would follow father on the footplate.

My grandfather, my mother's father, was born near Chiddingly, in Sussex, in 1850. He had finished with his schooldays by the age of nine and after the vicissitudes of those days he eventually became a master builder. The houses he built in Eastbourne are standing today. He bought the material, employed others, sold or let the houses himself, kept his own accounts and the State benefited not. He was 'regular Sussex' to his finger-tips and 'wouldn't be druv'. I deeply regret that in the years when I knew him I was too young to appreciate his qualities—contrary though he was.

One can read one book after another on crafts and village life and encounter men like my grandfather. Many or most were illiterate, yet they had in them something which all education cannot inculcate. One may now and again meet father, son, and grandson working together. Father, now approaching ninety, may be a trifle slow, but he has the inestimable asset of experience of the older techniques. His son will probably be the king-pin and business brain and therefore as much concerned with contacts as with the mechanics, while the grandson may be a school-leaver 'trainee' or the modern equivalent of the journeyman, depending on his age. Often his first employment will be with another firm in order to widen his experience, but eventually he will 'come into the family business'. In such a concern the 'old man' is good prestige. He might not pass 'time and motion' applications, but so long as craftsmanship cannot be computed he is as safe as his years. Were such a man to stop work he would become a memory in less than six months.

With an improvement in financial prospects there is today a greater incentive for son to follow father in the rural industries, wherein the prospects for the thatcher, for example, are now good. Against this, there is still in the country mind the enticement of 'city lights', even though they are but a façade. Village communities, though often inclined to regard 'foreigners' with suspicion, are less parish-bound than formerly. Whereas the countryman of the past looked to the sky over his village, he depends now too often on the 'forecast' over the radio.

In former times the thatcher was often a part-time hedger, ditcher, and odd-job man. His slender capital made it necessary for the owner of the house or property to pro-vide the materials, while the thatcher would price his labour and time according to the job. Usually this was a mutual agreement settled down at the local. Incidentally, the price is now reckoned by the 'square', of 10 ft × 10 ft, of roof area.

The blacksmith was a general factotum in iron, at every-one's beck and call, as subject as any workman to the temperament of the farmer, for better or for worse. The wrought-iron workers, whose names are part of the history of art, were a little better placed, but they were still subject to the integrity of the patron, whether it was the Church or the dilettante. If he were an enlightened man, dedicated to an idea, then those craftsmen who worked for him were in a better situation.

Craftsmen, like artists, are not necessarily 'businessmen'. In fact, artists and accountants are usually 'poles' apart, and it has often been impossible to combine the two in one person; 'sums' are a frightful bore to the one and a fascination to the other.

In those crafts which have always been essentially rural in character—the blacksmith, the carpenter or the thatcher, etc.—the worker in the past 'knew his place' and touched the forelock, but today there is a status of greater entitlement and with it goes an independence conducive to self-respect. The fundamental change *had* to come—or else.

Organization at various levels has proved of tremendous value in presenting a new image, which contrasts sharply with the picturesque figures of the past. These organizations have been instrumental in educating the public to reject past conceptions of the old status. In short, a man is no longer inferior because he is a highly skilled artisan.

It is clear that in the matter of survival certain crafts, such as thatching and pottery, are safe, because fashion makes no demands which require adaptation to a new style or the use of synthetic materials. Weaving, too, is on fairly certain ground. In fact, both weaving and pottery can exploit the hand-made qualities peculiar to their respective crafts.

Craftsmanship has had to contend, in the last 200 years, with a succession of dangerous encounters. The gaunt spectre of the Industrial Revolution and its attendant train, we have dealt with. Through it all certain crafts have come through largely unaffected. The crafts of hedge-laying and dry-stone walling have only to contend with barbed wire and electric fencing, neither of which by their impermanent and temporary nature can hardly be treated as dangerous rivals. The woodland industries as a group continue vital as suppliers of timber in various prepared forms and of a number of comparatively simple products which are elementary and indispensable.

The making of furniture presents a complex picture. There is a growing tendency in domestic life of subordinating activities to the 'telly' and of dove-tailing normal activities to the programme. The furniture of the room containing this Behemoth has so be rearranged to suit the ritual of watching. The set is cased in plastics and laminations and seems unhappy in the company of any period of furniture.

Concurrent with this is the necessity to counter the economic barrage and to make furniture to financial calculations' which too often result in a façade of all front, no back, and not very much side. One can receive more favourably the new resistant finishes and materials, which may better meet the demands of a faster pace of life. Much depends on the individual reception to plastics. The traditional tools and techniques have scarcely any place in what is virtually a new industry. For those who still cherish a piece of furniture there are craftsmen well able to express themselves in the contemporary manner.

Every movement contains the seeds of its own opposition; or expressed more simply, people get tired of a particular fashion and a reaction sets in. If the design trend of one decade is austere, then that of the next will be ornate. When that trend has worked itself into an orgy of excess, then the pendulum will swing once more. So far as all this concerns furniture, it means that plastic and lamina will have to meet the natural warmth and repose of the furniture-makers' craft.

A greater danger lies in the unbroken rise in the cost of living. The working-speed of craftsmanship is slow because it is impossible to apply 'time and motion' to the techniques. A firm of craftsmen employing a number of people cannot offer the wages with which other industries attract people. The present 'brain drain' is a phenomenon appearing in many industries. We have the odd spectacle of Englishmen going to Australia to join the police, and of Australians coming to Britain—to join the police. Everything really depends on the individual choice—to sell everything and prostrate himself at the new altar, or to cut his cloth and remain a craftsman. The man who makes the latter choice may not be worse off in the long run. The turbulence of the city ratrace is so violent that it is hardly surprising that country dwellers may catch some of the backwash.

We have now in the last twenty-five years a more insidious hindrance, in the shape of obstruction from the State, to which the enterprise of the small man is anathema. If the individual can 'prove' that he is vital to export, then the State may listen; if however, the individual wishes to make things difficult for himself, then the consequences are hardly the concern of the State. This obstruction cannot be touched, it can only be sensed.

Excepting the elementary crafts of rural life which through history have grouped themselves in each parish, the pattern of distribution over the country has been irregular. The source of supply has determined the situation of many, while others have been sited in this or that valley because of the presence of running water. At one time potters tended to work near the sources of their materials, but when the cost of transporting china-clay became less than that of kiln-fuel, then it became possible for potters to work elsewhere, and with the introduction of electric kilns the original bond disappeared. Nevertheless, there is a cluster of potters situated in Cornwall, well sited to cater for the intensive tourist industry. On the other hand, there has been an intermittent manufacture on a Roman site, in Suffolk, since the first kiln was fired.

At one time thatchers tended to be located within the regions in which the 'native' materials were to be obtained. Although they have continued the methods traditional to their regions, they are increasingly placing themselves at distant call. Bearing in mind that there are nearly 800 men working in this craft, it follows that they may now be located anywhere within the boundaries.

The closer one studies rural industries, the more it becomes apparent that after the mid-nineteenth century, those craftsmen who remained at work in the village community had of necessity to look further and further afield for business. We have considered the thatcher, and we find it no less true of those blacksmiths who have turned to and specialized solely in decorative wrought-iron work. By a hard-earned reputation they are gaining commissions from very distant customers. The Rural Industries Bureau[1] is performing a dual service; firstly by instruction through their own officers in various techniques and secondly by the compilation of registers of craftsmen and women at work in each of the industries. Such registers are of inestimable value to architects, house-furnishers and land-agents. They have also published a useful list of craftsmen for the benefit of individuals, and tourists. Craftsmen have by nature, individualist tendencies and some organization and 'channelling' of their output is advantageous to everyone concerned. Craftsmanship may suffer further casualties and changes, but it will survive as long as people are attracted to the hand-made product.

[1] Now known as 'The Council for Small Industries in Rural Areas' (CoSIRA).

5
Woodland and Coppice Industries

FELLING

There is, of course, much more to felling a tree than simply causing it to fall to the ground to within 6 in. of a predetermined place. Contrary to the usual practice on the Continent and in America, the foresters and woodmen of this country make the cut as near to the ground as physical adeptness and the root formation of a tree will permit. In fact, a good woodman will pride himself on this ability, for the more that goes down the less waste is left.

The first stage is called 'laying-in', whereby the buttresses or swellings leading to the roots are removed with an axe. When sufficient clearance has been made, a tapering gap is made on the 'face' of the trunk, that is, the part facing the direction of the fall. This takes away the support on that side. The axe is now dispensed with, and the third stage begins, with sawing on the opposite side or the 'back' of the tree, with two men using a cross-cut saw. Now, all the 'work' of a cross-cut is done on the pull-stroke, each man alternately pulling and releasing. Practices and methods of felling vary from one region to another; until a hundred or so years ago the entire felling was made with the axe, but it has since become usual to employ the saw and axe as described. When the axe alone was used it was customary to make the first opening at the face as nowadays, but the second opening on the opposite side was made a little higher, so that the tree went down more readily.

The larger sizes of cross-cut of 60–84 in., as mentioned, are not fitted with the conventional fixed handles, but have detachable doles which fit vertically at each end. The doles are made for removal, so that the saw may be withdrawn when wedges are used to 'follow' the saw in order to raise the trunk and increase the opening.

The wisdom of the woods was acquired very early in history, and foresters then considered they must fell during January and February, unless they required the bark of oak for tanning, in which case certain felling would be delayed until March or even April. More recent research has, however, disputed the winter-felling theory. At the same time one may feel they did not bring down the giants of the forest according to the calendar without some very good reason. They had been doing these things for some 3,000 years.

Once down, the tree can be cut into sections of bole and branches and trimmed of its projections. In this condition the bole and main branches can be manoeuvred with greater ease. A great deal depends on the condition of a deciduous tree, as to the extent to which it will break up by its own weight in falling. (I recollect seeing a beech flatten out on the ground like a pancake, but this was a single tree that had stood in parkland.) With the tree cut up, the volume of useful timber may now be determined, and there are various methods of making this estimation of a mass so irregular as a tree-bole, but they are all derived from ascertaining the midway girth, with allowance for bark, and the length.

At this juncture we should remember the term 'Standard', in both its uses. Firstly, there is 'standard timber', or that which follows its natural growth to produce the crown, by which we know the splendid trees of the forest and woodland.

Secondly, there is the 'standard' as a unit of cubic content of the average full-grown tree. This content is reckoned at 165 cu. ft.

For purposes of identity, each bole or branch is marked on the butt-end with appropriate signs and then it is manoeuvred by ropes and chains out of the forest, to join the rest. Until the advent of mechanical power all this movement was accomplished with horses, as many as were necessary. Once 'out of the wood', and on to the open dump, each trunk is carried away to the timber yard. This was done either by a timber 'neb' or a pole-wagon. In either case, trunks were and still are carried 'butt-first', in order to put the greater weight at the supported front end, and so minimize the 'swing' at the tail overhang. The neb was a massive two-wheeler, designed to carry a single trunk of the largest dimensions, underslung with the butt-end below a specially designed and extremely massive arched axle. At the centre of balance the trunk was suspended from a kind of 'jib', which could be raised and lowered. The pole-wagon, which was the forerunner of the present-day motor-hauled trolley, had iron stanchions at its four corners of two transverse beams, each above its respective axle. The distance between the transverses was and still is adjustable to suit the length of the trunks. The haulage capacity of the modern motor enables a number of trunks to be transported together, all securely chained.

In those days of horse-drawn vehicles it was still possible to carry several trunks at a time, but what was then a journey of great labour and much time can now be quickly accomplished, for the distance from the forest to the yard may vary considerably.

Within the last few years a fundamental change in the method of felling has come about. Chain saws have been devised and introduced, largely to displace the axe and the cross-cut. One may regret the passing of the 'ring' of the woodman's axe and the 'wang-wang' of the cross-cut. We have now, in their place, the agonized crescendo shrieks of the chain saw, which, presumably, has brought with it a new set of skills

Whatever tools have been used, the whole process has been generally known as felling. In Surrey, according to George Sturt, in *The Wheelwright's Shop*, they knew it as throwing, while in Herefordshire, it has always been falling. —'Tree-falling, a speciality', one wayside notice still reads. Reference to the *English Dialect Dictionary* will provide a positive mine of information which one may follow up.

Our forefathers and all the generations before them went into the natural woodlands and forests for their timber, selecting, felling, and converting as they went. When the population was still no more than several millions and supplies of timber were as yet seemingly inexhaustible, the foresters had no need of a comprehension of 'natural regeneration' or plantation. Today we may not realize the extent of those 'primeval' forests—that what we call Epping Forest, for example, is but the remnant vestige of a vast deciduous forest which covered all of North London, Hertfordshire, and extended right across Essex to the North Sea. Not for mere architectural essay were so many Essex churches built with 'lantern towers' to guide the traveller.[1]

Our forests were, however, subject to continual encroachment and denudation and in later centuries some legislation was made to protect these sources. It has not till the present century that the industry of forestry came into being. In the train of the industry there followed the sciences of timber and ecology. Because of this late start, our artificial, cultivated forests are therefore young, as forests and woodlands may be judged. Much research and arboriculture is being done at the arbreta and pineta.

[1] There is much to glean about this in *The Old Straight Track*, by A. Watkins, published by Methuen in 1923.

Generally, we do not accept sudden change. A long familiar wood is cleared and in great perturbation we 'write to the papers'. Or the Forestry Commission sets a plantation to cover some long-familiar open country and there follows another spate of letters, mostly from people who are sincerely concerned with the preservation of what we term our national heritage, which because of continued erosion by industry, by population 'overspill', or by the driving of motorways is dwindling in acreage to an alarming extent each year. Over-all, afforestation, either by softwood or hardwood, may be the least endangerment. Hilaire Belloc never got between the pines but he smelled the Sussex air. The Forestry Commission is as much concerned with equating production and erosion as it is with research, and it must be a difficult and additional matter to apply themselves to the unrewarding task of trying to satisfy the tastes of the population, each member of which has his or her own ideas of what is beautiful. It is the Commission's misfortune to have become associated in the public mind with an image, and that image consists of a blanket of monotonous spruce flung across an area of previously open mountainside.

It is proper that more than a word about fire risk be included in this subject. Those Forestry Commission notices, be they in English or Welsh, are there because fires can start, either by the wanton carelessness of certain individuals or by the excessively dry conditions consequent upon a prolonged period of drought. The larger plantations are purposely divided by fire breaks and rides, and in addition some access is provided by service roads which, though unmetalled, are adequate for the foresters. During some spells of intense heat, following a drought, one may walk in a forest or on an open, sandy heath, where gorse and bracken dominate the margins of a forest, and get a sense of impending danger, as though spontaneous combustion were about to occur. A forest or heath fire, one large enough to make nonsense of men's efforts at control and extinction, is a

Timber Bob, variously
known as a Drag, Neb
or even a pair of wheels.

Top-sawyer and partner, the pitman.

terrible thing, in both the phenomenal speed at which it covers the ground and the destruction of flora and fauna that remains in its wake.

CONVERSION

According to the dimensions and nature of the timber, various methods of conversion may be used. The division of the largest and heaviest timber into plank, baulk, or block form can only be accomplished by the use of saws; either the cross-cut, as in felling, or by the pit saw or hand saw. In medieval times, when timber in its felled state was but a little greater in section than the desired member, trimming could be effected by chipping with an adze or by hewing with a broad-axe. This type of axe had a single-sided taper and would therefore be ground 'right-hand' or 'left-hand', to suit the user. The adze, which in origin is contemporaneous with the other early woodworking tools, has its cutting edge set at right-angles to the haft. The blade has a shallow concave edge, enabling the user to chip away along the faces of the timber, producing the familiar dimpling, which is characteristic of medieval work. Some misguided 'romantics' have sought to reproduce this dimpling on wood which has already been sawn and planed clean. Now the adze, being a hollowing tool, its present-day use is largely confined to certain craftsmen who require a concave surface on some parts of their work—such men as those who make Windsor chairs and those who turn and carve platters and spoons. A larger type is used by shipwrights and makers of dock gates.

A great deal of timber may be divided by cleavage, that is by splitting the wood to follow the grain. This is possible with oak, ash, beech, and the softwoods, but never with elm. It can be done with all coppice-grown timber, to which we shall come later. Heavy cleavage can be accomplished with 'beetle and wedge' (see the delightful inn of that name, at

Moulsford, below Oxford), or the intermediate and the lighter stuff can be cleft with a fromard, which is started with a lighter beetle. With the smaller dimensions of timber, once the cleft has been started it can be 'followed through' by persuasive levering. The more slender the wood, the more important it becomes to preserve the fibres, though the straight grain and peculiar character of the various soft-woods permits their being sawn down to quite slender dimensions. This matter of cleavage does not cover the commercial deals, which are all sawn and are out of the sphere of this book. At the opposite end of the range of timber there is elm, which, because of its twisting grain, cannot be cleft. This very characteristic makes elm the best of all woods for constructional purposes, where extensive mortising must be made. We shall meet elm again, among the country furniture-makers.

Long ago men found that certain kinds of tree, when cut right back to the root, just above the ground, instead of growing again as a central tree-bole, would throw up a cluster of straight shoots which grew into usable poles. According to the nature of the tree, this process could be repeated at regular intervals until the tree or 'stool' eventually exhausted itself. Whole plantations of these 'stooled' trees were formed and today they cover many thousands of acres over much of the country south of the Trent. Such plantations are especially extensive in the Wealden country and much of Wessex. In some localities they are to be found in small coppices dotted about the counties. Alder, ash, birch, sweet chestnut, hazel, and the osier are so cultivated and cropped, each according to the nature of the material required.

Forestry and coppice-work each involve totally different procedures. Whereas forestry is, in itself, a separate in-dustry, the cutting of coppices is usually done by the crafts-men, each according to his requirements. The exception to this, however, are the makers of baskets and fish-traps, who buy their rods from various sources, surprisingly even from abroad. In coppice clearance, nothing else but the felling-axe need be used, since the heaviest poles are the ash and chestnut. But in order to produce a good crop of clean, sound wood, the ground must be kept clear of extraneous growth which can deprive the plantation of food and ventilation and induce parasitic growth. In some industries, such as those using hazel and where the cutting is made at comparatively short intervals, the crafts may work through the whole plantation, section by section, eventually arriving back at the starting-point. Hurdle-makers, especially, usually make their hurdles 'on the spot', likewise the 'chair-bodgers', so one may sometimes experience some difficulty in finding them in a large plantation, and may only 'stumble' upon them by chance. Their life is a simple, unencumbered one, their tools are few and simple and their lore nearly inexhaustible. They use no 'machinery', but the simple contrivances they make themselves, though the 'workshop' craftsmen, who have not to consider portability, will have appliances somewhat more complex and certainly more permament, such as setting-frames, breaks, and 'horses'.

These primitive arrangements do not always appear self-explanatory to the uninitiated, until one watches a steamed ash rod being bent and curved here, straightened there, or placed in a 'setting-frame', so when cold it may be extracted permanently set. So it is with the rakes, and trugs and hurdles; they cannot be improved, nor can machines be devised to manufacture them.

PIT SAWING

Nowadays, they saw up tree-trunks lengthways into planks or baulks by various power-driven saws, either circular or vertically reciprocating. But until well into the present century, from as far back as Roman times, this work had been done by hand, by two men, one standing atop the

5 HINGE-BANDS FROM ST ALBANS CATHEDRAL
TWELFTH CENTURY   *Victoria and Albert Museum*

6 FIREBACK FROM SUSSEX IRONWORKS 1582

Victoria and Albert Museum

7 CHANDELIER SUSPENSION-ROD SEVENTEENTH
CENTURY   *Victoria and Albert Museum*

8 STAFFORDSHIRE LUSTREWARE

Victoria and Albert Museum

9 WEDGWOOD ETRURIA POTTERY
Victoria and Albert Museum

10 LINEN QUILTED COVERLET 1703

Victoria and Albert Museum

11 CEILING-BOSSES FROM ST ALBANS CATHEDRAL
FIFTEENTH CENTURY   *Victoria and Albert Museum*

12 PANEL CARVING FROM ST SEPULCHRE, LONDON. SEVENTEENTH CENTURY

trunk and one below. In most parts of the world, the trunk rested on trestles, above the ground, but in this country it became customary from some time during the eighteenth century to work with the trunk supported over a longish pit. This pit was a permanent affair, slightly deeper than a man and up to 15 ft in length. They did not use the age-old large frame saw except for carved work, but a pit saw. Pit sawyers always worked and travelled as a pair, the man on the top of the trunk being the senior of the two, and it was his responsibility to set out the cuts and to arrange the work according to requirements. He also had full care of the saw. The pit man had to prepare the logs and help set them into position.

Where it was impracticable to have a permanent pit, as in the woodland clearings, a pit of similar dimension was excavated, two logs were laid along the top with two short pieces across each end. These were called strakes and sills. In view of the slowness of the operation and the consequent limit of production, the pit saw held its place for two reasons. One was the convenience where heavy machinery was impracticable and the second was that the 7 ft saw went through timber impossible for circular saws. Small firms could not afford reciprocating gang saws—which had a number of blades in a frame—so the simple, portable, adaptable, and cheap pit saw lasted a very long time.

There was a great deal more to their business than was apparent. Their craft rested on a well-set saw, and the greatest care in positioning the trunk and providing satisfactory support. The trunk was first hewn to provide flat surfaces on its opposite sides. One side provided extra stability in resting over the pit, while the opposite side, now the upper surface, provided both a clear face for marking out saw cuts and a sure foot-hold for the top man. It was then secured by iron dogs to the transverse bearers and the wooden sills which ran the length of the pit.

Accurate guide-lines, either chalked or blacked, according

to the colour of the timber, were essential for any work of the sawyers, and this was especially so when they were required to produce planks of equal and even thickness throughout. George Sturt says they used to 'split the heart', that is to make an initial cut dead in the middle and then to cut to either side, as this obviated what were known as 'ring-shakes', whereby one of the annular rings might be shaky and allow the older heart to separate itself. The remaining cuts could then be made and it was from this point that the art of the competent sawyers showed itself. As with all kinds of sawing, the angle of the saw was obtuse to the trunk, so that the weight of the saw did some of the work. The top man was the guide and pace-maker, for he, working in daylight, could see how things were going. The pit man, down among all the sawdust, with much of the light obscured by the mass of timber above his head, had to follow the pace, alternatively pulling the saw down and lifting, periodically applying oil by a rag on the end of a stick, from a pot which he kept in a recess in the wall of the pit. When the light was bad, as it so often was in winter, the pit man depended upon a candle, stuck on a piece of wood and conveniently positioned.

The saw they used was quite different from anything of a similar size. Generally about 7 ft in length, it tapered from about 10 in. to about 3. Uniformity in depth would have made it pit-heavy and unwieldy, but the severe taper obviated this. For the top man, the depth at his end, where the progress of the saw could be followed, was sufficient to ensure that once a good start had been made an expert pair could keep the course true.

The handles were completely different from each other. That for the top man was called a tiller and may be described as T-shaped, with the upright of iron, about 21 in. in length and having a slight curvature that set the user just that much back from his work. The double handle of wood made the cross of the T and varied appreciably in width, from 14 to

24 in. The tiller was normally bolted as a fixture, but most blades were made with alternative holes. The handle for the pit was called a box, and at a casual glance it might resemble a type of two-handled box-plane. Examined in the hand, one would immediately notice a deep centre-slot and a long, tapering key or wedge. The box was usually much narrower than the tiller. Once it had been properly positioned on the tail of the blade, the wedge was knocked home tight. It was made removable so that the saw could be drawn out at the end of a cut. This was essential because, with each positioning of the trunk on the bearers, all the plank cuts were made as far as possible, in a row, before the trunk was levered forward to enable the process to be resumed. And so the labour, the sweat and the saw-dust continued until the whole trunk was converted to planks.

As the kerfs deepened, so the emerging planks increasingly vibrated. To obviate the jarring to the sawyer's hands, a rope was thrown around the plank-ends, and as the kerfs still deepened, it became necessary to bang in shallow wedges to damp the jarring.

A word about sharpening. The top man did this, placing the blade, teeth uppermost, into three deep-slotted and stout wooden pegs which projected vertically from the horizontal beam of a trestle. This simple assemblage was called a sharpening-horse (that name 'horse' crops up time and again among the more 'primitive' crafts); it was of robust construction and looked the more primitive for the inevitable burnings and chippings over all its surfaces.

With the blade resting securely in its slots, the top man could occupy an hour or two, restoring the right edge to every tooth. Since the saw cut only on the 'down' stroke, the teeth were all inclined that way. Each tooth had to be dead level with its fellows, horizontally, and to project alternately left and right, just that fraction that the saw would clear itself in the kerf. And again, all the 'lefts' had to project equally with the 'rights', so that both sets should work equally and thereby produce a dead straight kerf. A badly worn or neglected saw having a bias would try to proceed in a curve. This tool was correctly known as an 'open pit saw' to distinguish it from the frame-saw, used either on curved work or 'above the ground' on trestle-supported logs. For curved work they alternately used a 'turning saw'.

So these two men and their saw usually travelled from job to job. Much of their summer work was in the woods and forest, converting felled timber for easier transport, or they might work at saw-yards. As winter approached they often travelled about the country, calling at wheelwrights to carry out the work required at the wrights' premises. Each kind of wood—oak, elm, or ash—as it was 'opened' up by the sawyers, revealed its character, even in the 'green' condition. Each had its own scent and response as the saw went in deeper. The man who had bought the timber as it had stood in the woodland directed his requirements of the sawyers—and learned at this stage whether his wisdom was sound or faulty.

Pit sawyers, it seems, were a race much on their own, uncommunicative and perhaps brutish. Yet not quite that, for brute force alone could never accomplish that which required a fine mixture of an inherited sense and good physique. They were not by any means the last of the 'primitives'.

For cutting out pieces which were curved, such as wheel-felloes, cart-shafts, or certain parts of a wagon body, the sawyers used the large frame saw, which can be found in the rest of Europe and parts of Africa and Asia, where the English pit saw is not used. This saw has a rectangular frame in which a slender blade is held under tension, between the end cross-pieces. With the type of saw any desired curve can be made.

Various simple notations were used to mark the ends of timber and one may sense a remarkable affinity between them and those which were similarly used by the medieval stone-masons as 'signatures' to their works. A table of these mason's marks may be seen in the Abbey of Tewkesbury. The two crafts are a long way apart, yet at some time in the past the two kinds of craftsman may have worked much closer.

COPPICE WORK—HURDLE-MAKING

There are two types of sheep hurdle, both of which may be used to quarter off a section of a field, so that a flock of sheep, usually of the Down breeds, may be 'folded' for grazing. This is done in order to confine the flock within an area to ensure good feeding off roots and that the soil will be well trod. As each area is cleared the hurdles are moved to quarter off the next section. This concentrated folding does not occur where the field has been sown as a grass ley.

The two hurdles used are the Gate, which roughly resembles a six-barred gate, and the Wattle, which is of woven hazel rods. Both have their end uprights extended downwards to points for insertion in the ground. Overall dimensions of both kinds may vary a little, but a length of 6 ft by a depth of 3 ft may be taken as the average. The method of construction of wattles has for many years been applied to large ones for the partitioning of country-house gardens; these may be as much as 6 ft in height.

The men who make these hurdles draw their material from different coppices. Wattle hurdles are made of hazel and the gates of ash, though in both kinds other wood, such as chestnut or willow, may be used if the necessity should arise. Both are simple and have not changed either in pattern or construction from the time they were evolved. Machines have not been devised to take the place of skilled men, who have understood, through a lifetime of experience and environment, the nature of the materials. Some men are solitaries, working in the depths of some coppice, and it is often the case that the wanderer shall only find them by accident.

Like certain other craftsmen, their tools are quite simple and few in number—a felling-axe; an adze, hammer-headed for banging in pegs; a fromard and bittel for starting cleavage; a brace with one continuous bit for drilling peg-holes; and a 'Horsham' billhook, for chopping and pointing. Of course, a Cotswold 'hurdler' will not use a Horsham, but something nearly the same. It is not the heavy-weight tool favoured by hedge-layers. Whether one finds one man working alone, or two or three together, they spend their working life in this environment, in close communion with all the moods of Nature, and so come to understand the qualities of the wood they use. Their year is in two parts; the winter, when the leaves and the sap are down, when all the cutting, selecting, and bundling is done; and the summer, when they make their hurdles.

During the clearance of an ash coppice the ash poles are felled and cut into sections from base to crown. The 'chopping-post' is simply the base of a tree left standing and cut off to a suitable height. As the hurdle-maker, gate or wattle, is a cleaver of wood, he uses material of coppice growth and dimensions, and in this winter work his days will be spent in felling, lopping, and splitting. On the left-hand side of the chopping-post, well chipped and burred by a season's work, is a row of several short, slender poles, set at one-foot intervals. This row provides a gauge by which the required lengths may be obtained.

Each pole is drawn from the stack of felled ash, and successively chopped with a bille into suitable sections, from foot to top, and each piece is thrown on to its respective heap, arranged fan-wise. Anything of no use goes on to a fire, which burns continuously, mostly smouldering quietly, or now and again flaring up as a fresh lot ignites and adds its own pleasant smell to all the damp scents of a coppice. The base of each pole makes hurdle-parts, and sundry poles, next comes stuff for bean rods and above that the crown for pea sticks. At the end of the day a considerable quantity of material has been chopped and sorted into respective piles, each of which is made into conveniently sized bundles. The largest are stacked pyramid-fashion so that all the material will be well ventilated. Those poles which are suitable for the parts of gate hurdles are cleft into halves or quarters. The cleavage is started with a fromard and beetle—or froe and bittel—and this is usually followed with a froe or an adze, with which the opening is levered. In all this work the worker is careful to have his bille safe off the ground and readily accessible, simply by bringing the tool-edge smartly down on the chopping-block.

Cutting hazel from the copse, follows a procedure similar to that for ash, but for hazel the cutting is made at shorter intervals, usually about seven years. Hazel will send up quite long, slender shoots and these, when cleft, provide the best material for the woven wattle hurdle. If ash and hazel are for hurdles, then sweet chestnut is the wood for fence paling. This consists of cleft sticks wired up, top and bottom, in a continuous row. It makes an excellent temporary fencing, as it can be rolled up like a mat, after manufacture and easily transported. The runners and pegs used by the thatcher are another substantial by-product of the hazel coppice. In rod form, they are bundled for dispatch to the thatcher, who makes them to suit his own requirements.

GATE HURDLES

Although gate hurdles alone do not provide the wind-break that is wanted for penning during lambing-time, they are extremely useful and light. Material for them is readily obtainable where coppice ash provides a plentiful supply. Poles of twenty to thirty years' growth from a clean, well-cared-for plantation will cleave well to provide uprights and bars. The uprights are made thicker than the bars, and are mortised sufficiently to receive the tapered ends of the bars, six of which are used for each hurdle. A vertical brace is added midway and two diagonals from the bottom outer corners to the top centre make up a rigid, yet resilient and long-serving hurdle. The six bars are not placed equidistant, but, as in the case of field gates, the distance decreases from top to bottom. This is a simple deterrent to the natural curiosity of sheep of all ages about the great big green world on the other side. During lambing-time, the shepherd augments these gates by adding straw-bales to form walls around the pens. Within such compounds in-lamb ewes can be accommodated and cared for. Generally they are made about 7 ft wide by about 42 in. high, and often used additionally for subdividing a large field into sections of 5 acres.

WATTLE HURDLES

Amid all the paraphernalia in the clearance, there will be found a block of wood a little over 7 ft in length. It is not straight, but has a slight curve and along its length will be found ten holes, spaced equidistantly. In between use it tends to become covered with leaves and scattered shavings. This is the hurdle mould and into those holes the upright hazel rods are placed, all heads down and eventual tails up. The two outer rods are usually called shores, while the remainder are the sails. The rods for weaving have all been previously cleft. The first is 'let in' three or four staves in and woven in and out of the staves, then around the outer shore, where it is given a 'half-twist and turn' before the weaving action is resumed. This peculiar form of bend is made so that the fibres in the grain will not be broken. As each runner, or rod, is exhausted, a fresh one is let in and the process continued until the intended height is reached.

At this stage the wattle, is removed from the mould and all the sails are trimmed just clear of the weaving. The end shores are left to exceed the weaving at the base by about a foot and they are chopped to finely-tapered points, similar to those of gates, for pushing into the ground.

The curve of the mould produces a corresponding curve in the finished wattles. These are stacked by the score where they flatten under their own weight. In this simple manner, the wattle is tightened up, because if woven flat, they would quickly go slack. It is usual to leave an unwoven space in the middle, especially in those made for shepherds. A stick thrust through this space enables a number of wattles to be carried at once.

By late autumn all this work will be finished for the year and the hurdler will be preparing for another winter's cutting.

WALKING-STICKS, HOOPS, ETC.

Hazel, ash, and chestnut provide material for several more coppice industries. In spite of some major changes in barrel-packaging, industrial hooping is still required for 'stack' barrels, intended to contain 'dry' goods like hard fruit and cheese. Makers of walking-sticks, the stout country-going types, use a lot of ash and sweet chestnut, usually cut at 'two years' growth and steamed or immersed in hot sand before being curved on a break. Alternatively the curve of the handle can be produced by artificial cultivation, which will compel the new shoot to grow in the shape of the required curve. In Wales, too, they select a suitable shoot and root-base and carve the crook of a stick from this, with distinction.

MAKING RAKES, SCYTHE-SNAITHS, AND FORKS

In spite of the appearance of some curious objects on the retail market, which are being passed on as garden implements, it is not surprising that the serious gardener will continue to demand the simple, centuries-old wooden rakes and scythes. A well-designed implement, nicely balanced, will make a minimum demand upon the user's physique.

There is nothing like ash for implement handles and the hafts of axes. Ash has resilience to the continuous vibration sustained by rakes and scythes and no less to the shocks which the axe-haft must absorb. Ash also lends itself to steaming and artificial curving and bending. The cheap rake has two bad faults; the steel tine-head makes it head-heavy and the handle lacks balance; together they result in an unduly tiring implement. The wooden rake was designed centuries ago and there has been no reason to change it. The unvarnished handle falls easily to the hand and behaves responsively. The head is attached neatly to the splayed division of the handle. This head is broad enough for about fifteen wooden tines and is set at a slightly acute angle to the handle. This stops the rake from 'jumping' when dragged over the ground.

Such rakes were at one time made in two sizes, the larger, called a drag rake, carrying about thirty tines compared with fifteen for the garden rake. The size of the drag puts a steel head out of the question. Hay-raking nowadays is done by a tractor-hauled rotary. In the days when the whole of agricultural field-work was performed by labour, male and female, there would be whole teams to do the tasks now done by machines. Various types of hook and sickle, the scythe, the flail or drashel and the rake, all varied a little, from county to county, so that even today we are still finding out 'how they did it'. There was a third type of rake in which the head was set at about 45°, so that the natural dragging action left the hay deposited in a line to one side of a cleared 'lane'. It looked a most odd implement and one might be excused for thinking it a damaged rake. It is this work which is done by the modern side-delivery rotary. Incidentally, what has, for simplicity, been called a rake-handle is, in fact, called a stail.

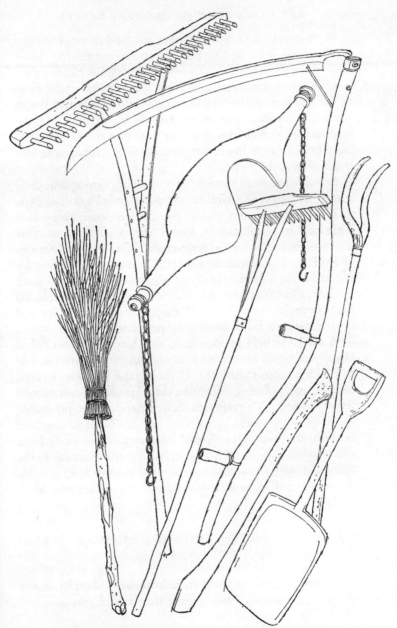

Some of the products of Woodland Crafts.

Scythes vary, like most implements, and in most designs are distinguishable by the double curvature in the handle, or more correctly the snaith or snedd. There is a decidedly Old-English, pre-Chaucer ring to these part-names which gives us a fair indication of origins. The southern, English snaith has a quite marked curvature, but the northern or Kendal type has slighter curves. We may note that the Dutch 'sith' has a dead straight handle of much heavier proportions, like those of central Europe.

Suitable poles are turned, after shaving, throughout their length, by means of a kind of box plane called a stail-engine, which is rotated clockwise as one does a pencil-sharpener. This kind of plane may be found among all those used by the carpenter, who uses a 'rung-engine' for turning the rungs of ladders. The snaith is rendered pliable for bending by immersion in a 'steam-box'. In this condition, fresh from the box, a batch is placed in the setting-frame, which holds them securely in the required shape until they are dry and cold, when their shape is retained permanently.

A scythe is held by two little side handles, called doles. Usually of beech and fitted to metal rings, they are wedged in position to suit the user. If the scythe is stood on end, blade up and pointing leftwards, the 'right-hand' dole should fall at hip-level. The left-arm, fully extended, should enable the fingers to touch the tip of the blade. The distance between the two doles should be about the same as from elbow to fist. The blade is attached in a manner similar to the doles, but with the addition of a small strut to keep it rigid. As an alternative to ash, the makers sometimes use birch or alder.

MAKING HELVES, YOKES, SHOVELS, AND PEELS, ETC.

These implements are made from 'standard' wood by reason of their dimensions. They constitute a varied group.

Once the Iron Age craftsmen had settled the manner of attaching the tool-heads to their respective handles, the way lay open for detailed improvements and refinements in both head and haft. A great many types of axe and, indeed, variations of each type were evolved, until by the middle of the nineteenth century every manufacturer of tools could show a remarkable range in the catalogue. Every type and variant had its own haft. While the American makers eventually settled for hickory, the British have found no substitute for the native ash.

Since it is imperative to 'follow the grain', these hafts are always cleft from the block and never sawn. When the initial cleavage has been made, rough shaving is done with a light axe until the rough shape emerges. The long, finishing stage is carried out with various kinds of draw-knife and spoke-shave, whilst the haft is held securely between two adjustable chocks. The present-day felling-axe is indeed a tool of superb balance and in expert hands is an extremely effective tool. These handles, or helves, deserve a separate study, but regrettably we must here be content with describing one or two which are representative of the family.

The conventional square-mouthed shovel, such as that used by council road-workers has a short handle with a T end, or a Y, for manipulation. This type can be found everywhere except in Cornwall and the west of Wales, which have a different kind of shovel. It is the long-handled West of England or Tipperary type which is to be found on the Continent. The blade, too, is different in being shallowly pointed or 'round-mouthed' instead of having a square mouth. Two such radically different tools necessarily require different methods of handling.

The shovel used by a maltster and the baker's peel were both made of beech, preferably cleft and shaven out of one piece. And when two pails of milk or water had to be carried by handle the shoulder-yoke was indispensable. Various woods were used, but the best of all was willow, because of its light weight. The yoke which was used when oxen were used on the farm was usually made of hornbeam, though oak and beech were alternatives. For many years an ox-yoke graced the front of the 'Tiger' inn, at East Dean, near Eastbourne. It was in this neighbourhood that one of the last ox-teams was used.

Until the advent of the threshing-machine, which in its original form was invented by Meikle, in 1786, all threshing of corn took place in the rick-yard or the barn. It was a slow, laborious process in which a quite simple device called a flail or drashel was used. These are but two of variant names for the same thing. The handle, usually about 30 in. long, sometimes more, was of ash. The swingle, the part which thrashed the corn, was quite stout and made of crab or holly. The very flexible joint, essentially the same as a universal coupling, consisted of two loops either of iron or eel skin, each loop, one within the other, being secured to the handle and the swingle. It has until recently, been a characteristic of farming practice that changes in the farm occurred but slowly, so we find that over a hundred years elapsed before hand threshing was eliminated. The advent of the combine-harvester has possibly effected the most rapid and revolutionary change in history. The combine has, in fact, obliterated the image of a thousand years.

MAKING BESOMS

You may, from time to time, in coppice country, notice here and there a stack or two of what appears to be brushwood. The stack will be regular in shape, with a 'pitched' top, like a roof. Quite close by there should be a lean-to stack of rough poles around a tree, though one might confuse this with the countryman's stack of winter fuel. These two kinds of stack together will be a sure indication of a besom-maker in the vicinity.

The besom is so easily, quickly, and cheaply made, and

so simple and effective, that one may be surprised that for use about garden and yard it is not universal. It will pick the autumn leaves off a lawn cleanly as nothing else will. The very lightness of the necessary action is invigorating to a well-cared-for lawn. At one time the Forestry Commission used thousands as fire-beaters, but their places in the strategically placed racks are now filled with a different kind.

To watch a man making a besom is to gain a false impression of his task. It all looks so easy; you just grab a bundle of birch cuttings, tie 'em up and ram a stick into the bundle—or so it seems. It's funny how unco-operative that wretched bundle can be in one's own hands. Among the 'primitives' it is a craft of considerable skill and not a few years of experience and woodcraft.

The best material for the heads is taken from the crowns of a seven-year plantation. Younger trees have too fine and thin a crown, but from the seventh year the birch will yield enough suitable brushwood. This cropping is usually done by a merchant who sells in quantity, all bundled, to the besom-maker, who builds up this supply into the stack we have noticed. The bundles are built up in layers, placed alternately across and lengthwise, each bundle head to tail with the next, so that everything beds down firmly into a rectangular mass, that will not collapse during seasoning. The stack is completed with a 'ridge' like a haystack, to carry off the rain and snow of winter. This work is done in the autumn, so that everything shall be ready by the following spring.

Early in spring the stack is opened and the bundles withdrawn as required. The cuttings are prepared for use with chopping and stripping-bittes for the coarse and finer work. The unwanted stuff from this operation is not wasted, but is later made up into bavins or faggots, to be sold as firewood. Country bakers like it for firing their ovens, as do farmers' wives. This preparation usually occupies an entire day to provide an ample supply for an unbroken spell of binding.

Binding the head of a Besom.   The method of stacking hazel

Making a Besom.

From long experience they know how much to gather for an 'armful', which is skilfully arranged so that the longer cuttings are in the centre. This is done, sitting astride a besom-horse, and facing a simple vice which can be closed and opened by foot-action. This vice holds one end of the binding material, which is wound around the stem-end of the head-to-be, at two places. The question of supply apart, besom-makers have various preferences concerning the best kind of binding. Some prefer willow or hazel, others like ash or oak. Any of these, when cleft into thin strips, will make a supple binding which has more 'life' and 'give' than the all-too-frequent wire. In some parts they like to use long strands of bramble or briar, which is shredded of its murderous thorns. The binding is secured by the same knot with which farmers secure sheaves of corn. The use of wire is comparatively recent.

Working with the first man, a second prepares the handles using ash for preference, or lime or hazel. Cut up into handle-lengths, the poles are prepared with various shavers. It is unnecessary to obtain 'finish' or dead-straightness. There is something about the 'feel' of a besom that is in keeping with the task it performs, and, of course, an 'unfinished' handle is less likely to slide out of the user's hands. The outer end is chopped to a blunt point, while the opposite head-end is given a gradual taper, both ends being done with a tool somewhat resembling a broad-axe. The blunt taper is made to prevent splitting when the other end is pushed into the besom-head and banged on the ground, the most effective method of putting the head on. Sometimes, they secure the head by knocking a slim, wooden peg into a hole drilled right through. A good man can make a besom-head in one and a half minutes.

The day's work is made up into bundles of a dozen, which are built up into a stack for storage, before dispatch. Besoms are made in several sizes, which are known by the circumference of the bound-head, 10, 11½ and 14 in. In some parts they make and use a variant of the type described. Like the besom, it has a head of birch, bound in much the same way, but is without a handle and is called a swale.

One may stand on the summit of Hindhead, in Surrey, and look down upon an extremely beautiful country. As the inquisitive eye looks about, an interesting pattern begins to emerge among all this Wealden complexity. In addition to the many houses of all shapes and sizes, one sees, here and there, a tiny cottage, mostly built in brick. The similarity among them is striking enough for comment. Until the turn of this century the Punchbowl was dotted with such cottages, for until then there was a population of some sixty people, following a way of life in surprising approximation to that of the crofters of Scotland. All but three of those cottages have disappeared. One is the Keeper's Cottage, where lives Mr Watkins, a one-time Navy man, turned landsman. His knowledge of nature is infinite. The second is now the Youth Hostel, and except for internal alterations, it is little changed. I write of a cottage, but, in fact, this was a 'terrace' of three, each of which was 'one down and one up'. The third, in a commanding position, has been considerably altered.

The people who had lived and worked here were the 'Broom Squires', a name that is sometimes loosely applied to all besom-makers, but my Hampshire informant had never heard of broom-squires. In this corner of Surrey, hard on London's busy doorstep, one may sense an echo from a long way back in history. Over this still wild heathland the road to Portsmouth has several times changed its course, uncertain, like a river.

MAKING FENCING, WEATHERBOARDING, SHINGLING

It has been customary to make field-gate posts of cleft and hewn oak. Such posts are 6–8 in. square and about 8 ft in length, of which some 3 ft are buried in the ground. A 'pyramid' top is left to enable rain to drain off rapidly. These posts are usually left rough and unhewn where they will be below ground, as this makes them 'bottom heavy' and gives them greater stability.

Bar or Rail Fencing

Cleft oak stakes are sufficiently strong that when their bases are axed to a fair point they may be driven into the ground without the preliminary of digging a hole. Gateposts, however, require a hole to be dug, as they are of larger section. Where wires are used they should be secured to the heart of the wood and not the sap. Such stakes, after cleavage, do not require creosoting, nor do they require a period of seasoning. End or corner 'strainer' posts are supported by diagonal struts, under compression, of similar sectional dimensions. Rail fencing usually consists of cleft or sawn oak posts set at 9 ft intervals, each mortised to take three rows of rails. These, likewise, are of cleft oak and about 10 ft in length with a diagonal cut across the ends so the meetings of the rails shall overlap within the mortise. Again such fencing, being of cleft timber, requires no treatment. The fencing must be put up section by section, so that the rails may be inserted in the mortises of the posts. Once in, they cannot possibly come out, or be extracted except by breakage.

Pale fence

This form of fencing requires the rail type as a foundation, on which a vertical row of thin pales is secured by pegging, each overlapping, in a manner similar to weatherboarding, but 'on it's side'. Though the pales, of best-quality oak, are 'wafer-thin', they make up a type of fencing far more durable than any ferrous type. Usually 5 or 6 ft high, they 'shut out' the outside world, a feature very much to be

Turning a rake-stail, making the tines and cutting them with a peg-knife

Weatherboarding on The Fox Inn, at Bramdean, near Alresford, Hampshire.

desired in many circumstances. Very often an additional lengthwise strip is added to the top to finish off this style, which, once erected and finished, will need no further attention for the next forty or fifty years.

The whole fencing is pegged, as is rail fencing. The pegs are of oak, square in section and knocked into round holes, an exception to the adage, because the corners of the square bite into the round walls of the holes. The entire process of making posts, pales, and rails is preferably one of cleavage, from the splitting of the 'round' into segments by beetle and wedge to the cleavage into strips by beetle and froe. These pales have to season, for which purpose they are closely bound into bundles, to resist any warping.

In Herefordshire, builders have traditionally made use of a form of paling to fill the interstices in half-timbered houses and barns. The resultant 'pattern' is similar to that of the punnets for strawberries. In the case of barns, this paling is left bare, but for houses it conforms to the principle of 'wattle and daub'.

Weatherboarding

Timber-framed houses and barns with 'weatherboard' or 'clapboard' facings have for centuries been built mainly in East Anglia, Essex, Hertfordshire, Middlesex, Surrey, Kent and Sussex. The timber used north of the Thames appears to have been principally elm, whilst the builders in the southern counties used oak.

In the case of elm, this was always prepared by the pit-sawyers, as elm will not cleave. The oak boards were usually cleft. Very often, the irregular 'waney' edge of the outside board, the board with the bark, was left by the pit men. It was usual to give the boards a thin edge and a thick, that is they were tapered in cross-section. This wedge-effect made the overlaps form better, the thick edge of each board being at the bottom and outside the thin top of the next board below. Nowadays the external faces of weatherboard walls may be either creosoted black or painted white, an external, linseed-based paint being used.

The resolute founders of the New England States took the idea with them, and brought it to an astonishing degree of beauty. Such buildings came to be accepted as the traditional style. In America, however, they used very fine softwoods, which were available to them in superabundance. The student of comparative styles and techniques will find many examples of adaptation of the original English to the new environment and materials of America. From ash to hickory and from elm to pine or chestnut and from yew to maple.

Shingling

As an alternative to roof tiling builders infrequently resort to 'shingling' with thin slats of oak. Usually each shingle is 12 in. deep by 8 in. wide and it is nailed to the roof battens in the same manner as slates. Here again a style of roofing found its way to New England, there to be greatly extended in usage. There, too, oak was replaced by red cedar. The Conestoga wagons brought back large consignments, much of which was exported to this country, where, in turn cedar has now replaced oak. The original oak shingles were all cleft with a 'shingling' froe, but the cedar shingles have always been sawn with a very fine circular saw.

MAKING CLOGS

In the Northern manufacturing towns, where *pavé* or stone setts have been universal, or on the mountain farms, it has long been customary to wear clogs for work. In primitive or extremely utilitarian standards of living clogs have been invaluable. In Holland and in France, as elsewhere on the Continent, clogs are worn by all farming people, who before entering their homes kick their clogs off and leave them on the threshold and 'go about the house' in heavily stockinged feet.

The traditional clogs of England, Wales, and Scotland consist of wooden soles of alder, and leather uppers which are strapped. Since the use of clogs is confined to Wales and the North, their manufacture is for the most part confined to these regions, though the craft has most certainly been carried on in other districts. Where the soil and the climate are favourable to the cultivation of coppice alder, in sufficient quantity, then it is an economic business.

The best material comes from poles which are 6–7 in. in diameter, at man-height from the ground. As with coppiced ash or hazel, these poles are the straight shoots from the stools, after cutting back. When suitable poles have been cut by felling they are cross-cut with a curious type of bow saw, which has a blade some 4 in. deep. This is worked by two men and converts the poles to short, workable lengths. These lengths are cleft down in rough shapes somewhat larger than the finished clogs. This stage is accomplished by beetle and short axe.

The shaping of clogs from these clefts is done with a stock knife, which is a remarkable instrument. It consists of a stout blade with a long projecting handle and is worked with a levering action. At the fulcrum end a hook engages with a steel eye fixed to a 'horse', which is a low kind of trestle. This stock-knife, ground very sharp, is essentially the same as the peg-knife used by a rake-maker for cutting the tines. The leverage gives a sensitive control in expert hands. The shaping process is all done with the stock-knife, and at the end of a day's work the soles are stacked in the form of a bee-hive, so that they may be properly ventilated. So stacked, the hives are left to season, during which phase they will dry right out and shrink slightly. The finishing touches can then be made with various knives.

The leather 'uppers' are secured to the soles by a row of metal studs and those clogs intended for the industrial use are fitted with steel plates. Both the French 'sabots' and the Dutch 'klompen' are made entirely of wood. This entails the scooping out of the interiors for the insertion of the feet.

The noise made by people wearing clogs on stone setts has inspired many 'clog-dances' from those parts both at home and abroad wherever clogs have been worn.

CHARCOAL-BURNING

When we have a bonfire of wood we find that the fire naturally leaves an outer ring of charred, unburned wood, and that when this charred stuff is thrown into the fire, it burns very hot and smokeless, with a short flame. The iron-masters at work before the Romans discovered this and applied it when they wanted the greatest heat possible in order to smelt the iron ore. When later they built furnaces with controlled, forced draught, even greater heat was obtained.

The use of charcoal for iron-smelting, the making of early steel and the fusion of the ingredients of glass and finally the production of gunpowder, continued unchallenged until the introduction of coke, which in turn gave still higher temperatures. We may note in passing that railway steam locomotives were fired with coke, until a satisfactory method of using certain grades of 'steam' coal were introduced.

In the beginning, the Iron Age masters produced a malleable iron which was forged by hammers into the tools and weapons of that time. Better furnaces and air-blast, enabled them to melt the iron so to draw it off into sand-moulds as pig-iron, for further reheating as required. Charcoal had, by this time, become the universal fuel in industry, which had arrived at a comparatively advanced state by medieval times, when water was the motive-power for operating the larger hammers, the equivalent of the modern drop-hammer. The mill-wheel shaft was fitted with a cam

Making clogs in the Severn-side woods of Shropshire.

Preparation for burning charcoal, in the old way,
in the Wyre Forest.

which, in rotation, raised a long beam at every turn. This beam was hinged at the far-end and carried the hammer at the rising and falling end. Control of the hammer was effected by opening and closing a sluice.

These early mills of the Weald were sited by streams which were dammed to provide a good head of water. The remains of these ponds may be found today, moss-grown and deep in the forests of Sussex. This industry lasted until, for several reasons, it gave place to the newer methods at Ironbridge and Sheffield. The inquiring traveller, aided by an Ordnance Survey map, may follow such clues as hammer-pond and furnace and spend happy hours 'digging'.

All the way through this long phase the charcoal-burners, almost a race apart in their forest-dwelling seclusion, were producing the fuel out of several kinds of wood. The best fuel of all was derived from alder buckthorn, though alder itself is quite unrelated to the buckthorn; to some extent oak and chestnut were also used.

The principle of charcoal-manufacture is that of heating wood in the absence of sufficient air to complete combustion. This eliminates all moisture and volatile elements, leaving a residue of black carbon in solid form. Charcoal is manufactured at the source of supply of the suitable wood, to obviate transport. After several months of seasoning, the wood is ready. A circular area in the clearing, some 15 ft in diameter, is prepared. In the centre a 'chimney' of split logs is arranged about a stake some 6 ft high. The logs to be charred are then placed around, sloping to the top. This is continued and so enlarged until a dome-like structure has been built up. The 'dome' is then covered with a deep layer of straw turfs and earth, to be followed by a second outer layer of logs, which are finally covered with leaves and earth. This shuts out almost all the air. The dome-like stack, now about 15 ft in diameter and some 5 ft in height, is ready for ignition.

The centre stake is withdrawn and some burning charcoal

is dropped down the 'chimney', followed by a few sticks of dry wood. When this is well alight the top is sealed, causing the fire to spread outwards. The process of charring occupies up to ten days, dependent upon conditions, and remains under the burner's continuous supervision, so he must live near by during the season, which occupies the whole of summer. He must take action if the wind should create undue draught or if lop-sided burning appears to be taking place, or if the fire should break through. From time to time he may dress the dome with more earth where a weakness might be developing. At one time, the charcoal-burner lived in a primitive cabin, constructed on the spot, but times change.

At the commencement of the process, the mound emits a great deal of white smoke, which soon gradually changes to a blue haze. This haze eventually dies away altogether. Experience tells the burner when the charring is completed. The mound is now uncovered with a rake and in so doing precaution must be taken against a flare-up, should the fire be still alive, and as a further precaution the charcoal is stored for a while before it is shovelled into sacks for dispatch. Charcoal-burners have, by calling, always been solitaries and are secretive about their work. Times change, and with the more modern methods of kiln-burning, only the principle remains. Modernization has, in some districts, been carried still further by wood-distillation, whereby all the volatile content, hitherto completely lost, can now be recovered—wood alcohol, acetic acid, tar, and creosote. Seven tons of wood will yield one ton of charcoal. In the best quality the granular structure of the log is more or less intact and the fuel is fairly clean to handle.

Supply and demand, the twin sisters who have provided most of the headaches and conflicts in history, seem to have reared their heads very much in regard to timber and who shall have priority—the shipbuilders, the glass-blowers, the iron-masters, or the makers of gunpowder. All made their demands and in the centre of this tussle stood the charcoal-burner, who was called upon to meet increasing demands in the face of legislation to conserve the best timber. Charcoal today is primarily an important ingredient in many things—in artificial silk, in ferrous metals, as a gas-absorbent and a heat-insulator, in the manufacture of deodorant, sugar, penicillin, and fertilizers.

6

Carpentry

THE CARPENTER

Perusal of the ledgers kept by a village carpenter will reveal the astonishing variety of activities in his business and indicate some of the things which an adaptable man can produce —travelling chests, ladders, cowstalls, doors, coffins, sash-windows, gates, staircases, pumps, all these and more, interspersed among a hundred and one 'bread and butter' jobs, often done at short notice, for it is to the carpenter that everyone goes for odd repairs in wood, as to the blacksmith for repairs in iron. Such men, whatever their craft, are the salt of the earth and a delight to meet and talk with.

In a carpenter's workshop we may note the variety of tools used and at the same time notice that while some of these tools are commonly used by any of the men others are the personal property of individuals, such tools as chisels, axes, and planes, that in years of use become so 'acclimatized' to their owners' hands, that they will not function in the hands of others. The handles and helves, especially, acquire indentations and a 'feel' that correspond to one pair of hands alone. This is especially so should a man be left-handed, and for this reason certain tools, such as axes and adzes, are made 'left-handed' and their edges ground accordingly.

Where a firm of carpenters and joiners has been long

established, through many generations, we are likely to find some real antiques in tools, some of them no longer to be found in the tool-makers' catalogues. An inquiry of these makers will elicit a great deal of information on such matters. Wooden stocks and their spoon-bits lie cheek-by-jowl with the modern ratchet-brace and 'twisty'-bit. Mr Capp, of Stewkley, near Leighton Buzzard, made his own rung-engines, in three sizes to give different tapers. They were very much better-made than the more familiar 'Stailengine', used for turning the handles of rakes and scythes. Mr Capp made his engines of box, I think, and finished them very well, with finely lathe-turned handles.

Out and about the yard stand butts of elm and oak, in rows of sawn planks, all ventilated for long seasoning by the long-established rule of a year for every inch of thickness, long enough for a pair of robins to have taken up residence and brought up several broods, long enough for the least-frequented and undisturbed part to have acquired an atmosphere of its own. Everything about the yard and the shop and the saw-pit, shallow-filled with darkened sawdust, the very tools and the speech of the men, all make short time of one generation. Here one will find a tangible link with a much older countryside.

Many of the tools, though made within the last fifty or hundred years, are likely to be much older in origin and and design, some indeed, such as the large frame saw, used at the pit, have stemmed from way back, even to the Conquest, and are distinguishable only by later refinements. These things belong to an age long before 'time and motion' study. There have been various methods of expediting timber conversion and there has even been some attempt, by artificial means, to speed up seasoning. Nature has not been conspicuously co-operateive in this matter and, in fact, has not modernized her ways in all the millenniums of her rule. You cannot compute the seasoning of timber, nor a crafts-man's satisfaction with his work, nor his ability to distinguish one wood from another, not by sight alone or direct touch, but by the transmission to his hands through the tool he is using. He may not know some tools by their sizes, in inches, but by the work they do, not as a one-inch bit but as a leg-bit, and so on. It is a little different now, in many respects, but the pride and skill remair .

Timber can be bought from the sawmill, or from the plantation as standing timber, or by auction before felling. In the first instance the buyer will select the timber in the sawn state, but by the latter methods he will inspect the trees before purchase. The larger and older the tree, the more mellow will the wood be and for some purposes can be left until a slight 'decaying' occurs, which, commencing at the base, will produce rich streaks, which they call 'figuring' and is much sought-after for furniture, but such wood cannot be used for exterior structural work. It can be used for furniture, and having a natural beauty will only have that beauty impaired by the super imposition of some forms of polishing which has been in vogue in the past. A staircase, having strings and risers of oak with elm treads, will look very well to the eye when finished with a wax-polish.

FIELD GATES

A well-made cleft-oak gate, untreated or unpainted, should with reasonable care outlast most of two generations of farmers. It is so designed and constructed that most of its weight falls at the hinge-end. When one looks at a gate in the closed position one notices that the hinge-post and the upright of the gate are not quite parallel. This is because the hingeing sets the post and upright a little further apart at the foot. When the gate is opened to a right-angle with the line of the fence or hedge, it should remain in that position, but given a push it should close of its own accord, whereupon the weight at the extremity will be taken by the catch-iron.

The man who makes gates may do his best and exercise every ingenuity, but farm usage is unavoidably rough, the fields uneven and often deeply rutted and hoof-trodden around a gate. Too frequently, the gate is neglected, or repair is put off for another day.

However much field gates may vary in detail arrangement of bracing, of hinges and catches, they are all the same basically. Two stout square-sectioned posts of oak stand a gate's width apart, having half their overall height sunk in the ground. This half is left untrimmed and in the natural form of the timber; this makes it bottom-heavy and much firmer in the ground. The gate itself consists of two uprights, a top rail and a brace, which runs diagonally from the foot at the hinge to a point about midway along the top rail. The great majority of gates have four rails below the top, a by no means inconsiderable minority have five below, and here and there, quite exceptionally, one may come across a gate with only three below. So we get the familiar five-barred gate, the less common six and the very rare four. Usually, these rails or bars are reinforced intermedially by two vertical braces and it is in the arrangement of this bracing that the great variation occurs. A 'double X' is extremely common, while in the Fishguard area of Pembrokeshire the bracing is arranged fan-wise.

The vertical at the hinge end, variously known as the harr, arr, or heel is $4\frac{1}{2}$ to 5 in. wide by $3\frac{1}{2}$ in. deep; the vertical at the latch-end, the toe, is usually $2\frac{3}{4}$ in. square. The top rail has an overall taper in both dimensions, the lateral thickness making it flush with heel and toe, but the vertical depth shows a more distinct taper from 5 to 3 in. The manner of the taper may vary from a straight line to some form of ornamented jowl close to the tips of the upper hinge-plates. The rails below are uniformly 3 in. deep by $\frac{7}{8}$ in. thick and are arranged closer together at the bottom in order to deter the youngest of lambs from exploring the great world that lies beyond. Farm dogs, of collie ancestry, can of course,

13 CARPET DESIGNED AND MADE BY WILLIAM
MORRIS   *Victoria and Albert Museum*

14 CUTTING OSIERS FOR BASKET-WORK *C. F. Snow*

15 STRIPPING THE WILLOW FOR BASKET RODS

C. F. Snow

16   MAKING A GATE-HURDLE   *Museum of English Rural Life*

17 MAKING A WATTLE-HURDLE

Museum of English Rural Life

18 USING A SHAVING HORSE FOR MAKING THATCHING SPARS

Museum of English Rural Life

19 STARTING A WELSH CROOK FROM THE ROOT OF
ASH   *Museum of English Rural Life*

20 FINISHING A WELSH CROOK

Museum of English Rural Life

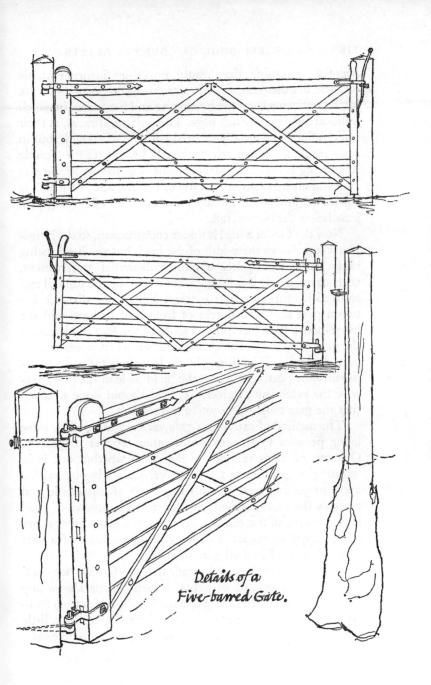

Details of a
Five-barred Gate.

negotiate anything that would prove an insurmountable obstacle to other animals. The various members of a gate are joined to the heel and toe by mortise and flat tenon, in which joints are secured by oak pegs. The rails and braces, at their intersections, are usually secured with clenched nails, but in some instances with small carriage bolts. Where the 'double X' bracing is used, the arrangement is to have a 'V' on one side and an inverted 'V' on the other, the apex of which is lap-joined flush with the top rail. Any kind of bracing projects below the bottom rail.

Now the foot of a heel is under compression, so the hinge-plates merely lap the width of the heel, but the head, being under tension, requires a more substantial arrangement, with straps nearly 2 ft long, extending along the top rail and secured by three or four carriage bolts. The distance between post and heel decreases from foot to head and the hinge-hooks therefore project more at the foot. This causes the gate to swing to the closed position when released from partial opening. The forged hooks have long tangs for banging into the post, and are on the 'field' side of the post, likewise the catch-iron, unless that field should slope so much that the gate must open out to the road.

The method of catching a gate varies considerably, some being peculiar to an area, while others appear irregularly. One can often determine by the catch whether one is in 'hunting' country or not, and the vertical spring-bar with a knob projecting well above the post is characteristic and perhaps the most efficient, but there are a number of good ideas in some of the catches. Even so, too many farmers are quite happy to secure a disintegrating remnant of a gate with a length of barbed wire or twine.

Field gates are commonly made in 'nine-foot' or 'ten-foot' widths, but a sample of actual measurements shows any width from 108 to 122 in., while the height varies from 38 to 46 in., and it may be noted that five barred gates are a little deeper than some six. Sometimes, one may find a double gate, essentially the same as a single, but having a greater overall width. Such gates are often secured by an iron loop, overlapping the toes of the two gates, being bolted to one and dropping over the second.

Unless gates are intended for a particular field, they are often made in numbers to standard sizes, during off-times. Traditionally, gates have always been made of oak, originally cleft, but latterly sawn, though one often comes across a cleft gate. They are untreated and unpainted, except in one or two areas such as West Pembrokeshire, where gates, ladders, farm doors and gambos are all painted orange. Some gates are now being made of soft wood, which must be creosoted.

WATER-PUMPS

Before they eventually turned to iron as a material, village pumps, the pumps in farmyard and cottage garden, were made of elm, as were the drain-pipes in the cities. They always had made them of elm, ever since men first applied the principle of raising water past one-way valves, by leverage or wheel. The vertical pipes of these pumps and the horizontal drainage pipes were fitted together by a water-tight conical joint, sealed with hot mutton suet. Most pumps were made in two sections, one above the other, and their meeting edges were coned to fit, the lower within the upper. The lower pipe had a two-inch bore and the upper one had a five inch, to accommodate the bucket.

They always looked for a good, clean butt of elm, clear of side branches, and boring commenced as soon as the tree had been thrown—or falled, or felled. Elm, the best wood for continuous immersion in water, will last far longer when bored in the sap condition. If it is left until after seasoning, cracks appear, which though of no account in structural work, would, of course, be disastrous for pipe work. At one time they squared the butt with adzes, but later they did this over a saw-pit. Squaring the butt provided stable baulk, and a clean face on which the line of the bore could be marked out with accuracy along two sides and the ends. The butt was raised on trestles and securely dog-spiked, on a slightly inclined plane, so that the 15 ft auger, set in line with the chalk-line centrings would have its handle set at a convenient working height.

Augers designed to bore parallel holes were of two kinds, the nose and the screw. The nose auger had to be 'started' by a 'centre' being made in the end face of the butt, with gouge and mallet, but once started would follow a straight line all the way, irrespective of any variation in the grain. On the other hand, while the screw auger would 'start' itself, its screw point tended to follow the grain. Any attempt to bore a 10 ft hole with a screw auger would have failed. The 15 ft shaft of the auger was mounted on its own horse and much preparation was necessary to 'sight' it with the chalk lines. Both the trestles and the horse were therefore made to massive proportions. Once the auger and lines had been correctly aligned, boring could commence.

The 5 ft handle gave a very good leverage, but it was a decided advantage to have two men on this long and arduous job. Every so often the auger head, was withdrawn, bringing with it an accumulation of shavings. Everything depended henceforth on accurate setting and once the head of the auger had disappeared in the depths of the butt there was no correction of any error. Each butt was bored from opposite ends, which met half-way with a tell-tale 'give' as the auger-head went through to the opposite bore. Like the men who bore tunnels, the meetings were never more than a trifle out. The top half of the pump had an initial boring of 2 in. diameter, and this was enlarged to 5 in., in two stages, the intermediate being about $3\frac{1}{2}$ in. This enlargement was made with tapered auger-heads, and to provide for these changes the heads were made detachable from the shaft.

Near the top of the upper pipe a tapered hole for the elm

spout was made and on the opposite side a slot for the handle was made. The lower half had a series of holes—small enough to keep out frogs—driven in above the sill-line. At the top of the lower half, inside its junction with the top, a one-way valve was placed. The bucket, likewise of elm, was made to a very close fit within the 5 in. bore. The water drawn through its centre was captured by a leather flange and retained by means of a lead clack. The bucket was turned to shape on a lathe and finished with chisels.

Positioning and erection of a pump was always carried out when the well was low. When all construction was complete and all the iron-work made by the blacksmith was fitted together, the pump was given an initial priming, and then, if it drew water which then died away to a trickle, all was well; but if during pumping the water stopped, then there was something wrong. In fact, the work was done methodically and with such care that such a thing rarely occurred.

The depth of these wells naturally varied, depending on the source of water, but unless the well exceeded about 20 ft, the pump was made in two parts, as described. But if the depth exceeded 20 ft, then the pump was made in three lengths, with the two lower ones identical in bore. In Shropshire these pipe-lengths are called 'trees'. It was not uncommon, in those parts where the elm flourished in numbers, for a tree to be selected from the farm-land itself, and so there was many a farm which had provided the timber for its pumps. The pump was a utilitarian piece of machinery, but that did not preclude some ornament on the 'jowl' which contained the fulcrum of the handle, which in turn often had some slight elaboration made by the blacksmith. It should be noted that a wooden pump or pipe was not subject to freezing during winter.

LADDERS

The man at the top of a fifty-rung ladder, or higher still at the top of a billposter's extension ladder, is obviously in a position to tell you whether an alloy ladder is better than one of wood. At best, an aluminimum alloy is a 'dead' metal, and some spring and life is a decided merit in any ladder taller than the relatively short ones of say twelve rungs.

Unless a ladder is made to be extended, in which case the sides must be parallel, it is made with a gentle taper from about 18 in. in width at the foot to about 13 in. at the top. This makes a ladder 'bottom heavy' and therefore easier to handle. The peculiar ladders used especially by the Kentish fruit-growers have a pronounced 'splay' at the foot, to about 36 in. These ladders are also more slender than the conventional type used by builders. The splayed foot provides for stability, where the placing of ladders is usually quite difficult, with the top of the ladder resting among the branches. Further, with a such a ladder, the fruit pickers can lean freely to either side, to collect the crop without fear of the ladder turning over.

It is customary to make the sides of spruce or Norwegian pine. A good, straight tree is sawn down lengthwise to produce two lengths, of hemispherical section. The flat, inner faces are planed smooth, but the curved outer faces are left with the bark intact in order to protect the wood during assembly. At 9 in. intervals holes for the rungs are marked off, with the two sides placed together, and then drilled with a tapered auger. The rungs, or rounds, as they are often known, are cleft from well-seasoned oak, though beech may sometimes be used. Each roughly cleft rung, is drawshaved and then finished with an 'engine' or box plane which is rotated around the rung to plane it smooth. Before assembly, it has always been customary to dry the rungs right out by leaving them exposed for several days, to ensure that no further shrinkage will take place after assembly.

One of the sides is laid, outer face down, upon two or more trestles, according to length, to provide a firm support at working height. We shall soon see why the bark has been left on, because by the time twenty or thirty rungs have been knocked in the bark will be appreciably bruised. Dropping the second side over the ends of the rungs is a task for three men, two to hold the side at each end and the third to ease the rungs into their holes, one by one along the ladder's length. When the two sides have been driven right home with a mallet, they and the exposed tips of the rungs can be cleaned up with a drawshave, which, of course, removes all the bark. At intervals of every six or eight rungs screwed iron stays are added, just underneath the adjacent rungs. These stays ensure that the ladders shall stay tight. The colours chosen for ladders appear to be determined by tradition and precedent. They may therefore be red, green, orange, or blue. We may take a cue from builders by storing our ladder either by several hooks along a wall or on several tie-beams of the shed-roof.

Ladder-makers may tell us, with a twinkle in the eye, that their products are priced at a farthing for the first rung, and double for each successive rung', but in fact there are two rates, one for ladders up to thirty rungs, and a second, usually half as much again, for ladders of over thirty rungs.

In times past a good carpenter and joiner could make the simpler furniture which country people could afford, though the further we journey back in time the more sparsely do we find homes to be furnished. What may appear now to be a sometimes 'crowded' room, was in those times much more roomy. A chest, a table, and several stools were sufficient for the needs of those days. Such furniture was well made and passed down from generation to generation. The later cabinet-maker would play no part in this order. Even later, when rural life was little affected by the Renaissance, the village carpenter continued to supply domestic needs.

7

Chair-Bodging

Chair-bodger—what a queer name for a sensitive if primitive craftsman. However one considers it, there seems to be a derogatory implication. Quite simply, a chair-bodger is a man who, 'on the spot', in the beech plantations of the Chilterns, produces all the turnery, the legs, spars and stretchers which are part of chairs of the Windsor style.

His raw material is beech, which by its nature turns very well when green, which enables him to cut and turn newly felled timber. Bodgers usually work in pairs, one chopping up the 'billets', the short logs, into suitable pieces for the second man, who works at the lathe. Like the hurdle-makers, they work at the source of supply, as this greatly simplifies their work. When one plantation has been 'worked out', they move to the next plantation, taking with them the lathe, the tools—very few—and the grindstone when they 'set up' again, as before.

It has been usual for the owner of the plantation to arrange for the felling and the lopping and topping. Such timber is worked on the 'selection' system, whereby, instead of a whole wood being cleared the trees suitable for work are selected for felling. The result of this is that in any plantation one will find trees at all ages of growth, intermingled, the older giving shelter to the seedlings. This type of woodland, of tall straight beeches, is characteristic of the Chiltern

Hills for many miles about the centres of the chair industry, High Wycombe, Stokenchurch, and Penn.

The first stage is of secondary conversion, from the felled tree to lengths of about 2 ft or so, by means of a two-man cross-cut saw. To raise a felled trunk to 'sawing-height' necessitated the use of the simplest form of leverage and inclined plane. This consists of two logs 7 or 8 ft. long, one end on the ground and the further supported on two short legs of about 18 in. The trunk is levered up this incline to the top, where it is held by pegs knocked into holes.

The sawn lengths are split into halves and quarters with beetle and froe and further reduced with a short-handled broad-axe into pieces suitable for legs, spars, and stretchers. These operations preserve the grain by cleavage and require a fine judgement to avoid waste. After chopping to a polygon, each piece is rendered approximate to the round by draw-shaving on a 'horse', which has a foot-controlled vice. And so, stage by stage, each piece of wood is transferred from the rough billet to the shape ready for the lathe. A good supply for the turning is always prepared to obviate any interruption.

The pole lathe is probably the oldest form of rotating device for turning. It must have well preceded the wheel lathe, which has a continual rotation, as long as the treadle is operated. The pole lathe has a treadle and a long pole, often of larch, having a strong spring in it. This is anchored at the butt-end and at a midway point it rests on a cross-piece, leaving the far end free. This end is joined to the tip of the treadle by a hemp rope, which is wound twice around the piece of beech to be turned. Now, as the treadle is depressed, against the spring of the pole, the wood is rotated 'toward' the turner and on release the pole rises, causing rotation to be reversed, 'away' from the turner. This means that all cutting or turning is made on the down stroke and the tool then withdrawn on the upward stroke. One might think it to be time-losing and less efficient than the continuous rotation of the wheel lathe, but the answer is partially in the aptitude of the bodgers. Most turners consider the pole lathe to be more sensitive, others prefer the wheel. Certainly the man who made the Windsor described later used a wheel lathe, as do most bowl-turners.

The lathe-bed consists of two baulks of timber, about 6 ft in length and 2 or 3 in. wide by 4 or 5 deep. These are securely bolted to two stout sets of uprights. The head and tail stocks, actually called poppets, of wood, have long pegs projecting down between the bed and can be adjusted. The left-hand poppet has a fixed mandrel, but the right-hand has its mandrel adjustable on a screwed rod with a handle on its extremity. As with all other kinds of lathe, there is a long bar along the front—the turner's side—on which his left hand rests while holding the cutting-tool near the ferrule—if it has one—while the right-hand maintains the sensitive leverage.

To watch a chair-bodger producing leg after leg with accuracy is an inspiration, like watching a blacksmith working on wrought iron, the more valuable as our environment is year by year encroached upon. Four or five types of cutting-tool are used; a deep gouge taking the first cut. The full width of the stick, leaving a coarse thread which is removed by a broad flat chisel ground with a slightly curved edge. The traditional rings, grooves, and bevels are marked with a parting chisel and formed with a narrow deep gouge and the parting chisel. Deep cuts are made with a skew chisel and the whole leg is finished off with the broad-chisel. A competent man can produce over 800 units a week, which means something like one unit leg or stick every four or five minutes. The bodger has the invaluable asset possessed by all craftsmen in that he can, at will, vary the patterns of his work, adding a little more bulge or taking a bit more out. That's how these traditional patterns acquire their regional characteristics.

At the end of a day at the lathe the pieces are stacked

four-square for seasoning and drying. Bodgers have always been specialists in making these turned parts; they have never made the complete chairs. To do this would entail a complete departure from the extreme mobility of their craft method, for in one sense they are almost nomads.

8

Making Windsor Chairs

The more one searches for the origins of this type of chair and investigates its history, the more one meets with evidence which tends to conflict. The suggestion that George III sat in one whilst sheltering in a house from a storm, may be placed with other apocryphal stories having much the same ingredients—a king, sometimes in disguise; a storm; and a poor man's cottage. In any case, these chairs were known as such some fifty years before George III became king.

The most sophisticated furniture of the seventeenth century was still fairly heavy and cottage furniture was correspondingly crude. By the general arrangement and the method of construction, the Windsor is likely to have had its origin somewhere in the latter part of the seventeenth century or the beginning of the eighteenth. The presence of cyma curves and the air of tightness seem characteristic of that period.

Until comparatively recently, the Windsor has always been a piece of 'cottage' furniture, rarely to be found in an environment more sophisticated than that of the moderate-sized farm-house. The elements were simple and could not have come out of the workshops of the cabinet-makers. With or without side-arms, it was clearly the work of the best carpenters, who were well equipped with tools and ability to make the simple styles of furniture. Since there is not a straight line in the entire chair, except the centre-lines of

Adzeing the seat
of a Windsor Chair.

legs and stretchers, a high standard of skill in manufacture has been demanded and therefore still is, since the tools and methods have not changed.

One has but to consider an armchair made by the best of craftsmen, to examine the seat and be surprised by an illusion of thinness produced by some skilful adzing and chamfering. That same chamfering, or bevelling, which on the old farmwagons not only made them appear lighter but did, in fact, eliminate as much as one-eighth of the original weight, though weight is not a factor in the matter of chairs.

One should cite the authority of F. Gordon Rowe, F.S.A., F.R.H.S., in definition of a Windsor Chair 'as a stick-back, wooden-sealed chair, with turned or plain legs inset to the seat, and often (though not necessarily) having a decorative splat in the back. The seat is frequently shaped, and more or less saddle-formed . . . back and legs alike are plugged into the seat.'

The best factories in High Wycombe are equipped to produce very good factory-made chairs, but with all the ingenuity in the world it is impossible to imitate the handmade Windsor—impossible, both mechanically and economically. It is the old story of the attention at every stage which the craftsman naturally gives. Made by machine, the seats appear thicker and are, the back- and arm-bows are thicker and square in section. The splats are elementary and lack the delicacy in the open work and they are left unchamfered. Recognizing this, one of the largest manufacturers has produced a range of chairs which is derived from the Windsor theme, in terms of the present techniques.

Windsors have been produced in such a variety of designs, in which the salient features have been cleverly interchanged, as to require consideration as a family. There are bow-backs, fan-backs, and comb-backs. The space in the back may be filled with a central splat and sticks to either side, varying in number, or there may be sticks alone, or splats alone. The designs of the splats are subject to considerable variation. The arm-bows may be continuous through the back, from side to side, or may simply project from each side of the back. The tips of the arms may be supported by a turned baluster or a plain stump which curves to form a point with the arm. All four legs may be turned, or the front alone turned and the back plain or thirdly, the front may be 'cabriole' and the back plain. The leg—stretchers may be arranged on the conventional 'H', or have the peculiar deep arc which joins the front legs, with plain short stretchers to the back. From three basic designs, there have derived a remarkable number of variations.

Contemporary with the English chair-makers, those of the New England states of America went very much further and because Windsors were very much in vogue during the eighteenth and nineteenth centuries they were to be found in the homes of some of America's most famous people. The makers went further, too, in producing various widths of settee, some of which had ten or even twelve legs, office chairs and cradles, according to the regional variations of the Windsor theme. While the overall proportions of the English chairs showed little variation, many American designers let themselves go. Some chairs were lighter and more graceful, while others tended to be much heavier, having legs and stretchers extremely bulbous and more acutely set, further in from the edge of the seat. Some had quite high backs, but all had the front legs projecting as much forward as the hind did backward. (English chairs all have their front legs at nearly right-angles to the seat.) Some of the American variations departed so far from the originals that, placed side by side, the family kinship seems very distant. Some of their makers may have seen few originals, but depended on a tenuous link, running through half a dozen states. A curious feature is in the finish they were almost invariably painted in various colours, thus obliterating the grain of the wood, whereas the English were either stained and glossy-polished—not French—or given a satin-wax finish which enhances the grain of the wood. This latter is a characteristic of the hand-made chair. Incidentally, factory-made chairs are often dispatched for later finishing, 'in the white' they call it.

Some of the features which distinguish a hand-made chair from a factory-made have been mentioned. The greater subtlety of line, the use of chamfering. There are differences in the woods used. Hand-made chairs may consist of yew, elm, beech, apple, walnut, oak or cherry. For the sake of the beauty of such woods, a satin-wax finish is fully justified. In the original 'cottage' furniture the woods used were elm for the seat, beech for all turned parts, oak for the splat, and yew for the bows. One may well imagine a customer and a maker having a chat about furniture the outcome of which was some departure from normal practice. It will be appreciated that however much the chair-bodger contributed he was not equipped to make a complete chair.

A well-made armchair has its seat so well shaped and the angles and distances of seat, back, and arms, the legs so nicely positioned, that the resultant chair is an extremely comfortable piece of furniture. A demonstration of this was afforded one when Mr Goodchild invited me to sit in two chairs he had made. One was as just described, but the second was what he delightfully called a guest-chair.

The tools used are developments of some of those used by the village carpenters, the men who often made farm-wagons, or who worked in association with the wheelwrights. Most of the tools came not from the big Midland or Sheffield tool-makers but were the joint products of the local black-smith and the carpenter, who turned up the wooden handle or the body, and the smith forging the blades to suit the individual user. These smiths, by making a spoon-bit or a drawshave, could get just that edge that made all the difference. Between them, smith and carpenter produced many a

tool not shown in the catalogues of the big makers. Even today, a Welsh bowl-turner has his peculiar 'outside' and 'inside' knives forged with a curl to his liking, the result of 'trial and error' between himself and the smith. Certain manufacturers, such as Henry Taylor, of Sheffield, specialize in making the complete range of wood-carver's chisels and gouges. But spoon-bits were the especial pride of some of those local smiths, who seemed able to overcome one of the defects of this tool, that of loss of diameter after repeated sharpening. They are forged in a number of sizes and each is fixed permanently in its own stock. Chair-makers say that such a tool is quicker in use and more responsive than the ratchet-brace into which a whole range of detachable bits can be fitted.

The use of a spoon-bit requires considerable pressure from the chest. A 'breast-bib' is worn, a broad piece of wood, curved to fit the chest and held there by strings around the neck and back. In the centre of the bib is a cup-like recess to receive the head of the stock. In the factories, the breast-bib was something of a 'badge of office' of the framers, who worked exclusively on framing. The bib was worn at all times.

The adze is as old as the axe and the type used by chair-makers is of great interest. The head is weighty and the blade turns up to a shallow concave and is maintained razor-sharp. This head, on a longish two-handed haft, gives a nice 'pendulum' swing that greatly assists in hollowing out the seat. One need not be a 'craftsman' to know the pleasure of using a tool that has served one well. The haft, in a lifetime of use, has long lost that 'shop-new' feel and has acquired the silken surface from use in warm, moist hands.

This chair-maker's adze, then, is used to shape the seat from the $1\frac{1}{2}$ in. blank. It's all done by sight, but the seat is not finished to its final smoothness. Instead, the legs and stretchers are fitted, when the seat is said to be 'legged up'. Smoothing off follows with a succession of shavers:—the

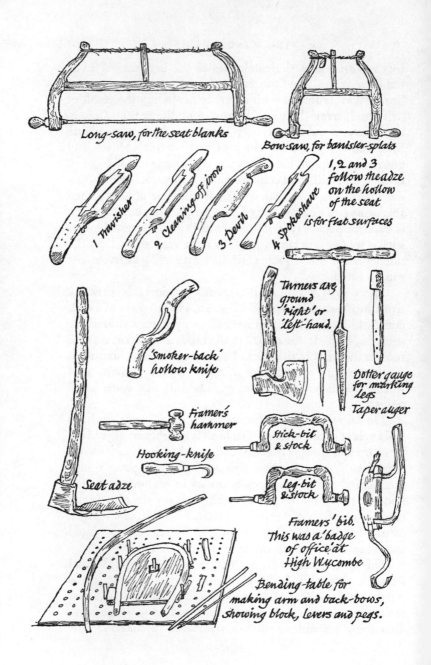

Long-saw, for the seat blanks

Bow-saw, for banister-splats

1 Travisher

2 Cleaning-off iron

3 Devil

4 Spokeshave

1, 2 and 3 follow the adze on the hollow of the seat

is for flat surfaces

'Smoker-back' hollow knife

Turners axe, ground 'right' or 'left'-hand.

Dotter gauge for marking legs

Taper auger

Framer's hammer

Hooking-knife

Stick-bit & stock

Leg-bit & stock

Seat adze

Framers' bib. This was a 'badge of office' at High Wycombe

Bending-table for making arm and back-bows, showing block, levers and pegs.

travisher, the smoothing-off iron and a devil, and a fourth tool, which may be described as a hybrid between spokeshave and the jarvis used by wheelwrights. This is a smoker-back hollow knife for shaving the hind side of bows.

Most craftsmen in wood, who have to bend it to a required shape, do this in two stages. First, the wood is rendered pliable by steaming, then it is either placed in a setting-frame, as with scythe-snaithes, or to straighten out bends on a brake. The bows are made of yew or ash and a more persuasive method is employed. A pattern blank of the inside contour of the bow, is bolted to a square, cast-iron plate, in which holes have been drilled on a squared pattern. The piece of yew or ash, is secured at one corner of the blank and coaxed by levers to the contour, and the whole is secured. It is usual to make a number of bows in one go, and this batch is stored together. As with any steamed wood, the shape is retained when 'cold'.

All bows are drilled to accept the back sticks. In the type of armchair most commonly to be found there are four long sticks and four short on each side, the long running the full heights of the back and the short ones stopping at the arms. All must be set equidistant or the appearance will remain constantly offensive to the eye. The banister-splat, present in some designs but not in others, is of oak or walnut and the design is cut out with a fret-saw. These designs are traditional, the 'wheel' being, perhaps the best known and most widely used. Others echo a Gothic tracery and all some skill in order to retain the symmetry of pattern. In the hand-made 'wheel-back' there is the vestigial hub in the centre, but for economy this is absent from the factory-made splat, as is the delicate bevelling on the back edges. One should look, too, for a bead all along the back bow edge. Some Windsors have their backs composed of a top piece like the back of a comb, supported by three identical splats in which an 'urn' motif has been incorporated in the design.

The seat, then, is the heart of the matter and the foundation of a good chair. Elm is chosen as it responds to the adze and is not prone to splitting; inferior wood has a tendency to warp, which is why a cheap chair will sometimes 'rock' diagonally. Look at a really good seat and see how many straight flat surfaces there are.

9

Farriery

In the beginning, in Celtic times, the farrier and the iron-worker at the anvil were one and the same person, although the two activities were separate crafts, each eventually requiring specialist attainments.

In addition to the work at the anvil, the farrier must possess knowledge both of the anatomy of the horse and of the differences between horses used for draught and for riding, whilst the shoeing of race-horses is even more specialized.

Basically, farriery has changed little since Roman times. What has changed is the shape of the shoe and a visit to a museum such as the Curtiss, at Alton, in Hampshire, will show the evolution. Shoes made by the Romans and the Romano-Celts were secured by three nails a side in counter-sunk holes, the making of which produced bulges. There was a calkin or cork at both points. During medieval times, and the Tudor period the shoe became flatter and broader. It was assymetrical and broader on the outerside, which retained the cork, while the inner tip lost its wedge. During the period down to the seventeenth century shoes developed a shape more like the present form, regaining the inner cork. The seventeenth-century farriers introduced the groove, which was not yet continuous; curiously, the cork was usually absent from both points. This design was shortly followed in the same century and the eighteenth by a

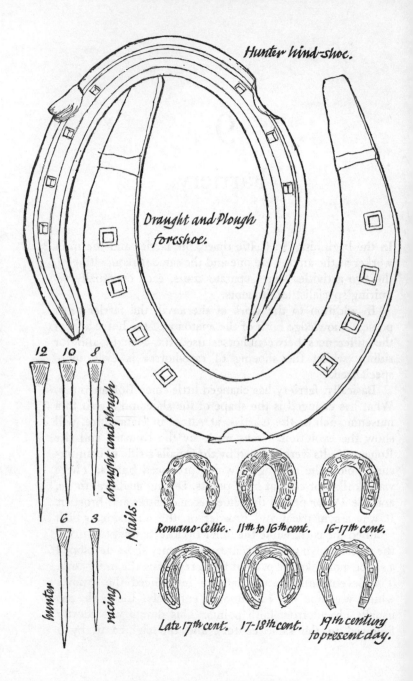

Hunter hind-shoe.

Draught and Plough foreshoe.

Nails.

12 10 8 — draught and plough

6 3 — hunter — racing

Romano-Celtic.   11th to 16th cent.   16-17th cent.

Late 17th cent.   17-18th cent.   19th century to present day.

'spatulate' appearance which contained an inner 'keyhole', and the groove was now continuous. It was at the beginning of the nineteenth century that the shoe attained finality in two forms—the draught-shoe, flat and rather broad, with no groove but an outside cork. The front clip was introduced to provide increased stability on the hoof. The riding shoe was made, as now, in various weights with a continuous groove. The clip was on the front for fore-shoes, but in order to avoid damage by the hind-hoof, at the gallop, the hind-shoe had one clip, each side, toward the front.

THE ANVIL

The English anvil has a flat, rectangular top surface, which extends to the left, to form the tapering, square-ended 'wedge'. The right-hand end is known as the 'beak' and has a roughly conical taper, the centre-line of which points up, to form a straight horizontal line from wedge to point of beak. Now the Roman anvil had no beak, so that it was not easy to remove the nail-hole swellings. In fact, this beak was not introduced until the late thirteenth century. An anvil weighs a little over 2 cwt and when tapped produces a bell-like note, which is music to the smith and indeed to anyone who can appreciate pleasant sounds. The block on which the anvil rests, is always of oak or elm, to give a bit of 'life', or the anvil would be 'dead', as a concrete road is dead.

The farrier may forge the complete shoes from the straight bar as received from the iron foundry, either flat or with groove, or he may buy shoes in various sizes already made. Such shoes require further work on the anvil to fit them to the individual horse. All this forging is done with a 'catshead' hammer, which is double-headed, one flat, the other convex. On each side of the head, next the haft-hole, are webs for making the clips. This clip, providing stability on the hoof, is of particular benefit to the heavy draught-horse in starting.

And when canal boats were horse-drawn the horse dug all four hoofs into the tow-path, putting all its weight against the tow-line in starting the boat.

Shoe weights vary. Those for heavy draught weigh about 4 lb apiece and are secured by four nails a side. Shoes for riding weigh from 14 to 9 oz and are secured by four nails on the outside and three on the inside. Shoes for a donkey have the points a little extended and turned slightly out. Likewise, there are various sizes of nail. No. 12's, for a plough-horse are 3 in. long. No. 6's for a hunter are $2\frac{1}{8}$ in. long and those for a race-horse, No. 3's, are only $1\frac{3}{4}$ in. long.

SHOEING

When a horse is brought in for shoeing the farrier must examine all hoofs, fore first so that the horse will not be nervous—it has already become familiar with the smells and sounds of the smithy. A particular 'nervy' horse must be felled and secured, and in Holland they still use a framework called a 'Hoefstal'. The farrier is usually assisted by a second man, called a 'doorman', who prepares the hoof. For this reason, a horse or pony which has never been shod is taken to the smithy with an experienced animal so that it may become accustomed to these strange surroundings. When its own turn does come, next time, it will not be difficult to handle, but will respond to the persuasive hands of the farrier.

The previously clinched ends of the shoe-nails are knocked off with a buffer and the nails withdrawn heads first with pincers. The hoof is rasped and picked clean with the buffer-point and pared with a special knife. Now the new shoe is tried for fit, as we try ours, and then fairly black-heated and held to the hoof to 'seat' it. The hoof is insensitive to this and the resultant clouds of smoke cause no alarm. It is especially at this stage and following, that the unshod young horse can become acclimatized.

The cold shoe is nailed on with a smallish shoeing hammer, starting from the front, then the nails are clinched at the points where they protrude. The farrier now runs his hand down from the hind-quarter to the hind-hoof which the horse, comprehending, will lift. Very often the farrier has had to work in the cold darkness of an early winters morning so that the horse shall be ready for the day's work. All the tools for the job are kept in a special box and never removed for any other purpose. The box contains hammer, pritchel, buffer, paring-knife, pincers and, of course, a supply of nails. A farrier knows all the farmers and people riding horses in his locality and keeps a stock of shoes in readiness for future shoeing, so that when a horse is brought in he has only to take a set down and get to work.

When shoes are made from the bar measurements of the hoofs are taken. The required length is cut off with a 'cold sett' and heavy sledge. The hot iron is forged on the anvil with the catshead. In the 'good old days' they even made the nails. Nail-holes are made with a pritchel, a kind of punch.

In the days when oxen were used for draught, they, too, were shod. But an ox has a cloven hoof, so the shoe had to be in two parts; these were fairly broad, thin plates which turn up on the inner sides, they were secured by three, four or sometimes five nails, which were short and broad-headed. The whole business of shoeing differed, if only because oxen are not like horses, either in anatomy or in temperament. Oxen also had their own type of harness, which is dealt with in the chapter on harness.

THE SMITHY

When we step into the interior of the smithy we may see little at first but the glowing hearth at the back. This hearth is usually constructed of brick with a flue at the back. It is about 6 ft × 4 ft and some 3 ft 6 in. high. The draught can be adjusted most sensitively by the old-fashioned bellows, though some smiths use a mechanical fan. The bellows, in capable hands, will keep the fire just as it is wanted, for too much air will 'blow the coal away'. To get the fire right he may sprinkle a little water and he will frequently use his queer little shovel which he calls a slice. What the smith likes is a clean steady glow that only dies away while he is working at the anvil and quickly responds to resumed work with the bellows.

At the front of the hearth, opposite to the chimney-end, there is a rectangular tank of water, sometimes called a 'bosh' —though I believe this to be 'Hertfordshire'. Any quenching of iron is done here, and of course, it is useful for cooling down tongs and other tools. All these tools are kept on a long rod along the front of the tank, but swages, flatters, and fullers all hang separately from an overhead position, on a beam.

A blacksmith requires a considerable range of tools and appliances, some of which, the anvil, mandrels, and hammers, are supplied by the big firms. The various tongs, on the other hand, are often made by the smith himself, to his own ideas, and it is better to follow his ancestors. This variety of tongs is necessary to provide satisfactory holds on iron, hot or cold, often of quite awkward shape. Some tools were made by 'travelling' smiths, men put out of normal business, but whose skill remained a by-word.

Stocks of iron, in various sizes of round and square and in sheet, will be found in the yard, and sundry 'old iron' lying in the corner in a tangled heap. To the uninitiated eye this may appear a confusion, but the smith has his own index, his memory, and usually knows just where to lay his hands on 'that bit of iron'.

With the almost complete mechanization of agriculture, the smith's 'day-to-day' work has changed to fit the new pattern, so in a separate shop we shall find power drills and an oxy-acetylene plant. However, the craft of smithing is not involved in this side. The metal used is normally

wrought-iron, or alternatively mild steel. Mostly, they prefer the 'grainy', plastic quality of wrought-iron, which makes it easier to handle. Its fibres lie in one direction and its strength lies along the fibres. Mild-steel is non-fibrous and equally strong in any direction and in its thinner sections of bar or rod may be bent when cold.

When wrought-iron is 'cherry-red', it may be bent, twisted, and hammered. At 'white-heat' it may be 'upset', 'drawn down', more extensively hammered. The 'grain', fibres or laminae must be preserved by forge-work. To turn down any part, on a lathe, would destroy the laminae. Mild steel, however, may be so turned.

The main processes of a smith's work are drawing down, upsetting, bending and twisting, punching and welding. When a smith reduces the thickness of a bar he draws it down, but to increase the thickness the bar is upset. The first is done with fullers and flatters, for flat bars, and with swages for round bars. Upsetting is done simply by striking the white-hot iron vertically end on to the anvil. Simply, that is, to the smith; I might try this and do no more than upset myself. Fullers, flatters, and swages are always in pairs; a top fuller, etc., in its own tongs, and an anvil fuller, which fits into a square hole in the anvil. Upsetting produces a thickening in any selected part of a bar. Any kind of bending is done either on the anvil at the wedge or beak end, or on the cone-like mandrel.

The lovely spirals in decorative work are made by twisting the bar from one end against the secured further end. The spiral is found in not a little of the work on field gates and wagons as well as purely ornamental work. This treatment may be rendered in the single square bar or in a bundle of bars, welded at each end and then cut off after twisting. But it requires considerable skill to obtain an even twist throughout and to keep the bar or bundle in a straight line. The remaining process is that of welding, or the joining together permanently of two pieces into one. Both pieces are brought to a white plastic heat, on the hearth, at the point of junction and hammered together on the anvil.

In addition to the spirals, all those scrolls and ornamental ends, leaf and hinge-work are executed by the processes described. The finest scroll-work has continuous curves and volutes which are transitional and are without those dreadful 'straights' which occur just where a nice transition should be.

In all these operations the smith must avoid 'burning' the iron by excessive heat. The sparks should not fly from a good hearth and it is in this that careful blowing with the bellows is so important. When the smith and his 'drummer' are working together at the anvil they do so by understood signals. A 'bouncing' hammer blow on the anvil is the signal to 'turn the iron over', without loss of rhythm, and when work is to stop for more firing the smith lets his hammer fall on the anvil. Bars can be severed by the use of 'setts' which are struck with a sledge. A 'hot-sett', comparatively slender, for the white-hot bar. A blunter 'cold-sett' for bars when cold.

The blacksmith, all through the centuries, has been the most important of the village craftsmen, for in the days before Birmingham, the Black Country, and Sheffield, it was the village smith who made all the hundred and one tools, especially the edge-tools, used by the other craftsmen, particularly those working in wood and stone.

10

Wrought-iron Work

The best men of today are well enough equipped in technique and aesthetics to be able to produce decorative and useful iron-work which is comparable with that of the past masters. It needs but the customer, who may sometimes be the business firm, to replace the medieval church.

While we are still in the smithy we may be able to follow the procedure in making a gate. From the original drawing, approved by the customer, a full-scale working drawing is prepared on paper, the back of which is afterwards rubbed with fine chalk. A tracing is now made on to a large flat sheet of 'rusty' steel. This surface will 'take' the impression clearly. Sometimes, the smith will draught a design straight on to the steel sheet with his chalk stick, after setting out the main structure of the gate.

The main elements of such a gate are the two uprights, called the back stile—the hinge side; and the front stile or toe bar—the latch side. The cross-pieces are rails or bars, top, middle, and bottom, or heel bar. The space between is filled with a number of uprights according to the size of the gate. At the bottom are additional 'dog bars'. The usual method of hinging such a gate; especially the largest gates, is by a journal at the top and a turning-cup at the bottom and the tail of the journal must be set in a stone or brick pillar. It is the usual practice to put a knuckle or heel on the bottom bar, where it meets the back stile, as a reinforcement.

Inn-sign bracket at Broseley, Salop

THE
NEW
CROWN

FREE HOUSE
A E DROMGOOLE

Garden gate made at Barley
Hertfordshire

WEST
HOATHLY

LONDON 38
TURNERS HILL 3
WYCH CROSS 4½

Village Sign
Sussex

THE
GEORGE
W. COLLINS

Balustrade over porch, at Winslow, Bucks

Some smiths rivet the framework, others weld it.

For all exterior work the iron must be protected against the elements and no expense is therefore to be spared. All rough scale is removed, likewise any rust. Then follows a priming coat, consisting of red-lead powder, gold size and turpentine, which dries matt. This is followed by an undercoat of flat lead-paint. There is a choice of several top coats, of which Berlin Black is the best known.

Indoor work and domestic appliances such as fire-irons and various kinds of bracket may be finished in the same manner or what is called 'armour bright'. This is much favoured, as it enhances the appearance of the metal, just as a satin-wax polish does woodwork. This finish is obtained by 'pickling' in an acid bath to remove all the scale from the iron. Work at the anvil must be done with a clean fire and hammer and anvil with smooth faces, free of dirt and scale. The iron-work is further cleaned with wire brushes, and washed. Polishing with emery follows all this and the work is completed by lacquering.

The modern smith obtains his iron in bar form, more or less ready for use. This has been so since the fourteenth century, before which time the smiths had to beat out bars. It is the resultant unevenness of texture which distinguishes the very early work, and which is sometimes sought after today. It is the height of insincerity to hammer machine-made bars to resemble the hand-drawn.

THE VOLUTE OR SPIRAL SCROLL

They were forging iron in the Weald and the Forest of Dean, and elsewhere, some 400 years before Julius Caesar paid us a flying visit, but because iron, unpreserved, will rapidly oxidize, we have scant evidence of any iron-work dating before the medieval. The spiral scroll was possibly the earliest decorative element, if only because the smith of some distant time took a thin bar of iron, heated it in his

21 FINISHING OFF AN AXE HELVE   *Miss M. Wight*

22 THE BESOM MAKER BINDING A HEAD WITH
WILLOW. NOTE THE SIMPLE FOOT-OPERATED VICE
The Times

23 CHARCOAL BURNING: BUILDING UP THE CENTRE
OF STACK   *Hubert Davey*

24 CHARCOAL BURNING: COVERING THE STACK

Bowden

25 MAKING A CLEFT-OAK FIELD-GATE. HEREFORD-
SHIRE   *Museum of English Rural Life*

26 MAKING PLOUGH-BEAMS

Museum of English Rural Life

27 TURNING CHAIR-LEGS ON A POLE-LATHE
Howard Evans

28 A CHAIR-BODGER'S SHOP IN THE CHILTERN WOODS. THE POLE AT FULL
DEPRESSION

Council of Industrial Design

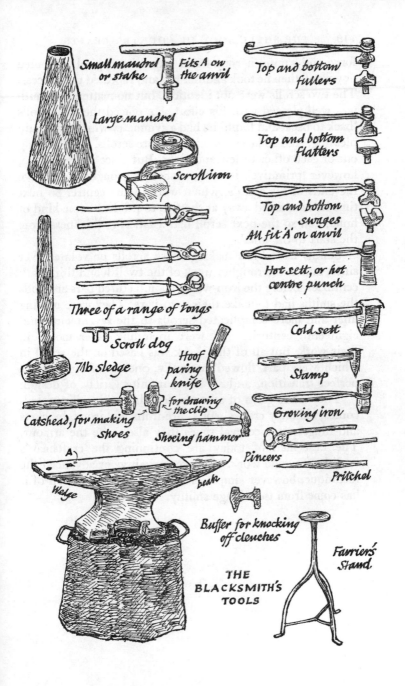

Small mandrel or stake

Fits A on the anvil

Top and bottom fullers

Large mandrel

Scroll iron

Top and bottom flatters

Top and bottom swages

All fit 'A' on anvil

Three of a range of tongs

Hot sett, or hot centre punch

Scroll dog

Cold sett

7lb sledge

Hoof paring knife

Stamp

Catshead, for making shoes

for drawing the clip

Groving iron

Shoeing hammer

Pincers

A

Wedge

beak

Pritchel

Buffer for knocking off clenches

Farrier's Stand

THE BLACKSMITH'S TOOLS

forge and wound it round and round in a spiral. It cooled down and then he took another bar and repeated the process. The two scrolls were not identical, but no matter, the smith was well pleased with his effort. He placed the two scrolls 'back to back' and found he had a symmetry which was again pleasing. And so he set to making more scrolls, some flowing out of each other to left and right. But since no craftsman, however 'primitive', is ever satisfied, he sought to improve the ends of his spirals, which were in the centre. So next time he hammered away at the tips to produce some kind of finial, and so the next scroll had a tapering thickness from the start to the finial.

Smiths have been making these scrolls or volutes ever since, and in the rougher work of the twelfth and thirteenth centuries, before the iron-works manufactured bars and rods the smiths had to make their own bars. They were making finer and more complicated scrolls in the seventeenth and eighteenth centuries and were including other motifs in their work. But all of that work was based on the scroll in which every part 'flowed' naturally, one out of the other in perfect transition, and all in an infinite variety of design.

They made gates of all sizes, together with railings, balconies, chimney cranes, spits, fire-irons and irons, brackets and hinges. In medieval times they also made the armour. The best men of today are continuing the craftsman's tradition of good work. However primitive or advanced the technique, however simple or elaborate the design, all of it has come from the village smithy.

11

Wheelwrighting

The harvest-wagon may have been derived from the stage-wagon, which came into general use for road transport during the latter part of the sixteenth century. The stage-coach was the express vehicle carrying passengers and mails only, and travelled at about 10 m.p.h., with 'stage' halts at posting-houses to change horses. All goods and freight was carried by the stage-wagon, which also carried passengers at low fares and proportionate discomfort. The carrier was completely different in design from the coach and was similar in appearance to the farm-wagon that we know, but provided with an overall canvas tilt for protection of goods and passengers. The stage-coach was always built by coach-builders and the stage-wagon by wheelwrights, consequently the two vehicles presented a radical difference, not only in design and arrangement, but also in finish. The coach, of course, had a form of spring suspension, but the wagon had no springing at all. Likewise, the horses used were quite different; the carrier was always hauled by a team of eight heavy-draught horses, and the wagoner, reputedly a jolly man, usually walked at the head of his team, though some men rode their own horse, dismounting to use the appro-priate brakes at the commencement of the descent or ascent of hills.

Such wagons usually took priority, by unwritten law, over every other class of transport. In medieval times, and indeed until the time of Telford and Macadam, the condition of the roads was such that road-wagons could not be run during the months of winter. All goods had therefore, at that time of the year, to be carried by trains of pack-horses.

The farm-wagon or harvest-wagon, for that was its principal use, was at first little different from the heavily built carrier, except that it was generally a little more lightly constructed, for field-work. It had no form of cover and was intended to be hauled by one, two or sometimes four horses. In the fields it was an advantage to use as few animals as possible, for the sake of mobility and turning. Originally, the ox was the universal draught animal on the farm, and remained so until it was displaced by the horse. The transition, however, from the ox to the horse was not complete until the middle of the last century.

While the road-carrier, together with the stage-coach, was put off the road by the advent of the railways, the harvest-wagon remained in increasing use until, in its turn, its place was challenged by the invention of the tractor. During this phase wheelwrights continued to make improvements in design, until the peak was reached during the 1870s. The tractor came to displace the horse, as the horse had displaced the ox, slowly at first, but at an increasing rate as it became more efficient. The use of tractors for the haulage of wagons was, however, quite illogical, and farmers increasingly used either properly designed trailers, or more frequently a botched-up contraption made of old motor-lorry parts. The methods of agriculture which had changed little since medieval times have gone now. These old wagons were an integral part of that way and there is no place for them amid a rural industry which is now totally mechanized.

The harvest-wagon was built by men who went out to the woodlands and bought their timber by direct selection. They knew that years would elapse before this timber would be thoroughly seasoned and ready for use. Generations of practice had produced a type of man and engendered a way of thinking in wood. As with everything else about their lives, the wagons they made changed but slowly, and with knowledge passed on from father to son everything was instinctively made to last. Into that making went something else that is hardly understood now.

So it was inevitable that the English farm-wagon, at the peak of its era, constituted one of the best examples of what we mean by the finest in craftsmanship. Generations of knowledge and custom went into the shape of a pair of shafts. They were shaped the way they were to suit the anatomy and gait of a horse. Shafts were tapered for balance, and to the practiced eye they looked right. And so it was with the wheels and the spokes.

While the surfaces of the roads, before Macadam, were bad enough, the by-roads, lanes, and farm-tracks were even worse. Many cart-ruts were so deep as to become permanent, with the result that the wheel-tracks of wagons, that is, the distance between two opposite wheels, had to be the same, or nearly so, for all wagons in a locality. Once these ruts in a lane or farm-track had been made, they deepened with the passing of each winter, and then, with the approach of high summer, they dried out hard. They became in effect, like the rails of a railway, and wagons had to be built to 'a gauge' set by generations of use. And because tradition had determined that the track of a Surrey wagon must be 70 in., that wagon could not be used further afield, where the 'gauge' might be 77 or 62 in. 'Taking the routs', they called it. If too wide for the 'rout', or too narrow one wheel would follow its rut while the other rode on top, enough to over-set the wagon, or turn it on its side.

For all the great variations in design and detail of wagons from one county to another, from the Yorkshire Wolds to Cornwall and from Kent to mid-Wales, these wagons were basically similar in their structures, in that they consisted of a body and an undercarriage, which, in turn, consisted of

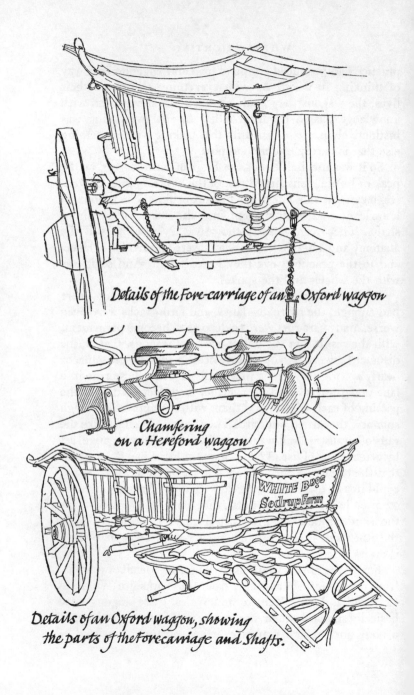

Details of the Fore-carriage of an Oxford waggon

Chamfering
on a Hereford waggon

WHITE Bros
Sedrup Farm

Details of an Oxford waggon, showing
the parts of the Forecarriage and Shafts.

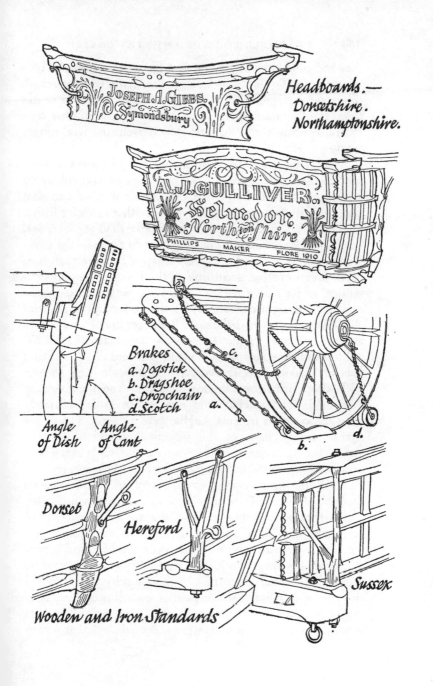

JOSEPH A. GIBBS. Symondsbury

Headboards. —
Dorsetshire.
Northamptonshire.

A. J. GULLIVER. Helmdon
North*ton*Shire
PHILLIPS MAKER FLORE 1910

Brakes
a. Dogstick
b. Dragshoe
c. Dropchain
d. Scotch

c.

a.

b. d.

Angle
of Dish

Angle
of Cant

Dorset

Hereford

Sussex

Wooden and Iron Standards

fore and hind pairs of wheels, fitted to axles and joined by a
centre pole. To the fore-carriage, the shafts were attached.
The two carriages were extremely robust, but the centre
pole, rigidly attached to the hind carriage, permitted considerable front-end flexibility for movement over rough,
uneven fields.

Except for some variation in number of spokes in fore-
and hind-wheels, it was in the body-design and colour by
which one came to know that this wagon was built in East
Sussex, that one in mid-Suffolk, and another in Oxfordshire.
One may feel that one design was better than another, and
yet know that a Sussex would look out of place on the Cotswold Hills, or a Hereford seem unhappy in Dorset. In fact,
each design evolved according to the topography and agriculture of its native region. The Kent wagons were quite
plain and straightforward, while the Oxfords had graceful
ship-like lines, as had those of Somerset and Dorset, with
arching rails over the hind-wheels, so enhancing these lines.
All through Northamptonshire and the Fens of the Holland
part of Lincolnshire, the wheelwrights made their wagons
with deep, capacious bodies and gave them elaborately
decorated head-panels. This exuberance ended abruptly
once the counties of East Anglia were entered. There, the
simple, robust lines of the wagons harmonized so well
among the quiet charm of the wattle and daub farms, which
to this day sport cocked-up gable-ends to their roofs.

The building of a wagon or cart involved the harmonious
thought and work of a team of men, each highly skilled in his
department of the whole craft. Carpenters constructed the
body and the under frame and it was another man's responsibility to make the wheels, while the blacksmith produced all the forge-work, the wheel-tyres or the strakes,
supporting standards for the body and sundry pieces. When
everything was finished the painter contributed his share,
to give the wagon its gay, proud coat of paint, so well applied
as to outlive a generation of farmers, even though that wagon

would spend so much of its life exposed to the heat of the harvest sun, the rains of Spring and the frosts of January. I remember a Sussex wagon, broad of wheels, on a farm near West Grinstead, which carried the date 1888 on its faded head-board. 'That wasn't when it was made', said the farmer, 'that's when it was last painted.' And into that last word went all the implication of a good job well done— sixty-five years ago! They ground their own colours in those days.

We have seen that the wheelwrights of the past selected their timber from the woods. Some wrights employed their own sawyers, while others called upon the travelling sawyers. They were a pair who worked 'top and bottom', sawing laboriously hour after hour down the length of a felled trunk, which was secured in position over a saw-pit. They worked none the less with infinite skill to produce planks of equal and even thickness. In the later years wrights more and more bought their timber, partly seasoned, from the merchants, who did all the preliminary work.

Seasoning was a long process, as it was usual to allow one year for every inch of thickness. Especial care in this was needed for the treatment of elm, which was used for the naves of wheels and for the axle-beds, etc. In the finished state, a nave roughly measured 12 in. or over in maximum diameter and some 15 in. from front to back. Elm was invariably chosen, because only this wood would stand up to the mortising of holes for ten, twelve, or fourteen spokes, together with the large, tapered hole, from back to front, for the axle. No other timber could have withstood the ultimate strains, after the spokes had been banged home, of years and years of wear without defect.

The framework of the body was made of ash and oak, with panelling and flooring of elm, though Scandinavian deal later came in for cross-flooring. Where a springy resistance to knocks and strains, as with the rails and ladders, was required, then ash was chosen. The heavy, transverse parts of the undercarriage were of elm, and called bed, bolster, and pillow, from bottom to top. The pole which joins them, front and back and maintains the wheel-base, was of ash, because plenty of whip was required. Three different woods were used for the wheels. Elm, for the naves, has been mentioned; then there was oak for the spokes and ash for the felloes, that is, the segments comprising the rim. Oak was always cleft with the heart at the back of the spoke, where the strain was greatest. The reason for cleavage, was that this quickly revealed any fault in the wood, which would not be disclosed by sawing, until too late, when the spoke split asunder with a bang as the wheel was shut tight by the contraction of the cooling tyre. Ash was also used for the shafts, which, being secured at their butt ends only, needed plenty of springy resilience at their free, toe ends.

It was usual to make the body and the undercarriage as two separate units, to be joined by two stout centre-pins, one at the fore-carriage end and the other at the rear. The front pin was also the axis on which the fore-carriage turned and it was therefore thicker ($1\frac{1}{4}$ in.). It will be realized that the whole wagon was expressly designed for movement over very rough, uneven ground.

In the earliest wagons all four wheels were quite large, both in diameter and in tread, but the trend in design was for wheels to decrease, especially the front ones, as attempts were made to improve the lock, or turning capacity. Whereas the early wagons needed 'half a field' in which to turn round, the last designs could be turned in their own length.

The wheelwright's skill and reputation was centred on his ability to make a wheel and to so perfectly construct the axle-beds that when the wheels were 'hung' the whole carriage ran as it should. Wheels were made with the spokes 'dished', so that when one looked at the wheel 'edge-on' it presented a slightly 'coned' shape. The spokes did not project from the nave at 90° to the axle, but at anything from $2\frac{1}{2}$° to $12\frac{1}{2}$° forward from the right-angle. This was done to make a wheel stronger than was otherwise possible, as a 'flat' wheel would shortly collapse either way under the constant stresses. The axles themselves, were set to point downward at a corresponding angle from the horizontal. These two angles, of spokes and axles, being identical, caused the load of the wagon always to fall in a vertical line to the ground, as the wheel, in rotation, brought each spoke to that vertical. The drawing illustrates this principle. The dished wheel may be analageous to the opened-out umbrella. It will be noted, too, that as the wheel 'leaned outward' there was more room for the body.

From a perusal of diverse writings of the past it is clear that the controversy over dished wheels was never resolved. Why were Herefords so deeply dished, yet the Essex, which had to encounter equally vile mud and ruts, so slightly dished. One may feel that regional precept determined everything.

When a wagon was under way one heard a continuous 'click-clack-click' from the wheels. The gait of a horse in the shafts causes a wagon to move along a slightly wavy course along a road. This tended to run the wheels 'off and back', on their axles. The dished wheel was designed to counter this movement and withstand the blows which were partly offset by the axle-arms being set a little forward, so that the wheels, seen in plan, appeared to be slightly 'pigeoned-toed'. The wheelwrights called this setting the 'foreway'.

The entire wagon was so constructed that any component part, wood or iron, could be extracted for replacement or repair. No part was ever secured by the use of glue. The whole structure was therefore skilfully designed. The parts of a wheel were shut tight by the tyre or strakes, which latter preceded the continuous hoop. Strakes were in segments of the same number as the felloes, each strake overlapping the felloe joints and being secured by four or five nails at each end. These nails, made in the blacksmith's shop, had flat shanks and square heads. The older wheels had two rings of strakes; in fact, the stage-carriers had even more, since their wheels had treads of up to 9 in. At the very end of the wagon era wheels were mostly shod with hoops and their treads varied from 4 to $2\frac{1}{2}$ in. The narrower treads were better suited to the lighter soils of the Cotswold; that is, anywhere from Golden Cap on the Dorset coast to the Wolds of Lincolnshire, but on the heavy Wealden clay of Sussex and Kent they favoured a 4 in. tread. Further west, beyond the Severn, the wrights of Gloucester and Hereford consistently built their wagons *and* their tumbrils 'broad-wheeled' right to the end, claiming that they held better on the heavy soils peculiar to that region. They were nearly all straked; even the few 'narrow wheels' were often so made.

Either way, straked or hooped, the tyres were made hot in a special furnace and put on hot, so that in cooling they contracted to the correct diameter, and thus bound the wheel tight as in a permanent vice. This circumference had to be calculated and measured on the flat strip by means of a 'traveller', something like a map-measurer, with a wheel 24 in. in circumference, though various sources indicate a variety of sizes. The final cold tyre had to be exact; too large, and it would be loose on the wheel; too small, and it would either buckle the wheel or snap some of the spokes.

The measured-out strip, cut to the circumference of the wheel, plus 'overlap' for 'shutting', was put through rollers which produced the hoop. The forge furnace had to be fired just right and clean to get the heat for shutting the ends of the tyre. The completed hoop was returned to the oven for reheating, so that thus enlarged it could be dropped over the wheel. This had been previously screwed down on the iron tyring-platform. There was a hole in the centre to admit the nave, and from this centre there projected a screwed rod with an iron turn-key. One may yet come across these circular iron platforms, the decisive evidence of a former wheelwright's shop. The tyre was extracted from the oven and carried by tongs or dogs to the wheel and lowered over it. It was quickly banged home with sledges, and helpers used watering-cans to extinguish excessive burning. And so, amid clouds of smoke, this age-old process went on. As the tyre cooled, the smith knew whether his calculations were correct, as the slowly cooling and contracting hoop increased its grip beyond that of any vice. With clicks and sundry bangs, the cooling proceeded, forcing home felloes and spokes far more than possible with any amount of blows with the sledge. No strakes could accomplish what a well-made hoop could do. George Sturt has described all this incomparably in his classic, *The Wheelwright's Shop*.

The wheels of the earlier wagons and tumbrils ran on arms of iron-hard beech, which were in one piece with the axle-bed, 6 in. or so square and getting on for 8 ft across from tip to tip. The axle part was tapered gently from a maximum diameter of 5 in. and was fitted with a iron cleat on its underneath, bearing portion. The whole piece was called an 'axle-tree'. Before the wheel was hung both the arm and the inside of the nave were well greased.

The later wagons had case-hardened arms, which were bolted to the elm bed. This had several advantages over the wooden axle-tree—comparative lightness, of course, simpler construction and, most important, replacements were easier. The smaller nave had to be 'boxed' with an iron core in order to run better on the axle. The difference between the two is noticeable, but the wheelwrights never settled their opinions as to which was the better.

The construction of a wheel, before the tyring stage was reached, required long experience in order to obtain strength and truth, though a good wagon usually outlived its original set of wheels. The naves were mortised with auger, buzz, and chisel, to receive the tenoned 'feet' of the spokes, the outer extremities of which were called tongues and were squared or rounded to fit corresponding holes in the felloes. Each felloe fitted over two spokes, and between each pair of felloes a dowel was fitted to keep the whole ring in a true circle. No process or device was omitted 'for economy' that contributed to the making of a perfect wheel. When the wheels were straked with two rings, the joints of front and back rings were staggered by about 2 in., so that they still came midway between the felloe joints.

It has been mentioned that wheels were always dished. Now, such a wheel had a correspondingly 'coned' tread; that is, the diameter of the wheel at its front edge was less than that at the back, otherwise a wheel would run on its front edge alone. Any hoops with treads in excess of $2\frac{1}{2}$ in. had to be coned to fit.

The blacksmith's part in the making of a wagon has been described, but it was on the iron standards which supported the sides of the body that he found some outlet for his artistry, especially when the wrought-iron was of square section. It was customary to heat these bars to a 'cherry red' and then to twist them round and round to make a spiral, before turning over to make a support for the outer rails. The sides were often secured to the headboard by ornamental 'fish-tails', finely splayed and tapered. Later wagons, built after 1850 or so, had round-section ironwork, so that spirals could not be incorporated.

Although the term *thread* was understood as long ago as 1674 (*O.E.D.*), those wagons which were built with iron supports had their parts secured by means of a wedge key fitting into a slot. Later came the use of the thread, but until the advent of the Whitworth thread, which standardized threads all over the country, it was the practice for smiths to tap their own threads, with the result that there were variations from smithy to smithy. This meant that there could be no certain interchangeability between the stocks, held by various smiths. There is a delightful little museum, founded by Sir Stafford Cripps, at Filkins, between Burford and Lechlade, where one may see these old taps and dies, and, of course, at the City Museum, St Albans.

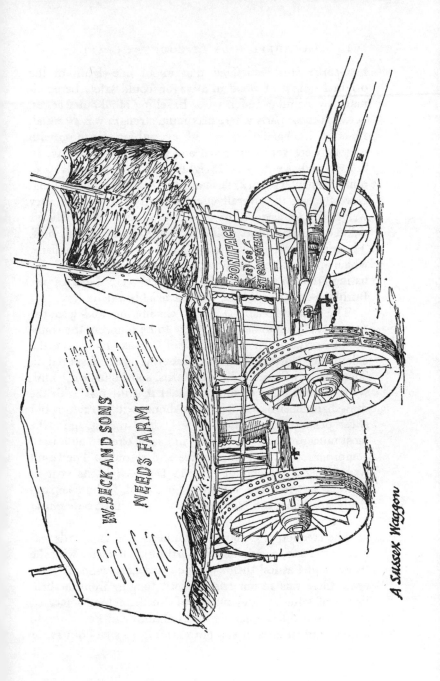

W. BECK AND SONS
NEEDS FARM

BONIFACE
18 88
ST. GILES, BONIFACE

A Sussex Waggon

George Sturt estimated that about one-eighth of the original weight of wood in a wagon could safely be eliminated by skilful chamfering, or bevelling of all outer edges, between those parts where maximum strength was essential. Practices in chamfering, as with everything else to do with wagons were very traditional and peculiar to a county. In Sussex and Kent, wheelwrights confined themselves to quite elementary work, no more than the merest bevelling. Nevertheless, the overall effect contributed to some very well-designed wagons, of which the Sussex were always painted Prussian Blue, while the Kents' were a creamy buff. The same simplicity was to be found on the East Anglians, which appeared in a variety of colours, still with blue dominating, though those of Essex which were built in the Burnham-on-Crouch area, were invariably a rich ochre.

The greatest elaboration in chamfering and also the gayest of all colour-schemes, were to be found in the counties of Northampton, Somerset, and Dorset. Orange was the colour for Northants, while blue was again favoured in Somerset and Dorset. The Herefords, some blue, some buff, were in some cases so finely treated that the man with the drawshare must have spent many hours with no return but sheer personal satisfaction. The Oxford wagon, quite the most numerous and widespread in usage, effected a pleasant compromise between exuberance and restraint. The result was a wagon which not only looked well in its coat of daffodil, but ran well, carried a good load, had a comparatively low floor, and was reasonably light in tare-weight at 18 cwt.

The creation of designs on the head- and tailboards was a craft in itself, comparable in forthright character with the 'Roses and Castles' theme on the canal narrow-boats. Here again there was an immense variety, ranging from the brilliance of lettering and motifs of Northampton, Somerset, and Dorset, the simpler charm of Oxford and Berkshire, to a quite utilitarian and spartan lettering in many others, or

even a total absence. It is just possible that the standards of wagon design and church architecture were not coincidental. One may feel that the churches along the geological Cotswold set the wheelwrights a challenge which they met handsomely.

The farm-wagon has been mentioned as a carrier of corn, hops, coal and gravel. At other times of the year there was manure to be spread, and for this the tumbril was designed. The body could be tipped up by releasing some device, enabling a bulk load to be deposited. It may be mentioned, too, that the wagon was also a ceremonial carriage, for weddings, funerals, and festivals.

All over Wales the extremely hilly terrain made four-wheelers impracticable and, of course, the farms have always been predominantly sheep ranges, with but little corn. There one will still find the gambo in considerable numbers. Essentially, the gambo is a two-wheeler, having a low platform, usually without sides, but fitted with guards, called stiles, to keep the load clear of the wheels. In the severely hilly country between Bishops Castle and Knighton, they used a heavily-built sled which ran on two wheels, designed to run free when going up hill, but locked by chains when going down. It had runners fitted to the nose-end of the side-members. Round about Clun, they knew it as a wheel-car.

Wheelwrights used a variety of tools and devices. Most of the carpenters' tools, augers, chisels, and drawknives, of course, but there were a number which were unusual and not used by anyone else. There was a samson, for drawing felloes together when the strakes were being nailed on. A jarvis, resembling a hollowed out, heavy spokeshave was latterly used for rounding the spokes. Down to about 1850 the wrights used a 'hollow' plane, like that used by ship-wrights on masts and spars. For cleaning out the corners of mortices in naves, a buzz was used; it was a heavy one-piece chisel of 'V' shape and had a fine point at the apex for accurate cutting. A traveller measured the circumference of a wheel, to be run off along the strip, prior to making the tyre. A spoke-dog was used for drawing two spokes closer so that a felloe could be fitted over their longest ends. The smaller axe, for cleaving oak for spokes, was a single-handed tool and was made with a left or right bias, according to the habit of the user, the blade having an oppositely ground edge with a haft made to suit. If made for a left-handed man, it could not be used by right-handed men, and vice-versa.

Not all tools came from the Midland tool-makers. Many villages had someone well able to make excellent tools, simply because by personal contact and trial and error, he knew exactly what was wanted. Likewise, the blacksmiths made many of their smaller tools, shaping them just to their liking.

Harnessing a horse to a wagon was known as 'shutting-in' and the reverse of this operation was 'shutting-out'. The horse was walked back between the shafts and harnessing was begun from the offside. The tug-chain from the collar was hooked to the long-staple near the toe of the shaft. This took the weight of the shafts and left the wagoner free to throw the ridge-chain over the back-pad, which forms the weight-carrying part of the harness. After which, the breeching-chain could be secured. Round the near-side, the end of the ridge-chain was hooked to the long-staple, so as to bring the shaft-points just below the tug-chain hook on the collar. This position was important, as it affected the horse's pulling capacity. When this had been done, the tug and breeching-chains could be coupled up. When 'shutting-out' a horse, the following order was observed. 1. Offside-breeching. 2. Off-side tug. 3. Near-side breeching. 4. Near-side tug. 5. The ridge-chain from the near-side.

Seen in elevation, a straight line may be drawn from the tug hook, right through the shafts and the fore-carriage hounds. If a second horse was used, in addition to a single

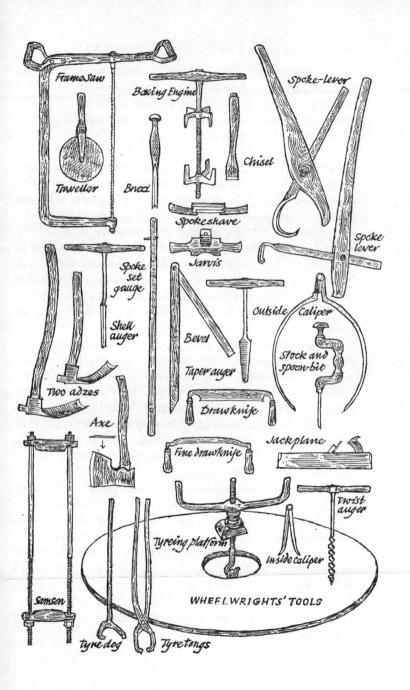

Frame Saw

Boxing Engine

Spoke-Lever

Traveller

Buzz

Chisel

Spokeshave

Spoke-lever

Jarvis

Spoke set gauge

Shell auger

Outside Caliper

Bevel

Stock and spoon-bit

Taper auger

Two adzes

Drawknife

Axe

Fine drawknife

Jackplane

Twist auger

Tyreing platform

Inside caliper

Samson

WHEELWRIGHTS' TOOLS

Tyre dog

Tyre tongs

shaft-horse, then it was harnessed 'in trace', tandem fashion. A trace harness had no back-pad, but had extra straps from the meeter-strap, on the horse's back, by which the trace-chains were suspended. Between the two horses, the trace-chains were kept steady by a spreader-bar.

The wheelwright's craft was one which could not adapt itself to the present revolution in agriculture, so with regret this chapter has had to be written in the past tense. With the passing of the farm-wagon there has gone a race of men who were artists to the tips of their very sensitive fingers. With them, too, has gone the head carter, who was responsible to the farmer for the draught animals, wagons and carts, harness and gear. Just as with the passing of the steam locomotive, there has gone another race, the driver and fire-man, the men of the footplate. I think we are the poorer for their going.

Most wheelwrights did not work by diagrams, but kept a stock of patterns for felloes and other curves. They always worked by an innate sense of what is correct, a quality and ability born of hard-won experience. They worked by sight and touch and by a long cultivation of this habit, were able to use their tools with accuracy. Only by this habit could they produce the subtlety of curves that went into a wagon, wherein the only straight lines were the transverse ones of the body and the underframe.

Many veteran wagons, some well over 100 years old, may still be found in farmyards and quiet corners of the farm. An enquiry of the farmer will disclose wagons and byegones otherwise inaccessible to the casual person. One will often be well received, for a few farmers keep an old friend, instead of chopping it up for firewood, as they will also keep an old shire horse.

Examples of restored and preserved wagons may be seen at the following museums:

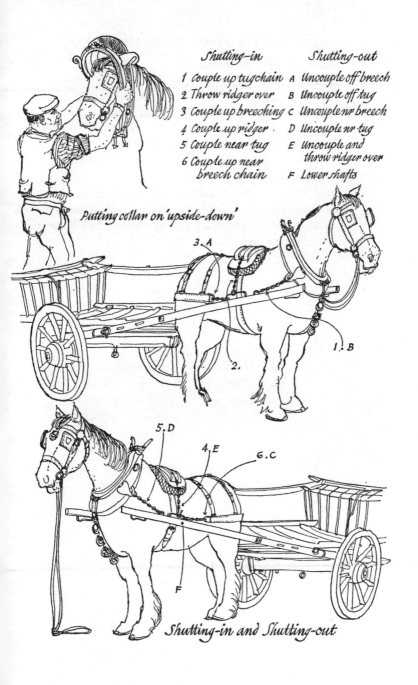

Shutting-in

1 Couple up tugchain
2 Throw ridger over
3 Couple up breeching
4 Couple up ridger
5 Couple near tug
6 Couple up near breech chain

Shutting-out

A Uncouple off breech
B Uncouple off tug
C Uncouple nr breech
D Uncouple nr tug
E Uncouple and throw ridger over
F Lower shafts

Putting collar on 'upside-down'

Shutting-in and Shutting-out

Alton. Curtiss Museum.
Bristol. Blaise Castle Folk Museum.
Halifax. Shibden Hall Folk Museum.
Huddersfield. Tolson Memorial Museum.
Leicester. City Museum.
Lincoln. Museum of Lincolnshire Life.
Norwich. Bridewell Museum.
Plymouth. Buckland Abbey Museum.
Reading University. Museum of English Rural Life.
St Fagans Castle, Glamorgan. National Museum of Wales.
Stratford on Avon. Mary Arden Agricultural Museum.
York. Castle Museum.

12

Millwrighting

From a distance a windmill made a fine focal point in the level landscapes of East Anglia, and it was not until one was right up to the foot of a windmill that the impact of its structure was felt. With the mill 'set in the eye' of a fair breeze and the sweeps turning eight times to the minute, it was the sight on land comparable, perhaps, with the square-rigged ship at sea. Eric Newby, in *The Last Grain Race*, wrote of the orchestra of the wind in the standing and running rigging. Standing by a mill one heard the bass rumble of internal machinery and the regular soft woosh, as each sail came down, round and up, to be followed by the next, down, round and up, that soft sound increasing, to die away and be drowned by the next rush. It is strange, now, that the applied power of wind and water produced few sounds that were discordant. Discord came when mechanical power invaded the fields.

In this country there are three types of windmill and three of sail, or sweep. The oldest mills, those in existence at the time of the Domesday book, were all post-mills, in which the entire mill could be turned to face the wind. During the eighteenth century the tower type was evolved. This consisted of a standing round tower of brick or local stone, which contained all the milling machinery. The cap, which housed the sail-axle, alone turned to the wind, rotating like a turn-table upon bearings between it and the tower. A later development of this was the wooden octagonal tower, called a smock, some say, by a vague resemblance to the country-man's smock of the nineteenth century. In Holland such a mill, either tower or smock, is called a 'spinnekop'.

The problem of keeping the sweeps or sails into the wind was originally met by manual labour at the 'tail-pole', or turning beam, either by sheer brute force or by leverage, windlass or even pulley and block. This problem was solved in 1746 when Edmund Lee, himself a miller, applied the principle of the fantail, a wheel of vanes, set on a horizontal axis and positioned at the back of the mill, either behind the cap, or behind the body in the case of post-mills. So long as the fantail was 'tailing the wind', the vanes presented no faces to the wind, but as soon as the wind veered and got on the side of the fan, then rotation commenced and by a train of gears propelled the cap or the body until the wind ceased to turn the fan. Curiously, such a device was never adopted in Holland, where the windlass is used.

The original form of sweep consisted of a light framework mounted on each stock, or sail-arm, over which a canvas sail was set or furled according to the wind. That could be quarter, half, three-quarters or full sail. It became known as the common sail, and each of the four had to be set separately, each sail being 'brought down' to the bottom for the purpose. In 1722 a Scottish wright, one Andrew Meikle, the same Meikle who, in 1786, invented the threshing-machine, devised the spring sail. In this type, each sail became a more robust framework containing a large number of slats, or shutters, all controlled by spring tension, which could be adjusted at the tip, according to the force of the wind. This principle was greatly improved when Cubitt (who was later knighted), an East Anglian engineer who accomplished many things in his life, transferred the control from the sail-tips to the centre, through cranks to a pin, which ran through the centre of the sail-axle, as does the centre-sweep of a watch. This was the patent sail and enabled adjustment to the wind to be made without interrupting the milling.

Development in sails appears to have been so uneven that we find post-mills equipped with patent sails and fantails, as at Great Chishall, near Royston, where the hills of Hertfordshire fall away to the spacious lands of Cambridgeshire, or on the coast of Suffolk, at Thorpeness. In Lincolnshire, they developed the six-sailer, and at Peterborough they went still further with an eight-sailed mill. Both types of sweep, common or patent, have a feature in common. When seen from the side, one notices that the 'plane' of the sweeps have a gradual twist from the tips toward the centre of the heels. The force of a given speed of wind, striking the sails, will do more work at the tips than at the centre. If, therefore, the face of the sweep is gradually inclined toward the centre, then the advantage is increased. This is known as the 'weather' of a sail, and also reduces strain at the extremities. Seen again from the side, it will also be noticed that the sails point a little 'skyward', that is, they do not turn on a horizontal axis. They are, in fact, inclined on their shaft at an angle of 15°, in order to throw as much weight as possible back toward the centre. The weight of the shaft and gear-wheel behind the front bearing help in part, and the body of a post-mill is set well behind the axis, which altogether balance the entire weight as centrally as possible.

The original construction and erection of a mill, whether for wind- or water-power, together with the installation of the machinery, was the work of millwrights; though a certain amount of subsequent maintenance and repair was in some instances carried out by the village carpenters.

Putting up the centre-post, the cross-trees, and braces of a post-mill or constructing a brick tower was to such men a relatively simple matter. Their contemporaries, the master masons, were doing far dizzier things with blocks of stone. But the manner in which the wrights manoeuvred the stocks or sail-arms up and into the centre cross-eye makes the contemporary mind feel very humble. By the time they were building the tower-mills there was better tackle available, but since each of the four arms was about 30 ft in length and some 14 in. square at the inner end, one can but feel those wrights to have been a dauntless race of men. Each arm had to be lifted to the vertical 'big' end uppermost, which was inserted in the cross-eye and then turned through 180° to the top so that the opposite arm could be similarly dealt with. Today a couple of men with a mobile gantry will pull several levers, wave their arms and shout and, apart from tea-breaks, that will be that. Even the Egyptians had 10,000 slaves.

From the sail-axle a crown-wheel, having cogs radiating on its face, drove a second spur-wheel, rotating on a vertical axis, and so to the shafts turning the millstones, the gear for shaking the shoe distributing the seed to the stones and also for raising and lowering the loaded sacks. It was the ultimate practice to have engaging teeth of iron and wood. All the wheels were built up of segments and spokes of oak. The iron for the crown-wheel teeth was cast in segments and bolted to the wheel, to engage the spur-wheel, wholly of oak and mortised together and to the oaken octagonal shaft and bound by iron plates. Sometimes, the wheel bearing iron teeth was wholly made of units of cast iron. Each wooden cog had a long, tapering shank, the tail of which protruded through the stout rim of the wheel to the inner side. The shank and its corresponding rim-mortise had to be an exact fit on all four faces. Only by this and a series of good heavy blows with a beetle or a sledge would the cogs remain tight during their working life. It was a matter of craftsman's pride that they never came loose. Such exacting work as this could only be done by men of the same calibre as the wheelwrights. And since carpenters, millwrights, and wheelwrights were on common ground where timber was concerned, it is quite conceivable that a wheelwright might on occasion turn millwright. At first glance, those old wheels looked pretty rough, but this, in fact, merely belied the fine workmanship in the cogs.

The cogs were all driven in *before* the teeth were cut to shape. Had this shaping been done beforehand, the teeth would have been damaged by the blows. The marking off of the height of the teeth was done with an iron scribe, in much the same way that wheelwrights marked off the spokes. This business of shaping the teeth entailed equidistant marking and equality in thickness and taper. No matter if the shanks were right, centre to centre, if the teeth themselves were unequal, face to face, then there could only be trouble from the outset, starting with a faulty engagement which worsened until it set up a train of damaged cogs. If all the wear of engaging cogs is taken by the wooden ones, then it becomes a matter of periodic replacement. It was also considered that iron and wood engaged better than iron and iron and that quieter and smoother running was obtained. Millwrights certainly knew their job and for those hardworking teeth they used one or more of several woods, apple, hornbeam, beech, or oak. One may presume this would depend on the timber available, for while hornbeam is common enough in the vestigial remnants of the great Forest of Essex, it is rarely met with in other parts.

The primary gear-wheel in a water-mill turned in a pit into which water was continually finding its way, so the teeth were invariably of oak. It was usual to construct the water-wheel of oak or cast-iron in segments and to make the floats of elm, as that wood kept well when continuously wet. The 'picturesque' ruin of an old mill, long stationary and choked with weed and moss, will have lost most of its floats from the rot of inactivity, while the head-water spills uselessly from the broken leat.

Whenever possible corn was ground by water-power, as generally being more dependable than wind and certainly less fickle. Days of calm on the one hand, or wind-storm on

Postmill at Great Chishall, near Royston, Hertfordshire.

Undershot Mill at Rossett, near Wrexham.

the other could immobilize a windmill, whereas even in times of drought a well-sited water-mill could depend upon a reasonable head of water. It was not necessary to have a 'raging torrent', rather the reverse, in fact, where the land fell away reasonably. Rivers like the Thames and its tributaries and the Bedfordshire Ouse abounded in good sites.

The use of water-power was developed for a variety of purposes; for grinding corn, fulling cloth, operating forge hammers, mine-pumping, sawing timber, the manufacture of gunpowder and paper-making, and was not displaced until displaced by steam, though many water-mills continued almost to the present time. The limit to the practicable size of a windmill possibly prohibited its development beyond the tower type. One has but to compare examples of this type with such water-mills as Fakenham and the Isabella wheel at Laxey, in the Isle of Man.

Whatever the use to which a mill was put, the wheel was known by the point at which the water flow actuated it. So there were overshot, undershot, and breast wheels, each type being installed according to the site of the mill and the fall of water. Originally, the undershot wheel was not as efficient as the over- or the breast-shot, but during the first half of the nineteenth century Poncelet, a Frenchman, by using the *velocity* of the flow of water, instead of its weight, greatly improved the undershot type, which was simpler and easier to construct. Such wheels were usually of smaller dimensions.

The overshot wheel was used where there was a higher fall of water and was intended to turn by the *weight* of the descending water against the buckets or floats, and was designed to retain the water until its 'work' was done; to lose water too soon was to lose power. By the end of the eighteenth century Smeaton had so improved the overshot that it became practicable to transmit the increased power by shafts and belting to a number of machines. One such wheel, at a blast-furnace at Merthyr Tydfil, had a diameter of 50 ft and a width of 6 ft. It was installed during 1800.

Breast-shot wheels eventually became more common than overshot. These wheels, like the overshot, utilize the weight of the water, which was arranged at about midway. The wheel thus rotated in the same direction as the undershot and therefore opposite to the overshot. The order of the internal gearing was arranged accordingly.

Mention must be made of tide mills, which were sited on estuarine creeks, where the water of the rising-tide could be captured and then discharged *after* the turn of the tide. While we find them on the coasts of Suffolk, Essex, Sussex, and Hampshire, they were also to be found on the Tamar, and the Looe, in Cornwall. By the retention, by sluices, of the sea-water at high water, a head of water for nearly six hours' milling was obtained. As soon as the pressure of water behind the sluices was greater than the sea-ward, then milling commenced and continued until a little before slack water. The spell of each turn of milling thus depended upon the state of the tides each day or night. St Osyth Mill, known to have been sited in 1413, and then belonging to the abbey, had a supply pond of over 30 acres.

Reputedly of Norse origin, there were at one time a large number of horizontal wheels, some 500, sited in various parts of Scotland, wherever the Norse people had settled. Both the wheel and the runner stone were on a single vertical shaft, giving a direct drive without gearing. The output of such mills was necessarily low, each being sufficient for only a few households.

During the nineteenth century millwrights and engineers, notable among whom was Fairburn, evolved a set of ideal dimensions related to the supply of water and the work to be done. The speed of a wheel at its periphery came to be established at 4–6 ft per second and the buckets or floats to be set at intervals of 12–18 in., those of overshot wheels being set closer together.

Wind-power was utilized where sufficient water was not

available, so in Lincolnshire, all of East Anglia, Essex, the Downland of Sussex and Kent, and elsewhere, hundreds, even thousands, of mills were built. I regret, now, that my only recollection of working windmills is in Sussex; there was one near Heathfield, not so far from my grandfather's home, from which house one could see all the way to Hastings. A few steps away from his house was a second mill, of which I have clear recollections as a small boy, of being scared out of my wits, one dark night, as the great sweeps came down, one after the other, out of the night, with a ghostly feathering swish. I was too scared to notice that they were rotating anti-clockwise.

Millstones were arranged in pairs, the lower one, called the bedstone, being stationary, while the upper one, called the runner stone, rotated face down under the control of apparatus which kept it the right distance from the bedstone, a very fine adjustment indeed, to ensure the best milling. If the runner stone were to make contact with the bedstone, then damage ensued. Mills had several pairs of stones, one for flour and one at least for meal—one for man and one for the beast. They were made from either the Peak stone of Derbyshire (the old quarried stones may be found today, abandoned on the lonely peaks about Hathersage) or of French Burr, which is extremely hard and is much more expensive and which came from the Paris Basin.

There were various arrangements of the grooves in the stones, and what was known as a common dressing had these in ten groups or 'harps' running tangentially from the centre, each 'harp' containing four grooves, furrows or 'stitches', making a total of forty. Between the furrows ran a series of fine grooves called cracking. Each furrow had a vertical side and a sloping, so that when the runner was rotating the furrows met with a scissor-like action. From hoppers positioned above, the corn poured through a flexible spout or shoe, kept in continuous vibration, in a steady stream, like the sand in an hour-glass. As the corn was milled it ran away from the stones and down to the floor below, where it was continuously collected in sacks. It was usual to grind wheat by French Burr and barley, oats, beans, and peas by Peak stones. Amid all the fine white dust, and the shaking, roaring pulsation of the 'crude' heavy machinery, one might well have been bewildered, but that's the way our forefathers made flour for bread, before 'efficiency' and 'hygiene' reared their awful heads.

Periodically, the stones must be 'dressed'. This work was at one time a craft on its own, performed by travelling dressers. Most millers have preferred to do their own dressing, which as an indication must be done about every ten to fourteen days with the harder French Burr. This dressing is done with a 'mill-bille; an edge-tool of high-carbon steel, pointed at each end and wedged into a handle called a thrift. The bille is removable in the same way as the iron of a carpenter's plane. Extreme accuracy is necessary for the furrow depths and the milling surface, and this is gauged by moving a staff, rubbed with 'raddle' over the surface, thus revealing any irregularities. 'Raddle' is a mixture of red oxide and water. The task usually occupied two or three days and a 'traveller' charged about 30s. Where an inexperienced man might tap too gently with his bill, or too hard, the skilled man exercised the greatest sensitivity, graduating the cracking from the deepest at the 'skirt' or periphery to almost nothing midway. The best men could make sixteen cracks to the inch.

A stone of 48 in. diameter and in section convexo-plano weighs about 35 cwt and, of course, requires some form of apparatus for lifting and turning. This may be 'block and tackle' or a sort of gibbet with hooked bars. The initial running of the millstones was the responsibility of the dresser, who knew how to set everything finely balanced.

If the wind miller was dependent upon the vagaries of the wind, the water miller had his troubles, such as interference with the supply of water by other users, or actual diversion.

29 WINDSOR ARM-CHAIR, CHIPPENDALE INFLUENCE
LATE EIGHTEENTH CENTURY

Council of Industrial Design

30 WINDSOR ARM-CHAIR. YORKSHIRE DESIGN

Council of Industrial Design

31   FARRIER 'SEATING' A HOT SHOE
Museum of English Rural Life

32 FARRIER NAILING A SHOE

Museum of English Rural Life

33 FARRIER FINISHING OFF A SHOE
Museum of English Rural Life

34 THE FARRIER'S TOOLS, SET OUT WITH THE BOX
IN WHICH THEY ARE ALWAYS KEPT

Museum of English Rural Life

35 THE BLACKSMITHS FORGE. VARIOUS TONGS IN
FRONT OF THE QUENCHING TANK. THE LARGE
SWAGE BLOCK IN FOREGROUND

Museum of English Rural Life

James Arnold

36 AN ESSEX WAGON, BUILT AT BRADWELL

Water-craft, too, required a sufficient depth and width of water for navigation. Both were reputedly 'jolly' and 'dishonest'. By the 'Right of the Soke', it soon became the practice in the early Middle Ages for corn to be ground by the miller for the tenants or villeins of monastery or manor, and this put the miller in a strong position, one which was aggravated by the dishonesty of some, who took more than was their entitlement.

While the foremost millwrights, who were mathematicians, had established the 'rules' during the eighteenth and nineteenth centuries, there were still the old millwrights who by their village schooling, knew little of mathematics and less of geometry.

Where engineering entered into the construction of the last water-mills, the windmill, at the height of its development must have been the work mainly of carpenters and masons. It has been a characteristic, common to so many of the old craftsmen, that by arbitrary standards they were often illiterate. It is possible that, equipped with an innate simple philosophy, they were able to face the slower world of their time. Time they certainly had, yet they wasted little of it.

How does a miller 'start' his mill going? A windmill is held by a kind of shoe-brake, acting on the sail-axle. When released, the sails will commence to revolve. A water-mill can be stopped or started simply by closing or opening a sluice in the mill-race.

In recent years, during the fifties, I saw scores of mills in Holland, where some comparison may be made. They were pumping water, grinding corn, and sawing timber. Those for pumping varied considerably in size and in some places were grouped by the dozen or more at various levels of land. In general arrangement, the sawmills presented an astonishing spectacle. They were wholly of timber, having a 'smock' tower superimposed on a long wooden shed which was open at both ends. The butts of timber entered the shed at one end, on rollers, to be converted by a massive gang-saw, and emerged as commercial planking at the far end. 'Unicorn' Mill, just outside Haarlem, and situated by the river Spaarne, is a fine example. It is indeed a sad paradox that one must visit a country more progressive and harder working than ours in order to see and examine those things which in this country have been abandoned to the 'past'. Even in Holland, however, the mills are disappearing—there must be rather less than 1,000 left now.

'Union' Mill, at Cranbrook, in Kent, is, or was, still doing 'part time' as a working mill, and is an excellent example of a smock mill, with patent sails and fantail. It was built in 1814. Syleham Mill, in Suffolk is a fine representative of the post-mill at its final development, having patent sails and fantail. Brill, one of the best known of post-mills, has common sails, but has to be turned into the wind by tail-pole or turning-beam. The Dutch windmills all had common sails and apparently neither the spring nor the patent sail was adopted. The Society for the Preservation of Ancient Buildings has a Windmill and Water-mill Section. Their address is 55 Great Ormond Street, London, W.C.1.

13

Thatching

Join a thatcher at the top of his ladder, pass him a yelm of straw or a bunch of reeds, and we shall quickly appreciate what a windy day or a dry one means to this craftsman, as he works with his weight balanced between padded knees and feet. He works to a quiet unobtrusive method, usually with a second man on the ground, whose task it is to prepare and maintain a supply of material. Like most 'outside' workers, he expects to encounter every kind of weather and to cope with them all, where possible. His 'enemies', of course, are January frosts, March winds, and August rains. Frost stiffens the straw so that it is unworkable. High winds play havoc and render the straw unmanageable, while rain makes it wetter than the required degree of dampness. The dry, sunny days of any time of the year are his aids, likewise the soft damp, days of mist hinder him not, but can assist in the preparation of straw, called yelming.

The craft of thatching is one of the few that has not had to adapt itself to drastic change in the way that others, such as smithing, have. In fact, the method of laying the material, whether reeds or straws, has not changed since they were first used, when people sought some form of roofing more substantial and more permanent than foliage or herbage. The changes have been in the perfection of laying and securing the straw or the reed, all of which have resulted in a more effective and weather-tight-covering and above all in increased longevity.

There are three materials in present-day use; Norfolk reed, long-straw and combed wheat-reed. Norfolk reed, so named because the method evolved in that county utilizes the common reed, which is the tallest of our grasses, the *Phragmites communis* of the naturalist. It is generally considered the best, both for a weather-tight covering and for durability. Elsewhere in the corn-growing lands, in the Midlands, all through Wessex and much of the Home Counties, long-straw from the farms is generally used with great effectiveness. What is called combed wheat-reed is, at least to outward appearances, a hybrid, in that the straw of wheat is used unthreshed. Instead, it is 'combed' and then laid in a manner similar to Norfolk reed, to produce a 'texture' resembling the latter. It is often referred to as Devon reed because it originated in that county and is commonly found in the south-west to the Tamar. Formerly, the 'combing' was a tedious manual process, and one usually delegated to women. It is now done by an appliance fitted to the top of a thresher. The wheat is fed into the comber, thereby producing the unbroken straws which pass out of the thresher altogether, while the ears of wheat continue through the normal process of the thresher.

We may remember that many centuries passed, during which there had been an assured supply of material suitable for thatching, centuries during which there had been no fundamental change in agriculture to affect the supply, neither in the Saxon open-field nor the four-course rotation. With the invention of the thresher there still continued a supply, even into the present century. Not until the advent of the combine-harvester and the development of shorter-stalked varieties of wheat did there follow a shortened supply. On the other hand, the common reed is now being methodically cultivated and cut, while the old erstwhile neglected reed-beds are being cleared of the choking accumulation of natural decay.

There was, at one time, a marked decline in the number of houses thatched and in consequence, the number of thatchers at work, but with a swing of enlightenment and some 'field-work' by the *Rural Industries Bureau* and *The National Federation of Master Thatchers Associations,* there is now a considerable demand for craftsmen's time. To the present-day traveller in South and West Wales, it can be a revelation that most of the simple country houses were roofed with thatch until the advent of the slate industry and the spread of railways brought about an overwhelming competition with the new rival, which also displaced the stone-slab type of roofing. Readers of *The Old Farm House*, by D. W. Williams, published by Harrap, will learn many interesting things about the way of life in a small part of Carmarthenshire.

Where a decline takes place in the use of a material or a product, the craft will decline in consequence, and in turn there is a time-lag while new craftsmen are trained and before demand and supply can be set in motion. Today, there are 700 or 800 thatchers at work, specializing in either straw or reed, and they are much travelled. Whereas, at one time, a style of thatching and the material were regarded as peculiar to a region, the demand now for craftsmen often entails their travelling considerable distances. Reed thatchers are especially called upon in this respect.

The solitary exception to all this healthy resurgence is in agriculture. It is only recently that the thatched rick and stack have ceased to form a part of the rural landscape of England. The combine-harvester now produces the threshed corn in bags, while the baler follows to pick-up the residual straw and likewise the hay. The straw is deposited in wire-bound rectangular bales, which are then stacked in box-like formation and covered with plastic sheeting. When, in former times, the harvest was stored in ricks and stacks, one knew by the shapes which part of the country one was in. Considered aesthetically, the best of those stacks and ricks were to be found in northern Hertfordshire and the outward surrounding parts. The stacks were quite large, and oblong with apse-like ends, and they were very well thatched. In the rick-yard it was common practice for the thatchers to crown their work with an ornament of plaited straw. There was a considerable invention in the ideas. They should not be confused with Corn Dollies, which have a different significance, though the origins of both lie very far back in history.

Long-straw thatch is laid in courses or 'lanes' from eave to ridge. These 'lanes' are laid in naturally comfortable working widths of about 30 in., and at the completion of each lane, the ladder is moved leftward for the next lane. Some thatchers, incidentally, finish and tidy the thatch as they go, while others complete a whole side first and then with that part covered against possible rain they finish and clean off. Much appears to depend upon the weather at the time. The Norfolk and Devon men lay in courses along from right to left, proceeding, course by course, to the ridge a whole section or a side at a time.

With long-straw some preparation of the material is made beforehand, in which the straw is spread out on the ground and damped with water. Successive layers are added and damped and the whole is turned over with a fork to ensure uniform treatment. The whole process, together with that of grading and gathering into easily manipulated bundles, is generally known as 'yelming', and when eight or so of these bundles have been placed in the pronged fork, called a 'jack', the whole is called a burden, and that is a suitable working load to be carried to the man on the roof. This lengthy preparation is not entailed with Norfolk reed, but some water-spraying does take place with Devon reed.

Whatever, the material, thatchers always work from right to left.

Since thatchers are craftsmen of an exacting order and are by nature strongly individualist, it follows that their methods of working and their equipment are likely to vary in detail. Some secure the thatch by hazel runners held by iron pegs, some fix the runners by hazel pegs into the old thatch, yet again others use a large iron needle to sew the thatch with tarred twine. This last method requires the constant assistance of a second man 'inside' the roof. When an old thatch is being renewed all the loose, rotten stuff is combed out and removed together with the moss. Sometimes it is possible to make a satisfactory patching, but if the old thatch is generally poor, it is completely covered with fresh material, all pegged in with pegs and runners of hazel. The making of these is a coppice industry, but the thatcher always points them himself. The 'hairpin' of the pegs is formed by giving a half-turn and a twist, whereby the hazel is doubled without breaking the fibres. The runners are made up in lengths of 2–4 ft, or even more.

Standing back from a house, one notices that long-straw has a looser, more plastic appearance, compared with the stiff, 'close cropped', brush-like texture of reed. As the lanes of straw are laid, so they are trimmed and cut, but reeds are constantly dressed and coaxed home with a special tool called a leggat or legget. The Norfolk leggat consists of a handled square board containing a large number of studs on its face. This gives a good adhesion against the reeds. The Devon leggat, however, has diagonal grooves instead of studs. For use in difficult angles an extra leggat is used, having a shoe-brush handle to make it easy to use in those awkward places. Even in the matter of mallets for driving pegs, there are variations. I watched one man at Long Crendon driving home his pegs with a flat oblong board: this had a spade-like handle and was called a 'spud'. This

At Waterstock, between
Oxford and Thame

At Felsted near Gt. Dunmow
Two examples of longstraw thatching

Longshaw thatching in progress at
Long Compton, in the Cotswolds

A round tower of flint, and nave-roof thatched with
Norfolk Reed, at Barsham, Beccles, Suffolk.

same man had trimming- and eave-knives made from an old scythe blade cut in half and each provided with improvised handles—there was yet enough Belbroughton steel to serve a new lease of life. There are often several right ways of doing a job and we have noted that some men 'trim as they go'. The Sheffield firms list a variety of hooks and knives designed for thatchers, some for cutting gable-ends, some for the eaves and dormers. What one man can effectively use may fall unhappily to the hands of another. As in other crafts, it is often a case of the craftsmen and the blacksmith 'putting their heads together'. The yoke or jack, by the way, is nearly always 'home-made' from a piece of forked hazel.

The style of finish or ornamentation derives partially from the character of the material, but also from regional tradition. Whether in reed or long-straw, they finish off quite ornately in the region between the Thames and the Wash and westward to the Bedfordshire Ouse. Particularly in Essex, the gable end is not cut to an edge, but is turned round and pegged with runners to form a definite 'barge' and the peak is cocked up in a most distinctive manner. In the Vale of Aylesbury and in Wessex, too, they thatch with hipped roofs and apply a very neat thatch to yard and boundary walls which are made of 'wychert', a mixture of puddled straw and clay which must have originated in very early times indeed. Long-straw thatching is always secured by distinctive patterns of runners and spars just above the eaves, but reed requires no such treatment.

People who are prepared to engage a thatcher to roof their houses should not be guided solely by what is picturesque, but by the sheer practicality of a method and its appropriateness to the style of the house, the results of which are both pleasing to the eye and are durable and effective. When a house is built the angle, or pitch, or rise of a roof is arranged according to the material used, which may be thatch, tiles, stone slabs, or Welsh slates. Slates, being relatively light, wafer thin and flat, require but a gentle pitch and at that pitch are effective against wind and rain, though along the coasts of West Wales they do take the precaution of cementing over the slates. Stone slabs are heavy and so must be more steeply pitched in order to take as much weight as possible off the framework of the roof. Quarried stone will not fracture in flat wafers and must in any case be more steeply pitched to be effective against wind and rain. Pottery-fired tiles fall between these two extremes. Thatching does not weigh heavily on any structure, but must be steeply pitched in order that the rain will drain down off each reed or straw. This is what happens when the job has been well done. The water descends from reed to reed in its descent to and off the eave. So it is usual to have a pitch of about 50°, or in builder's terms a rise of 16 in. to a span of 12 in. The same roof will have well-projecting eaves which 'throw' off the rain and will not let it run back to the wall.

If it is intended that the roof is to be rendered proof against fire, then the reed or straw must be treated previously to being laid. It is useless to attempt proofing an existing thatch, simply because if well laid then the solution will behave exactly as rain will. When prejudice has been met and the whims of sentiment disposed of, there remain some practical features of a house with a well-thatched roof. Firstly, there is good insulation against both temperature and sound; combine thatch with walls of natural stone some 2 ft thick and half the battle is won, for such a house is quiet within, warm in winter and cool in summer. The life of thatch will vary from a minimum of ten to twenty years for long-straw to fifty or sixty for Norfolk reed.

In order to preserve long-straw thatching against the attention of sparrows, it is often customary to pin down a complete covering of galvanized wire netting.

14

Wood-carving

Of the many kinds of craftsmen working in iron, wood, textiles, or leather, none uses such a range of tools as the carver in wood. His complete range will run into several hundreds. Not all of them are in constant use, some are used but rarely, but none the less those rarely used must be there to hand for the task which cannot be performed by a substitute. One may pick up two pieces of wood, one of them is a plain rectangular block, prepared for work, but as yet untouched; the second is the finished carving with all its figuration, reliefs, moulding, and recesses. Between these two will stand many hours of careful and patient artistry, during which the carver must make his initial cuts and then in the course of the ensuing stages follow on with a succession of many types of chisel and gouge, struck persuasively with the mallet of lignum vitae, or 'eased' round with both hands.

Carvers of today work in a variety of woods greater than ever before, as the possibilities of the new materials are exercised. The wood longest in use is, of course, oak, while mahogany came in to use as 'lately' as 1725. Or they may work in lime, burr-walnut, yellow-pine, and rosewood, and many more. Each will be chosen according to the purpose to which the finished work will be put. While oak is still the best for exterior work because it will withstand exposure, yellow-pine is much liked for ornamental frames, because of

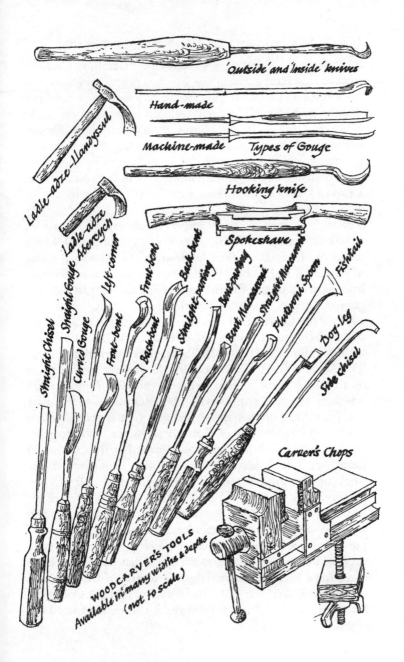

'Outside' and 'Inside' knives

Hand-made

Machine-made   Types of Gouge

Hooking knife

Ladle-adze—Llandyssul

Ladle-adze Aberoych

Spokeshave

Straight Chisel

Straight Gouge

Curved Gouge

Left-corner

Front-bent

Back-bent

Back-bent

Front-bent

Straight-parting

Bent-parting

Bent Macaroni

Straight Macaroni

Fluteroni Spoon

Fishtail

Dog-leg

Side chisel

Carver's Chops

WOODCARVER'S TOOLS
Available in many widths & depths
(not to scale)

its ease and smoothness of working. Grinling Gibbons worked in several woods, lime, box and pear, though his best work is associated with lime. Some very fine work has been done in pear, though box will respond to the cleanest work; it is very 'stable'. In the contemporary preference for unstained work each wood is left to render its own texture and colour, which in some work can be enhanced by the use of more than one wood. Walnut, laburnum, holly, gean, or yew, a carver knows by feel alone what he is working in.

The earliest work of Saxon and Medieval carvers, nearly all in oak, is recognizable by a comparative simplicity which called for fewer tools than later work. There was a purity of treatment and feeling for the wood which came to establish the work of the English carvers as the best in contemporary Europe. Compared with the generally 'shallower' work of the Continental carvers, the English was characterized by being more deeply cut, with some parts of the design 'behind' the outer parts. In short, they worked in depth. The French work, and especially the Italian, tended to be on the same 'plane'. Then again, in the idea, English work was very free and expressive. The later Renaissance work was formal and often symmetrical and greater attention was paid to the perfection of form. The looser, evocative expression of English carving was achieved at the expense of formalism. In this feature there is a direct similarity in the work of the stonemasons of the time, who delighted in portraying all manner of incidents and situations which we may now observe in so many of our churches, large and small. A strong vein of humour ran through a great deal of the carver's art, one which was no less capable of the most sublime beauty. The two trends, of England and the Continent, have been symbolized by the motifs of the vine and the acanthus. We may note, incidentally, that the Continent favoured walnut, which did not reach this country until the eighteenth century.

While Gibbons was working on the large carving there had been, in Tudor times, others using box-wood for the smallest carving. The Romans in their time, had understood the quality of box, and among other things used it for their combs, using an ingenious saw which had two blades, one in advance of the other, so that when the first cut was complete the second had been started. This quite simple method, ensured the equal spacing of the teeth. Such combs continued to be made until the seventeenth century. In Tudor days it was customary for young men of fashion to present such combs to their ladies. The exceptional density of box permitted some fine carving on these combs, which usually contained some appropriate motif.

When the art of engraving in wood was developed it was box again which was used. It may be noted that the engraving was, and still is, made on the end grain, while woodcuts are made on the face.

The Welsh carvers of the last century produced a great deal of fine work, amongst which were the celebrated lovespoons, which, like the medieval combs, were tokens. They were made by the donor himself. In various forms they were carved out of a single piece of sycamore, even to the chainlinks which joined the two spoons. This was indeed painstaking, skilful work.

The range of chisels and gouges, or irons, which in medieval times was quite extensive, was considerably augmented during the Renaissance, when many Italian carvers came to work here, some of whom did so under patronage. The work of this movement came less and less from the mind of the carvers, but increasingly from the new design books which were coming to this country. With the Italians came the new tools to mingle with those of English origin.

In the carver's workshop, and prominent to the visiting eye, along the back of the bench, lie many of the chisels and gouges; at least, there are those in most frequent use, because all 300 or so of the entire range could not be accommodated here. Enough though to indicate the variety: front-bent, parting, left-cornered, straight, veining, bacaroni, fluteroni, dogleg, fishtail, each kind in a range of sizes. Some of them come directly from Sheffield, while others have been hand-forged from the bar by a local smith and tempered in whale-oil. The larger irons are usually machine-made, but most of the finer are hand-made to individual requirements, so once again our old friend the blacksmith has his place in the order of things. Machine- and hand-made are distinguishable. Those made by machine have ferruled handles and 'shouldered' irons, and unseen to the eye is the pointed tang. The hand-mades have neither shoulder nor ferrule, and the blunt tangs are set in gutta-percha. Most carvers lay the row with cutting edges pointing toward them for easy recognition, but a further aid to identity is in the variety of handles, in box, yew, beech, holly, ash, ebony, and rosewood. Some have round handles, with various turnings, and among them we find octagonals also variously shaped (the octagonals keep the rounds in their place and prevent them from running away). All about this vast array are coping saws, bow saws and set-squares, bottles of linseed, shellac, and two kinds of mallet—the lignum vitae, already mentioned, which is for free-work, and the square-headed one, of bronze, used especially for lettering. This latter is Italian in origin and is less 'persuasive'. An indispensable device is the carver's chops, which may be described as a wooden vice, capable of being rotated and secured in any desired position, to enable work to be more easily modelled. In addition to the chops, work may be secured by a couple of 'holdfasts', which are clamps set at an incline.

Among the great variety of work which the carver of today is called upon to execute is lettering, often of a commemorative nature. This may be either incised in the flat surface or set in relief against a recessed ground. Really good lettering calls for a skill possibly even greater than the

modelling work, wherein some deviations may only enhance the quality of the work. Not so lettering, which
requires in the first instance a historical knowledge and
appreciation of alphabets, a sense of the appropriate and
an innate sense of spacing. The oft-quoted Trajan Column
is so 'perfect' that to some of us it is lacking in character
and personality, and since it lacks a 'lower-case' it cannot be
a universal arbiter. Carvers therefore look less to this celebrated column and observe more closely the work of Gill
and Johnstone.

15

Wood-turning

Considered under the collective head of 'treen', a word of Saxon origin, the products of the wood-turner have for a long time found a welcome place at the table. Platters, bowls, ladles, and spoons continued in use down to Tudor times, for it was not till later that people used other than their fingers. Treen and horn retained their places till gradually displaced by pewter and even then continued in domestic use in the cottage and farm-house of the remoter regions. Pewter in its turn gave way to its successors. The contemporary trend is very much in favour of a partial return to treen, so that platters and bowls are reappearing in new forms.

The work of the turner falls naturally into two groups. The larger consists of the hundred and one articles which must be turned on a lathe, while the smaller group comprises the various things which are produced by various methods of shaving, in which the turner and the carver naturally overlap and are sometimes one and the same person.

A considerable variety of woods is used by turners. For all the utensils of the kitchen, used in the preparation of food, sycamore is always chosen, because it has neither taste nor smell. For ornamental ware, of course, every kind of wood may be used to obtain the variety of colour and grain—walnut, lime, beech, elm, cherry, box, laburnum, plum, ash, yew. Boards and platters for cheese and bread, where used at the table, may be of sycamore, while egg-cups, cruets, and pepper-mills are of walnut. The turning of the bobbins for lace-makers was almost a line on its own, for a variety of woods were used: plum, spindle, hazel, apple, ash, maple, willow, birch, and dogwood. Where especially beautiful 'figuring' was required, then a piece of burr-walnut was not to be surpassed (burr-walnut, is a growth, on the trunk of the tree, of incipient twigs). Two kinds of finish are given to the finished articles. For interior carvings and all turnings not connected with food beeswax is applied, but for such articles as salad-bowls, spoons, and forks, then teak-oil is used. The comparatively simple way of life and the harder living in the remoter parts is reflected in the wares and implements. None the less it is true to say of Wales that in the homesteads one may find a fine standard of turnery and carving. Food-bowls, crocks, mugs, mazers, and love-spoons are still there, though their domestic importance is not so great. Maple or burr-maple was much favoured for the mazers, the etymology of which, according to the O.E.D., is obscure, but the name for such a drinking-cup seems to have been derived from the burr of the maple. In times past the Welsh drank their *meddyglyn* from mazers. It was a form of mead, which was spiced to give healing properties. Even in more recent times they partook of a kind of gruel of mead.

A similar kind of bowl, for drinking purposes, was used in parts of Scotland, and was known as a quaich, from the Gaelic '*cuach*'—a drinking-cup. It differed very much from the mazer of Wales, which was, and still is, turned, because it was built up with staves, on a round base and secured with a hoop of split willow, on the same principle as a barrel. This cup had a handle on each side. For partaking of brose and porridge a larger bowl known as a caup was used. These were the traditional uses, but today the last turners to make them, in Dundee, are now producing caups and cuachs mainly for the souvenir trade, in sizes from 3 to

Welsh Nursery Stool

Salad Bowl

Welsh Crock

Welsh Dinner Set

Highland Quaich or drinking cup

8 in. in diameter. They follow the tradition of having the alternate staves in light and dark wood. The traditional makers were known as caupers. A 'lost art' is that of inserting a thin 'feather' of wood between the stave-joints.

Whether a turner uses a pole-lathe or the treadle type seems a matter for individual inclination. Where a great deal of turning has to be done on any one article it would appear that continuous rotation has its advantages. The extremely primitive pole-lathe came firstly with a primitive society, but its retention appears largely due to its simplicity and easy portability. This was essential to the chair-bodger, who worked in the plantation and was accustomed to moving on as ready material from the vicinity was used up. Bearing in mind that the pole-lathe turner makes his cuts only on the down-trend, the permanent set-up of a workshop would leave the turner free of this impediment. Perhaps one should state this cautiously, because a competent workman may be sufficiently accustomed to the peculiarities of his tools to overcome what might appear to be a disadvantage. A man who can turn a nest of bowls on a pole-lathe cannot be lacking in any skill.

A variety of knives and chisels is used, but by reason of the flexibility of use this range is small, compared with that of the carver. All the cutting-tools used at the lathe have very long handles, whereby a very sensitive 'leverage' can be obtained against the resistance of the rotating wood. The greater the diameter of the turnery, the greater the resistance. The straight chisels and gouges, of various width and depth are usually supplied by the big edge-tool makers who specialize in this work, but all the curiously hooked knives used for working on the interiors and exteriors of bowls, particularly the deeper kind, are the work of 'combined operations' between the turner and his friend the blacksmith. These 'inside' and 'outside' knives are not listed in any catalogues and in consequence they are as individual as their owners.

Generally, this work is 'low-speed' turning with the tool just 'kissing' the wood, but I have seen 'high-speed' turning in which the conventional chisels and gouges were being used. The turner was 'masked' and worked in a cloud of wood dust, which covered everything. In fact, his working produced no shavings at all. He was also working more 'in line' with the axis of the lathe, whereas turners normally 'face' the lathe.

One has but to stand in front of a lathe, with the 'bowl-to-be' set in the chucks, to realize that shaping the outside, the convex of a bowl is an operation which *can* be performed with 'front-cutting' tools. If the bowl be set for interior cutting, then the interior will be facing the turner, while the exterior will face away from him, so short of resetting the bowl it is easier to turn the outside with hooked knives. In any case, the interior of a deep bowl cannot be turned with the conventional chisel. So we look around to the turner, who smiles gently and hands us this strange contrivance, which at first glance looks for all the world as though some enraged person had bent the end right over and back on itself. Except that the person concerned was in anything but a rage, that is exactly what has happened. The turner showed the blacksmith a circular block of wood and described how he wanted to transform it into a bowl. The eventual result, after a great deal of experiment was this strange knife with a cutting edge ground carefully on that curl. This then became the 'inside' knife. Once the precise shape and curl was established, all they had to do for the 'outside' knife was to reverse everything. Instead of a curl to the right, it was made to the left, remembering that in all lathe-turning the rotation is anti-clockwise, or towards the turner from the top.

Most workers in wood, as those in other materials, can show a few neat antiques among all their tools, old chisels or planes 100 or more years old, and with which they would part in no circumstances. 'They don't put an edge on 'em like that nowadays'; that being a chisel which has known perhaps half a dozen generations of firm, coaxing hands. When a single tool is being made the smith will be entirely engrossed in his work; which probably explains the qualities which such tools have possessed.

16

Weaving

We have seen, in the Introduction, how weaving evolved from its primitive beginning to become a vital cottage industry and how sheep established the wealth of medieval England. With gradual changes in the methods of manufacturing the finished article, the craft continued as a cottage industry until the revolutionary inventions of the eighteenth and nineteenth centuries. Weaving in England experienced a major interruption and set-back, so that by the turn of the present century there were hardly more than half a dozen weaving-sheds at work, whereas the folk industry in the remoter parts of Celtic Britain survived by an inherent vitality and continuity.

In England, the craft had now to benefit from the lessons of William Morris. It fell to his redoubtable disciple, Ethel Mairet, and a handful of weavers, equally dedicated, to lift the craft from the trough of arty-crafty debasement to its present healthy status, where it coexists with the best of machine-manufactured products. These leaders set standards and gave tuition to pupils and founded the modern craft, which demands a high technology from its practitioners, that is; a knowledge of fibres and yarns and their potentialities; of dyes, both vegetable and chemical; a critical appreciation; a sense of the appropriate use of materials; a historical and cultural background. Together with pottery, weaving may be considered the highest culture in all the hand crafts. Weaving is certainly the most complex of all the crafts, if only because of the number of processes which take place from start to finish and because of the variety and nature of the fibres. The pupil who plies the shuttle at the loom must previously have been schooled in each of these processes; he must handle the fleeces and understand their qualities; he must understand the differences between the colours obtained from vegetable and mineral dyes. The high technology of the master will follow if it is based upon a sound training.

Originating as a means of eking out a hardy way of life among the crofters of the Highlands and the islands of Scotland, the cottage weavers of today have the backing and expert advice of the Highland Home Industries, who can attend to the selling of the products which today enjoy a very wide market. All the processes from spinning to finishing are done by hand, and the dyes used are all derived from vegetable sources. From the rocks, lichen gives a warm brown; other colours are derived from the tips of heather (ling), peat-soot, willow-leaves, and bog-myrtle. In the Shetlands and the islands of Orkney, the wool, a silky and warm lightweight yarn, is used to weave an excellent tweed. The wool is of several natural colours—white, cream, grey, brown to a near black, and it is therefore left undyed. The real picture of spinning and weaving in these 'distant' parts is many times removed from any 'romantic' image and it is the business of the industry's officers to keep their fingers on the pulse of the market.

THE FIBRES

The earliest known fibre was linen. This is the inner part of the stalk of the flax plant. Flax was cultivated in Egypt and further east as long ago as 2000 B.C. and was brought to Europe by the Phoenicians, who then had trading contacts

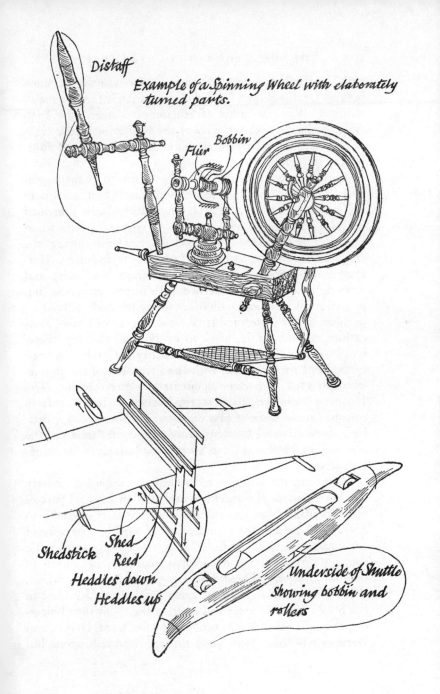

Distaff

Example of a Spinning Wheel with elaborately turned parts.

Flier

Bobbin

Shedstick

Shed

Reed

Heddles down

Heddles up

Underside of Shuttle showing bobbin and rollers

with the Celtic peoples of Britain. The weaving of linen became established in Ireland where today it forms a major industry. With an influx of Huguenot weavers, the Irish craft received a great impetus at the beginning of the eighteenth century, with improvements in the methods of cultivation, in spinning and weaving.

Cotton, which was introduced to England at the beginning of the seventeenth century, was known first in India in 800 B.C., and until the nineteenth century India remained the chief producer and exporter of cotton manufactured goods. The industry developed in England during the eighteenth century to become a machine industry. Hargreaves (the Spinning Jenny), Crampton (the Mule), and Arkwright were each concerned with introducing new, improved machinery and with overcoming the early difficulties peculiar to the cotton industry. The climate of humid Lancashire caused the industry to evolve and develop there. Until the end of the eighteenth century the craft had been carried out by hand, but with the invention of the power-loom, in 1787, it became dominated by the machine. The Jacquard loom was the last expression of hand craft in cotton. Looms were at first operated by horse-power, then by water-mills and later by steam. From that time on, the weaving of cotton became almost exclusively a machine-industry.

Throughout the history of this country the wool industry has been part of the rural life and was an integral part of our agriculture. Our climate has been especially amenable to sheep-farming and the manufacture of wool and because of the remarkable variation in soil and grass within our climatic range, we have been able to evolve a considerable variety of breeds of sheep. These may be grouped as long-wools, short-wools, and mountains. Long-wool sheep are bred in the bleaker, wetter areas and include the following; Leicester, Border-Leicester, Cotswold, Lincoln, Kent, Devon, and Dartmoor breeds. They yield a long, coarse, lustrous but in elastic staple. Short-wool sheep are generally bred in the warmer and drier areas. They include the following: South Down, Hampshire Down, Oxford Down, Dorset Down, Suffolk, Dorset Horn, Shropshire, Clun and Kerry. Generally, they produce a short, fine, and elastic staple. Mountain sheep, as their name suggests are bred in the high and exposed areas, of Wales, the Cheviot Hills, and the Scottish Highlands and include Exmoor, Welsh, Radnor, Cheviot, and the Blackface; incidentally, the last breed is the most difficult to drive and to contain within a walled field. Of the mountain breeds, the Cheviot is very much sought after for its wool is beautiful and can be easily spun.

Sheep of the Down breeds produce a fine and elastic staple which is suitable for light-weight materials. For coarser and heavier cloths, such as blankets and flannels, the Welsh breeds are favoured, though the mills use a variety of wools. The cottage weavers of the Scottish Highland and islands naturally use the wool of their own breeds. In Ireland, Donegal has established itself in the making of tweeds.

In addition to the natural yarns there has been an increasing use of synthetics, which may be interwoven with each other or with the natural yarns. The contrasts of textures offer a challenge to the skill and invention of the hand weavers, who not only produce weaves for their own market, but perform an indispensable service in experimentation for machine manufacture. Considered in either service, it will be realized that the craft of hand-loom weaving is not just an arty-crafty survival, but a vital part of the life of the country. The weaving industries of England, Wales, Scotland, and Ireland each have their respective characteristics, which we have appreciated.

THE WELSH MILLS

The history of weaving in Wales is of especial interest. In many of the mills a continuity has been established through generations of one family, each producing its own tradition of style. At some of the mills weaving on a small scale was combined with farming, so that both the farmer and his labourers were weavers only during the slacker farming time of winter. In fact, workers were employed as much for their abilities in weaving as in agriculture. Nowadays, however, the mills are all wholly specialist in weaving all the year round. In the section on weaving, there is a description of a hand loom and a comparison between its operation and that of the older types of machine loom, both of which are essential to the quality of Welsh weaving.

The mills are all sited by rivers giving an abundant supply of water-power for the fulling and finishing. The fuel for the dye vats is, in some mills, and was, in others, provided by alder-waste from the clog-makers. Peat, at one time dug by the miller, gave the heat for pressing the finished materials. Very often, these concerns were quite small, and by industrial standards may still be regarded as such, but by specialist production are able to produce some quite distinctive weaves. In addition, the gradual transition of the industry from the 'cottage' to the 'mill' has enabled the Welsh weavers to suffer less from the impact of the nineteenth century.

It is in the nature of wool to respond readily to either natural or chemical dyes. Natural dyes—vegetable or animal —are known as adjective or mordant, or substantive or non-mordant, according to whether they require preparation of the wool or not. The earliest of the vegetables used were woad, indigo, and whortleberry. Generally, the longer the boiling process the deeper the colour, which could be affected by the mordant used, such as iron, allum, or tin. With natural dyes, there was a limit to the range of colours. A considerable variation resulted from the time of the year at which the plant was picked. There was a certain amount of 'guess-work'—not in itself necessarily a bad thing, if the dyer was really expert—and most of the recipes for dyeing were, in practice, passed down through the generations. My wife is a brilliant pastry-cook, not 'because she follows the directions' but because she can 'feel the right amount in her fingers'. It is one of the marks of craftsmanship.

The first synthetic dyes were not produced until 1856 and became increasingly available during the next decades, until by the turn of the century all the larger mills were using them in preference to the natural dyes. By the late 1930s only a few remotely situated millers were continuing to use the old natural dyes. The manufacturers can now obtain hundreds of synthetic dyes, all constant in their colour-values. Nevertheless, for certain forms of weaving, the natural dyes undoubtedly have their charm.

Some vegetable dyes and their colours:

Dark brown. Wall lichen, red-currant, bracken, sorrel, walnut-shell, blaeberry.

Tan and light brown. Other lichen, sloe, elder, birch, broom bed-straw, heather.

Blue. Blaeberry, elder, indigo, woad.

Black. Gall nut, oak bark.

Green. Gorse, iris, broom, blackthorn, birch.

Purple. Blaeberry, blackberry.

Yellow. Apple, ash, buckthorn, hazel, bracken, birch, lichen, dog's mercury, gorse, heather, bed-straw.

Orange. Bramble, ragweed.

Magenta. Dandelion.

Red. Bedstraw, madder tormentil, foxglove, cochineal, lichen.

By the admixture of mordants and the intermixture of the dyes, a considerable variety of each colour was obtainable.

After dyeing, the wool must be disentangled, by loosening or 'opening' the matted fibres, in preparation for carding, which is a continuation of the loosening. In this teasing, or willying, not only is the wool loosened, but the colours may be mixed, for example, black wool and white are variously mixed to produce greys, for flannel. This process is facilitated by the admixture of vegetable oil. The thoroughly disentangled wool eventually emerges from the 'willy' to be collected by a comb.

Carding was formerly done by women and children with the heads of the teazle or with combs and cards. The latter consisted of fine wire teeth set in leather fillets. No fault occurring at this stage can be subsequently corrected. The carding machine was introduced for the cotton industry and later adapted to the needs of the woollen industry. Another machine, called a condenser, reduces the thickness of the wool strands.

The wool, as received from the final process in carding, is still too weak and too thick to be used for weaving. The slivers have to be sufficiently strong and elastic to bear the strain and friction which occur during weaving. There are two consecutive processes; firstly twisting and compressing so that each individual fibre is entwined and secondly the drawing out or extension. In spinning, the sliver increases in length as it decreases in thickness. In the hand craft this is accomplished on the spinning-wheel in which a 36 in. wheel drives a $1\frac{1}{2}$ in. whorl, so that the latter revolves very fast indeed. In any factory, this is done on a mule, which may have as many as eighty spindles. It has been a feature of Welsh mills that they use older patterns of machinery, eminently suited to the size and output of the mills. Most of this machinery dates from the last century and much of it has come from the Davies workshops at Llanbrynmair, Montgomeryshire. It is also a feature of the training of employees that they 'go through the mill' and so become familiar and competent at every stage.

Woven cloth consists of the warp or lengthwise threads and the interwoven weft or crosswise threads. Preparation of the warp varies with each intended weave of material

37 INTERIOR OF A MODEL OF THE POST MILL AT
SPROWSTON, NORWICH   *Science Museum*

39 LONGSTRAW THATCHER, AT ST MARYBOURNE, HAMPSHIRE

James Arnold

40 NORFOLK REED THATCHER AT STOKE ORCHARD NEAR CHELTENHAM

James Arnold

41 LONGSTRAW THATCHING AT GOOD EASTER, ESSEX

Rural Industries Bureau

42 NORFOLK-REED THATCHING ON A BARN AT SUDBURY

Rural Industries Bureau

43 WEAVING ON A SMALL POWER-LOOM IN THE WELSH TRADITION

Museum of English Rural Life

44   HAND-LOOM WEAVING IN WALES

Welsh Folk Museum

and its pattern and it is therefore the foundation of good weaving.

There are two units: a warping frame or mill, on to which all the threads are run, and the creel or swift, which contains up to thirty bobbins, according to the colour. From the creel or the swift the yarns are arranged in two rows and feed through a warping-bat, held in the right hand, from which the yarns are guided to the pegs on the frame. The threads are crossed to go alternately above and below the pins. This lengthy process sets the pattern of the weave and once it is completed that pattern cannot be altered. The process continues until a sufficient amount of warp has been prepared. The same process in hand-weaving is called raddling. Removed from the frame, the warp is chained into slip knots to secure it against any risk of tangling until it is placed in position on the warp-beam, which is situated at the back of the loom. This placing is called beaming and the greatest attention is required to ensure equal tension in every one of the warp threads, in order to avoid subsequent unevenness in the material. Because of this great care the woven material, when finished, will lie flat.

WEAVING BY HAND AND BY MACHINE

The looms used are of two widths, producing cloths of 54 or 88 in. weft. In a hand loom, or foot loom the heddles are operated by pedals, and are suspended in a harness containing four sets of heddles—one for each thread of the warp. The warp threads run off the beam at the back, through the eyes in the heddles to the front of the loom, under the weaver and so doubling back on to the cloth beam, below. The four sets of heddles are connected to respective pedals, the depression of which causes the sets to be raised or lowered from the normal position, according to the plan of the pattern. So each depression of any of the pedals produces an 'opening', called a shed, in the raised or lowered warp

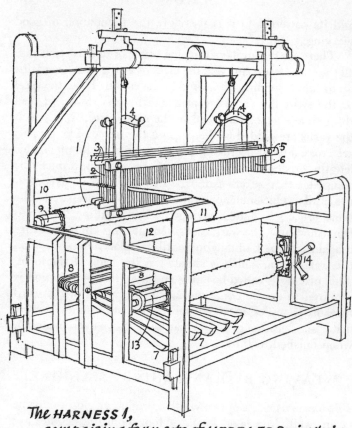

The HARNESS 1,
    comprising four sets of HEDDLES 2, in their
    SHAFTS 3, all suspended from HORSES 4.
The BATTEN 5, holding the REED 6.
The SIX TREADLES 7, connected to four LAMS 8,
    in turn connected to the heddles.
The WARP ROLLER 9, and WARP BEAM 10.
The BREAST BEAM 11, the CLOTH BEAM 12,
    the CLOTH ROLLER 13, and the WINDLASS 14.

The principal parts of a FOUR-SHAFT LOOM.

threads. The weft thread, previously wound on to bobbins, is contained in the shuttles, one shuttle for each colour in the weft. At each change of the openings the shuttle is passed deftly from one side to the other, each pass producing a line of weft. At frequent intervals, the weaver releases a heavy batten which beats and compresses the growing weave, which is wound on to the cloth beam by a windlass on the right-hand side.

In a machine loom every one of the foregoing hand movements has to be reproduced by remarkably ingenious machinery. The sequence of raising and lowering of the heddles is set by tappers and the passing to and fro is performed by levers which alternately 'discharge' and 'catch' the flying shuttle. The 'beating' of the weave and winding on are all mechanized. All this must be supervised continuously by a qualified operator, who must watch the shuttles so that the bobbins may be fed in. The contrast between the quiet of the hand-weaving shed, in which the soft sounds are only broken by the intermittent thump of the batten and the positively deafening racket of the machine loom must be experienced to be appreciated. In the one shed there is normal conversation and in the other little more than sign-language. Hand or machine, however, the principles and the sequence of operations are the same. An endless range of patterns is made possible by the setting of the warp, and the use and number of shuttles. Some weaves have a 'front' and a 'back' to the material, others have warp and weft equal on both sides, all depending upon the warp or the weft being 'dominant', or equal.

FULLING AND FINISHING

While many of the small mills are equipped to do their own fulling, this has always been done by a fuller, who receives the woven cloths from the hand-loom weavers. A fuller made this a full-time job, catering for all the weavers for a considerable distance. Careful inquiry in East Anglia, in the Cotswolds, and in Wales, may reveal the original purpose of an ancient and abandoned waterside building. In Wales, we have a useful clue in the word 'Pandy', for there are many place-names containing this stem.

The earliest form of fulling necessitated 'walking' the cloth whilst it lay in running water, that is the clear water of a fast stream. From the fourteenth century onwards this walking was reproduced by a set of wooden mallets actuated by tappets turned by the water-wheel. So this operation had to be performed not by the weavers who had always 'walked' the cloth, but by a new operator, the fuller. When all the processes, from dyeing and carding to spinning and weaving were 'cottage' industries, the fulling-mill was the only 'factory' process. It was introduced by the Flemings into Pembrokeshire, whence the practice spread all over Wales. The Flemings concurrently influenced and advanced the craft in East Anglia and elsewhere, though it was not until the middle of the nineteenth century that Welsh mill-weavers did their own fulling, so the fuller must have been to weaving what the miller was to the baking of bread.

When the processes of fulling have been completed, the cloth is dried by sun and air and stretched out on tenter frames; each frame large enough to hold a finished length of cloth. After the drying, the cloth is 'hot-pressed'. One may stand on the splendid bridge over the Teifi at Pentre Cwrt and be fascinated by the endless surge of the river in its mad tumbling haste from the curlew heights above Strata Florida to the sea beyond Cardigan. There can be no purer water than from such rivers as this.

In the Welsh Folk Museum at St Fagans Castle, near Cardiff, one may make an immediate comparison between the products of about twenty-five of the Welsh mills. The articles are principally, blankets, coverlets, and flannelling, etc., and in a while one can detect, within the characteristic weaves, the subtle variations between this and that mill. In the grounds of St Fagans an old mill, Esgair Moel, from near Llanwrtyd Wells, has been re-erected and is producing weaves for the market.

17

Bow- and-Arrow-making

At Agincourt, the French went down under a rain of arrows which fell on them at about 25,000 a minute, while their mercenary crossbowmen vainly sought to give support. Something like it had happened before, at Poitiers and Crecy. At Hastings, the Saxon axes, single- or double-handed were used at close quarters, while their wielders were behind the 'shield-wall'. This strategy was intended for defence against the normal low trajectory of arrow-flight. When the Normans, playing their last card, gave the order for high trajectory fire, the shield wall, held above the head, could only be partially effective and wholly cumbersome. In the débâcle which ensued we lost our last Saxon king.

Many primitive peoples, such as the Veddas of Ceylon and the Bushmen of Africa, for example, who are among the last of the true 'Stone Age' hunters, have for a very long time been expert in the making and use of bows and arrows, designed for their especial needs. The Bushmen now very often fit iron tips to their arrow-shafts, wherever that metal is available, but formerly they had always used stone tips, skilfully flaked to produce an exceedingly sharp point, and set in a mass of resin to secure them to the shafts. Such arrows were fairly small, as were the bows, and in order that they would be lethal against large animals, the tip was dipped in a poison from vegetable or animal sources and intended to remain in the victim, should the shaft break off and fall away.

In the Andaman Islands, too, the men, who are fairly small of stature, use comparatively large bows and their arrows like those of the African Bushmen, have tips which are detachable from the shafts, for the same reason. They use this weapon for hunting animals and also for fishing in the fast waters. The Veddas, of Ceylon, use a bow taller than themselves, for hunting, and the arrows are notable for the diamond-shaped iron tips. Whereas the Bushmen were accustomed to hunting in a dry, open country and had learned to use the bow at comparatively long range, the Veddas, living in heavily wooded country, learned to stalk their quarry at a close range, closing often to within a few yards before loosing their arrows. While the Veddas hold their bows in what we might regard as the orthodox manner, the Bushmen appear often to hold their bows very much out of the vertical and with the bow fingers extended.

The bow and arrow was the traditional weapon of the Red Indian peoples of America and the many tribes of Asia and Mongolia. The warriors of both these continents used the bow whilst riding their horses at speed, a tactic at which they were particularly adept, relying upon their own speed to render themselves difficult to hit.

Legend usually derives from historical origin, which being passed on from generation to generation acquires not inconsiderable embellishment and even transposition and some aura. We may read the story of the greatest of all outlaws, Robin Hood, who lived in the forest of Sherwood, and learn of his reputed prowess with the bow. Certainly, in the Middle Ages many men were outlawed for one reason or another. Robert, Earl of Huntingdon, or Robert Fitzooth of Locksley, or just Robin Hood, remember him how we will, was one of many such men in Plantagenet days. In the *Annals of England*, 1580, Stow wrote:

'Reign of King Richard the First. In this time there were many robbers and outlaws, among the which Robin Hood and Little John renowned theeves, continued in woods, disploying and robbing the goods of the rich. They killed none, but such as would invade them, or by resistance to their own defence. The said Robert intertained an hundred tall men, and good archers with such spoiles and thefts as he got, upon four hundred (were they never so strong) durst not give the onset. He suffered no woman to be oppressed, violated or otherwise molested, poore men's goods he spared, abundantly relieving them with that which by, theft he got from Abbeys and the houses of rich Carles: whom major blameth for his rapine and theft but of all theeves hee affirmeth him to bee the Prince, and the most gentle theefe.'

It is probable that 'Resistance' and 'Underground' had not then acquired their present-day connotation, but nevertheless, the head of many an appointed sheriff doubtless ached with the fruitless problem of oppression.

They still follow the craft of the bowyer in Sherwood, making bows and arrows both according to the traditional form, of yew and ash, or by a more recent technique, in which the bows are built up with laminations of various woods and glass-fibre and the arrow-shafts made either of aluminium alloy or glass-fibre tubing. The possibilities of completely reshaping the entire bow have been exercised, and the middle part, held by the left hand, and called the arrow-pass or arrow-plate, has been redesigned to provide a grip shaped to the hand. This revolutionary change can be appreciated in the drawing of an archer. This type of bow has to be built up on a specially designed jig, on which all the laminations of exotic woods and glass-fibre are placed together with adhesives and clamped until they are set.

The woods so used may be Canadian hard rock maple, Indian laurel, or Brazilian rosewood. When the laminated bow is set, there follows the skilful shaping with draw-knives and spokeshaves. This is 'worked-down' and finally polished. The arrow-shafts are flighted with selected turkey feathers, whilst the strings are made of three-ply Dacron.

In the times when the bow and arrow was both a weapon of War and of the chase, it was the yew which was so sought after, that for lack of sufficient natural supplies, much of it was imported, very often from Spain. It became necessary to legislate that every wine cask had a stipulated proportion of yew staves. This suggests that even at that time, it had become customary to make each of two sections, joined to make up the length, where originally each bow had been of one piece.

'Every bowe is made of the boughe, the plante or the boole. The boughe is knotty and full of pruines; the plante is quick enough of caste but is apt to break; and the boole is the best. If you come into a shoppe and fynde a boole that is small, long, heavy, stronge, lyinge streighte, not wyndynge, nor marred with knottes, gaule wynshake, wern freat, or pinch, bye that bowe on my warrant.'

Roger Ascham, *Toxophiles*, 1544.

With that classic instruction in mind the intending bowman or archer may consider his purchase.

Some of the best bows even now are of one piece, up to 6 ft in length and tipped with horn. As far back as the sixteenth century, however, a Manchester bowyer, one Kelsall, laid a strip of ash along the belly of his bows and so became a pioneer of lamination.

Hobbies are often begun and followed by some accidental origin. Roben Hardy, the actor, played Henry V in the B.B.C. production and was so personally involved in archery that he became in his own words, 'obsessed totally by the Battle, by the English archers and especially by the longbows with which they won such remarkable victories'.

His search for suitable yew ended when he ran to earth a traditional bowyer, not in England, as one would reasonably have expected, but in far-away Oregon, at a place called

Ullrich. One may wander through the largest yew forest in Europe, at Kinley Vale, near Chichester, and be surprised, but yew in the wild state, in this country rarely provides what the craftsman seeks, which is perhaps well, that this remarkable forest shall retain its eerie silence.

Having obtained several bows from the American bowyer, Mr Hardy decided that it would be easier and certainly more satisfying to make his own. His bows are made of two pieces, 'sister-split', from the same billet of yew. These pieces are joined at the centre by a double fishtail. As with most crafts involving any cleavage, the billet is split with an axe, which in this case was forged by 'the local blacksmith', who appreciated Mr Hardy's problem. The shaping of the two-part bow, still but roughly hewn, is made with an old draw-knife, found 'rusting away in a builder's yard'. It had belonged to a wheelwright and underneath that coat of rust there was still good steel that responded to some patient hours with a stone. As the shaving progresses the bow is 'tillered', which is to say that the string is tightened day by day and held on a 'tillering-board' until a deep arc has been obtained. The last stage consists of sanding and polishing until the white sapwood of the back—the outside of the arc —shines like ivory. The inside, where the heartwood lies, is known as the belly.

Even the traditional form of bow had a 'shaped' part for a good hold, though in no degree suggestive of 'streamlining' as in the laminated pattern. It is said that the medieval bow had no shaped hold, though some people would disagree and aver that some shaping was made. There is good evidence that the military bows ranged in weight and size from around 75 lb. draw-weight to as much as 120 lb.— certainly a man's weapon. Nowadays they consider that 60 or 65 lb. is too heavy, and, in fact, for archery, 40 to 50 lb. is usual. Men lived harder then, ate harder and drank harder, especially the military bowmen.

According to W. Gilpin, in *Remarks on Forest Scenery*,

1791, 'the secret of the greater efficacy of the English archers lay in the fact that the Englishman did not keep his left hand steady and "draw" with his right, but, keeping his right hand at rest upon "the nerve", he pressed the whole weight of his body into the horns of his bow'. Hence probably arose the phrase 'bending a bow' and the French one, of 'drawing a bow'. Those archers were drawn not from the playing-fields, but from the plough-fields of England, and so, fighting under their own lord of the manor, established themselves as a dependable source of man-power.

Mr Hardy makes his arrow-shafts of ash, which are turned and shaven, and then flighted with turkey or goose feathers. At one time the bow-string was of flax or hemp, but nowadays it is customary to use either a linen thread or Dacron fibre. Either material is plied into a strong string.

Archery meetings are held separately and jointly for the traditional long-bows and the modern laminated, in the latter meetings the events are separate. Up to a range of 200 yards the bow has, in capable hands, sufficient accuracy and force to render it lethal.

18

Making Coracles

The English word 'coracle' is derived from the Welsh *corwgl*, the diminutive of *corwg* and also from the Irish *curach*. This fascinating little craft, regarded by some people as quaint has a very distant origin. It existed and had evolved centuries before the Romans came, since which time the various designs have changed but little.

For the kind of water on which coracles have been used, they have been efficient, easily navigated—for those who were practised—and above all portable, and comparatively quickly made from material readily to hand.

The fast-running waters of the Teifi and the Upper Towy, almost all of the Wye and the smaller rivers of Wales; the wider calmer waters of the Towy below Carmarthan, the Severn below Welshpool and the Dee—all had to be used by people who were farmers or fishermen, or simply ordinary folk who wanted to cross rivers where they were too deep to ford. This type of craft was also used on the shallow marsh waters of the Fenland, both by the Iceni and by the contemporaries of Hereward. By means of such a craft it was possible to penetrate the vast acres of common reed. We may note, too, that in Ireland both the round coracle and the long design, the curach, were commonly used. The curach survives today in a more robust construction with a fairly conventional arrangement of oak ribs, but having the characteristic covering of cowhide or heavy canvas, heavily

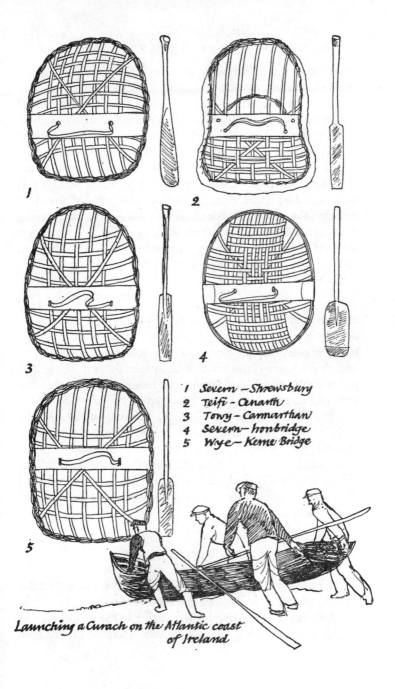

1 Severn – Shrewsbury
2 Teifi – Cenarth
3 Towy – Carmarthan
4 Severn – Ironbridge
5 Wye – Kerne Bridge

Launching a Curach on the Atlantic coast of Ireland

coated with pitch. They are used especially by the islanders of Aran and are usually rowed with three pairs of surprisingly narrow-bladed oars. My wife and I found such a craft in a cove near Strumble Head, in Pembroke, where there is likely to be contact with Ireland additional to the steamers from Fishguard. This particular craft was in conformity with the accepted pattern and had the familiar prow, rising from straight sides. It was about 18 ft in length with a 4 ft beam and had a flat stem. In an early narrative, of the sixth century, the curach is described as a sea-going craft, having a wicker framework covered with cowhide. A mast was stepped amidships, carrying a square sail. A simple form of rudder was provided. The rising prow was very effective against the long swells of the Atlantic.

Not surprisingly, the most familiar photograph of a Welsh coracle is that of a man carrying one on his back, looking, from the rear, very much like an enormous beetle standing on end. A slack strap athwart the seat permits the craft being slipped over the shoulders, leaving the hands free, though some men will carry the craft, by this strap on one shoulder. Easy portage is an important feature, because it allows the coracle to be used and stored easily. A coracle is never moored at the water's edge in the manner of a conventional boat, but is carried away to the owner's house. It is a kind of boat specifically designed for use on the waters mentioned above, where the conventional shape of oared boat would be impracticable.

TYPES OF CORACLE

When one pictures a coracle in the mind, it is usually of the Teifi kind, which is perhaps the best known.

The Teifi has a flattish prow, curving to the widest part of the craft, from which the sides gently decrease in width to the middle, where the seat is positioned. Aft of the seat the shape is semicircular. In cross-section, at any point the boat bulges below the gunwale and appears to lie deeper in the water than the other designs, for it must be capable of carrying the owner over very turbulent water.

The craft of all the other rivers are shallower and seem to lie more lightly on the calmer, more slowly moving waters, and in the words of one builder have been designed to 'skim' quickly over the water. The Towy, so far as is known, was designed rather later than the Teifi, and in plan may be described as very broadly egg-shaped, but with a flattened prow, and in section somewhat saucer-like. It has no waist, and is used on estuarine water. The Wye coracle, as constructed at Hereford, is generally similar, but the Severn types, that at Bridgnorth and the better-known one, used by Harry Rogers, at Ironbridge are dissimilar, the Bridgnorth being very deeply oval in plan, while the Ironbridge more resembles the Towy.

The dimensions vary appreciably, though there is no significance in this, as each coracle is made expressly for its intended owner, whose height and weight must be accounted for. In use the frail structure tends to lose its original shape, so precise measurements are not easy, but a Teifi can vary in length from 60 to 72 in., with some maximum of 40 in. across the prow and 34 in. across the seat. The depth varies from 12 to 16 in. The Ironbridge type is about 65 in. long by about 47 in. wide, with the depth about 14 in. The front edge of the seat is about midway between prow and stern. The average weight is 30 lb.

Generally, the paddle consists of a shaft with a bulbous top for manœuvring and a parallel blade inserted, but the Bridgnorth has a very well-made paddle which follows the line of a canoe-paddle. The length varies from 40 in. overall for the Teifi to 54 in. for the Ironbridge. Ash is usually selected as the most suitable wood.

CONSTRUCTION

Except for the construction of the gunwale of the Teifi, it may be said that in principle all coracles are similarly built. The framework consists of a number of cleft willow laths, laid lengthwise and crosswise and all alternatively woven. The numbers vary, but the Teifi has six lengthwise and eight or nine crosswise, spaced along almost the full length and width, while the Ironbridge has eight each way, but grouped closer to the centre. The Bridgnorth has seven each way, but set a little more widely apart. All types have two additional diagonals. This woven framework is not secured or nailed, so as to avoid friction with the outer covering and to obtain resilience. From this foundation the extremities of the laths are turned up and secured by a gunwale of willow laths for most types over which the frame-ends are turned and nailed. These nails at gunwale level do not affect the watertightness. The Teifi and the Towy have gunwales of woven unsplit hazel rods. The resultant structure can be described as having a basket-like texture. Except for a froe or similar tool with which to cleave the willow and a hammer, hardly any tools are necessary.

The earliest coracles had their frames of wicker covered hide secured with leather thongs, but for a very long time down to the present day this covering has been of calico similarly stretched tight over the framework and bound over into the gunwale. Whether of hide or calico, the covering was heavily coated with pitch, though it is not known what was used before this by-product of coal was obtainable.

PROPULSION

At first glance it is not apparent that the blunt end is the prow and that when the man is seated the stern tends to rise a little from the water. Only one paddle is used and the

Framework of a Teifi Coracle

Easy Portage

The normal paddling
action

Shaving the willow laths on a horse
(note the efficiency of this
simple vice)

normal paddling action can be described as a 'figure of eight' from side to side over the prow. It is possible to manœuvre quite large barges by a single very long oar used in a similar manner from a 'rowlock' over the stern. Thames lighters are frequently moved over short distances in this manner. By means of the 'figure of eight', an expert can propel a coracle with surprising speed. When fishing with rod or with net a single-handed action is employed to keep the coracle steady. The normal propulsion is a 'pulling' one, rather than a 'pushing'.

USE

Coracles are not registered, though on the Teifi they bear numbers, which are painted on both sides in large white figures. The Fisheries Board is not encouraging net fishing and fresh licences for this purpose are no longer being granted. When demonstrations of net-catching of salmon are given it will be observed that the net is 'trawled' between two coracles, whose owners hold the net at each end across the salmon-run and maintain their position with the free hand. The primary use, for a coracle, now, is for fly-fishing and sheep-dipping. The coracle is particularly suited to the latter task, as it can be manœuvred among the sheep—an impossible task with any other craft.

On the Teifi, between Cardigan Estuary and Llechryd, which is above Cenarth, there are sixteen fishermen operating, but upriver, from Llechryd to Newcastle Emlyn, there are only two men. Below Cenarth Bridge there is no limitation to the number of licences granted, but above Cenarth, the licence 'dies' with the licensee. As no new licences are being granted, net fishing on the upper stretch of the river will die out.

On the towy and its tributary, the Taff, there are twelve licences for operation below Carmarthan and two below St Clears. Fishing is permitted between March 1st and August

31st and during the hours of darkness, or when the rivers hold alluvia in suspension, that is, when they are heavily opaque from flood or springtides. No week-end fishing is permitted.

The coracle is a light and cheaply constructed craft with a normal 'life' of about two years. While detail repairs may be made from time to time, extensive renovations are not considered worth while; because of the simplicity of construction a new coracle is built about every two years.

WHERE TO SEE THEM

One can see coracles in museums, such as St Fagans at Cardiff, the Museum of English Rural Life, and at Bridgnorth, but even better is the chance-encounter with a 'coracle-man' either on his local water or outside his house. It is all a matter of traveller's luck and a nice reward for making a leisurely journey.

One can, however, be certain of an interesting and stimulating day by attending the Cilgerran Festive Week, during which the Coracle Races and Aquatic Sports are held on the third Saturday in August. There are events over 100 or 200 yds.; 'open' events for all coracles and separate events for Towy and Teifi, and again for women and boys. There is a Challenge Cup for the best handling and finally there are demonstrations of coracles in use. One comes away from this meeting with the realization that far from being 'quaint', the coracle is thoroughly practical and efficient, and, of course, it is a part of the rural life of Old Wales.

19

Pottery

The art of the potter stemmed from man's discovery that certain earths, those having a heavy clay content, became plastic when in a wet state, but dried out quite hard, though brittle, when exposed to the drying heat of the sun. By further experiment, some of this clay was extracted and made by manipulation into some suitable shape and placed in the centre of a hot, glowing fire. This was the initial step and the most important, because it was the basis of the craft. Those early pots were extremely crude, of course, and were quite porous and fragile, but were none the less useful in daily life. As time went on, it was found that some clays were better suited than others. There was no chemistry then, but men were learning, the hard way.

In the civilizations of the Euphrates and the Nile they made pottery of terracotta, which was porous but which was made capable of carrying liquids, by application of a heavy glaze. It may be noted that the Greeks gave their work a 'fine lustre' by applying a thinner glaze. This work was 'thrown' on a rotating wheel, but many centuries passed before the principle reached this country, during the era of the La Tène Celts.

This wheel pottery was obviously a tremendous technical advance on the crude and erratic work which began by being 'built-up' with coils of clay to the required shape. Greater strength was obtained by first weaving a willow 'basket' and then impressing the wet clay into both the inside and the outside of this foundation. The wheel enabled the potter to do two things; firstly, to produce a true round form and, secondly, to do it much more quickly. Concurrently, they were improving the consistency of the body and devising techniques of controlled firing. The Romans, who in pottery as in other arts and sciences, were consistently brilliant technicians, devised a means of making pottery in moulds. A mould having the required outside shape and surface of the pot-to-be was prepared beforehand, in two vertical halves, in which, could be incorporated any embossed, or incised design which was 'in reverse'. This mould, when fired, would retain permanently the required shape and dimensions. When the mould was cold the clay body was moulded to the inside of each half, trimmed off, and the two halves clamped together. From the very beginning it had been realized that when clay loses its water content in drying it shrinks, and the Roman mould simply exploited this. During the firing in the kiln the pot shrank within the mould. On extraction the pot was cleaned up and burnished on a lathe fitted with various abrasive wheels. The pot was finished with a lustre similar to that employed by the Greeks. The Romans had thus taken the first step towards repetitive production.

During the Dynasties of Han, Sui, Tang, Sung, and Ming, that is, from 185 B.C. to A.D. 1643, and during the period of K'ang-Hsi, 1667 to 1722, there was a high technological and aesthetic standard in Chinese pottery, in which Sung may be associated with beauty and Ming with the manufacture. The Chinese produced stoneware and porcelain, and during the last phase they used a remarkable range of metallic glazes.

In this country after the Roman departure, there was a long quiet period with little advance. Medieval pottery was mainly in the form of lead-glazed earthenware of a high aesthetic standard and was known as faience or majolica.

During the seventeenth century the Staffordshire potters were producing a slip-ware of a very high-standard. This kind of ware consists of a 'cream' of potter's clay, applied on a porous earthenware body which has previously been fired. A second firing produces the finished article. The slip may be 'trailed' to a deliberate design or the pot immersed in slip and a design then 'scratched' by the process known as *sgraffito*.

English slip was unequalled outside this country and reached a quality peak during the seventeenth century, when the Brothers Toft were producing their finest work. It is to be found in many places, especially the Fitzwilliam Museum in Cambridge and the Victoria and Albert Museum, in London. Slip-ware is therefore essentially 'English' in character and some of the decoration may well be considered a form of 'popular' art. By the end of the eighteenth century English fine slip-ware had displaced both faience and majolica; this latter had a 'coarse' body and was usually glazed opaque, dark brown or black. In 1650, some Dutch potters established themselves at Lambeth and in Liverpool; majolica or faience had been produced. Concurrently with the demise of faience-majolica a fine salt-glazed stoneware was being made in Fulham.

The first stoneware in this country, came to us from Holland and Germany during the sixteenth and seventeenth centuries and manufacture commenced at Fulham in 1672. This kind of ware, which carried a white salt-glaze, reached a high level in Staffordshire by the middle of the eighteenth century. It was about this time that there occurred one of those accidents whereby in this context the potentialities of china-clay were appreciated by a veterinary surgeon, and so the first use of this ingredient was made in pottery where a white body was designed.

Generally, pottery 'bodies' are composed of four ingredients which are mixed in proportions which vary according to the kind of ware and the nature of the individual pottery. This variation applies also to kiln temperatures

Lower Ninestone China Clay Mine, Stenalees, north of St Austell.

and much of the skill and the features which distinguish good potters are derived from their knowledge of how to 'break the rules'.

Both earthenware and stoneware have essentially the same body, consisting of ball-clay for plasticity, china-clay as the main ingredient, feldspar as a flux, and flint to keep the shape during firing. Some potteries use clay alone and by skilful preparation and firing produce the kind of ware they like. Not all use china-clay. When the clay body is fired at temperatures up to 1100°C. it becomes very hard, but remains porous unless subsequently glazed. If, however, the body is fired glazed up to 1350°C, the whole will fuse and become dense and vitreous.

Porcelain has a white translucent body, which is dense, vitreous, and therefore impermeable. The body has the same ingredients as stoneware, but has a higher proportion of china-clay. It is this translucence which distinguishes it from stoneware. There have been two kinds of porcelain, one 'hard' and the second 'soft'. Hard porcelain, already glazed, is fired at 1300°–1400°C., causing complete fusion. The Chinese and Japanese porcelains were hard. Soft porcelain, unglazed, is fired at 1200°–1300°C., after which the body is glazed and then fired a second time at 1050°–1150°C. What is known as bone china is treated similarly to soft porcelain, but bone-ash is substituted for the 'glass-frit' which is contained in the soft porcelain body.

The potteries which produced hard porcelain commenced work as follows: Plymouth, 1760; Bristol, 1774; Lowestoft, 1751; Liverpool, 1755 (transferred to Burslem); Wedgwood, 1757.

The potteries which produced soft porcelain commenced work as follows: Bow, 1744; Chelsea, 1730, joined with Derby, 1784; Worcester 1751; Coalport, 1780.

The solitary pottery working in bone china was Spode, 1805.

In 1757 Josiah Wedgwood established himself as a producer of quality in quantity, and when confronted with the problems of package and transport first of all arranged to have his own canal constructed to link the pottery with the English canal system. Not only had he a line of communication providing shock-free transport from works to destination, but he also went further and solved the container problem by getting basket-makers to manufacture special baskets of hazel. These baskets were worked out to a specification and indeed this form of container is still woven from 'seven-year' hazel.

Pottery by Wedgwood revived the classic precepts in design and decoration. In addition to the astonishing blue with which the name is inseparable, there was some fine work in oxide on a black ground and vice-versa. Work which had begun at Burslem in 1757 was transferred to Etruria in 1769, whence fine ware have come ever since. By the end of the eighteenth century earthenware as produced by Wedgwood had completely supplanted faience (which had an opaque glaze). Wedgwood died in 1795, but his work and tradition live on.

At this juncture it is convenient to summarize the kinds of ware.

Terracotta. Has an unglazed, porous body, fired at low temperatures.

Majolica-Faience. Has a porous body, glazed with an opaque tin enamel.

Earthenware. Has a glazed, porous body, fired at medium temperatures.

Slip-ware. Is earthenware with a decoration by slip-cream.

Porcelain. Has a vitreous, translucent, glass-like body, fired at high temperatures.

Bone china. Similar to the softer porcelain, but contains bone ash and is fired at a lower temperature.

Stoneware. Has a vitreous, dense, non-porous body, and is fired at high temperatures.

The kinds of ware must be described in detail:

Permeable ware. 'Heavy Clay' covers all commercial and industrial products, such as bricks, tiles, piping, sanitary ware, pipings, and insulators, etc.

Terracotta. Is unglazed, and is softer and more porous than earthenware and is fired at lower temperatures. The colour varies from oxide and yellow ochre to brown.

Earthenware. Less porous and harder than terracotta, and fired at high temperatures, after which the glaze is applied and subject to a second firing.

Impermeable ware. Porcelain and bone china have been described.

Stoneware. As stated previously, when a clay body is fired at temperatures above 1150°C. it fuses and becomes vitreous. Unlike porcelain, it is completely opaque and in colour varies, according to the source of the clay, from pale ochre to grey and brown.

Heavy clay is obviously an industrial ware.

The large potteries of Staffordshire and elsewhere produce various kinds of earthenware, stoneware, and porcelain.

The studio potters produce various kinds of terracotta, earthenware, slip-ware, stoneware, and saltglaze.

By the late eighteenth century the pottery industry was well established in Staffordshire and main provincial towns and indeed several places about London. In Cornwall and in various quite rural environments elsewhere there came into being a different form of production where the concentration was on quality and individuality. At first, these individual potters worked in the vicinity of the clay they used. With a solid-fuel kiln of brick construction the earlier potters were tied to the ground, but the invention of the smaller electric kiln meant that, with easy transport of materials, a potter could set up business where he lived. So today, in addition to the cluster of potters working in Cornwall, there are many to be found in other parts of the country, where trade will be catered for. The best continue to point the way ahead and eschew meretricious decoration and gimmicks. Like their fellow craftsmen in weaving, they are producing a class of product which would be impracticable, as well as impossible for the large-scale producers. In this matter, they are thus working parallel to, rather than against the big potteries.

Since it would be uneconomical for the small potter, sometimes 'one-man', to mix and prepare his ingredients, it is customary for him to receive the clay in a prepared state, whereupon he will 'wedge' the clay in order to remove every air-hole. We should therefore have an idea of what has taken place beforehand. After excavation from the open mines, the clays are prepared either by the quarry or by the big potteries. The clays are first exposed to the weather and then crushed in mills. Cornish stone and flint are extremely hard in their natural state and must be thoroughly ground down to powder form and cleansed of impurities. The four ingredients are mixed until they reach a state of uniform consistency and plasticity. Finally, the mixture goes through a pug-mill, where it is churned up, to emerge as a fairly solid but not hard block. It is in this condition that it reaches the 'studio potter', who will wedge this material as he or she requires it. The greatest care must be taken to remove every air-hole or impurity which may remain, and that the pottery to be thrown will fire evenly. Badly wedged clay will show air-holes, pittings and irregularities after firing and will often go out of shape in the kiln. Perfectly made wares are classed as 'firsts', while those with *slight* imperfections are 'seconds'. Anything else will be broken up. It is natural that a first-class potter will produce an absolute minimum of seconds or rejects. Though 'accidents will happen', most potters will, in fact, have few failures of this kind.

Studio potters use either the kick-wheel or the electric wheel. Some prefer the old wheel, which revolved slowly, for throwing the larger pots. The first electric wheel had a minimum speed which was too high for wares of the larger diameters. The later patterns of electric wheel, however, are very much more responsive and will rotate at a very slow speed indeed, and give a smoother and more even rotation than is possible with the kick-wheel. This type is worked by a horizontal treadle, coupled to the cranked lower end of the vertical shaft carrying the turn-table. The speed of the electric wheel is controlled by a weight-balanced pedal, which causes a cone to rise or fall against a friction-wheel, which is attached to the motor shaft. This motor is flexibly mounted to take the movement of the cone, in much the same way that a dynamo is mounted near the wheel of a bicycle. Some patterns of wheel have a 'two-cone' drive to obtain the same result. All wheels rotate anti-clockwise.

The turn-table is contained within a deep tray, having a flat end at the point furthest from the potter and a wedged end in front and next to him. He sits on a projecting 'saddle' which usually gets 'upholstered' by the addition of an old cushion. The pedal is on the right. Some potters judge measurements by a plain ruler, while others use the simple jigs or gauges—necessary where any repetitive work is being done.

From experience, potters know the density or weight of the clay and use a simple pair of scales to obtain the right amount when 'throwing' any piece of ware. This piece is placed, or even thrown down with moderate force if it is a big lump, and grasped with both hands for centring if it is large. From this point onward to the completion one can watch the original lump of clay, submitting to the firm, persuasion of the potter's fingers. If anything such as a pot, jug, bowl, or cup is to be made, then after the initial manipulations the right thumb is pressed into the rising column, while the left counteracts any tendency to 'bulge' undesirably. Once a deep hollow has been formed the potter usually 'changes hands' and using the left fingers on the interior, keeps the right-hand counter-acting on the exterior. The intended shape is thus gradually formed and any 'wayward'

tendencies curbed. One may watch this process time and again and never loose one's fascination for the response of the rotating clay, between the potter's fingers, now rising, now swelling and now contracting. To form the narrowing neck of a pot exterior finger pressure is exerted, which causes the pot to contract and extend upward. All the time during 'throwing', as the whole operation on the wheel is called, the potter must frequently dip his fingers in water to prevent them 'sticking'. The whole operation is indeed a wet one.

If a pouring lip is required, then rotation is stopped, and the lip formed by depressing the clay rim between the fingers. With frequent wetting of the fingers, water has accumulated and this is removed with a sponge. At the conclusion of throwing the pot, or whatever is being made, is cut from the wheel with a 'cheese-wire', and it is now in the clay-state, in which condition it will join its fellows on the racks where all the day's output will be stored to dry naturally. If the ware is to have handles, they will be shaped separately from strips cut from the wedged clay. They are laid on a wooden board and shaped by finger-pressure, and attached one by one to the body of the pot while both are wet. Some of the large potteries fire the shaped handles and pots separately and stick them afterwards with 'slip-cream', but the studio potter, being something of a specialist in quality production, will fit the handles after throwing and then fire as one piece. One can only expedite throwing and drying at the expense of quality. A pot which has had its handles fitted *before* firing cannot lose them, because fusion has taken place. If the handle of a 'favourite piece' has come away in your hand, then you know why. Again, any attempt to expedite drying can only result in failure during firing.

While all 'round' ware can be thrown on the wheel, any kind which is square, rectangular, or any other shape than circular, must be cast in a mould. This mould is made of plaster of Paris to the shape desired by the potter. It is rectangular in shape and about an inch or more larger all round. The clay to be placed in it is rolled flat to a uniform depth, rather like a piece of pastry-dough and well dusted with finely powdered flint. When laid in the mould it is impressed to the interior shape and any part remaining above the level of the mould is trimmed off from the middle outwards. A board is placed on top and the whole is inverted, when the mould can be withdrawn.

At one time potters had to depend on kilns using solid fuel— wood, coal or coke, and for some kinds of ceramics, kilns of this sort are still used. Essentially the kiln resembles an ordinary domestic oven—minus the external frills and gimmicks—but with the interior lined with fire-brick.

Many modern pottery kilns are heated by electricity, town gas, liquefied petroleum gas ('bottled gas') or by light fuel oils. Open flame firing, that is with the hot gasses in direct contact with the ware, is quite common, the ware being protected as necessary by placing it in fireclay boxes called saggers.

Glazes are applied in a liquid state, either by immersion or by brush-work; this is called trailing. A glaze may be defined as a vitreous or glass-like coating on any ceramic ware, and has a mineral composition which varies considerably according to what effects the potter is seeking. Among these minerals may be mentioned silica, borac, lime, various oxides, potash, and salt. The last is generally used on its own, not by immersion but by being thrown into the kilns, to produce the peculiar effect on much of the stoneware. Glazes may be applied on the bare clay body or on top of slip. Any decoration may be applied before or after glazing, according to the effect desired. By applying a 'wax resist' of water and paraffin, the surface of the body may be preserved, as in batique-work, from the adherence of slip or glaze which would produce a reversed image of the design.

At the Fownhope Pottery, in Herefordshire, they concentrate on stoneware, and use a clay from that part of Leicestershire near the coalfield, without flint or feldspar. Such clay dries out very hard and before firing considerable pressure with one's fingers is required to break it. A thrown piece of ware will retain its shape during firing with the addition of flint, and as there is only one ingredient feldspar as a flux is of no use.

As an example of a potter using 'local' clays, we shall find the Surrey man using gault. This is a stiff, dark clay, bluish in colour and to be found in a thin bed, below the chalk and above any green-sand.

Whether the individual potter throws pots on a kick-wheel, or whether he or she fires by solid fuel, electricity, gas or oil is clearly an individual decision. Every sincere potter is working with the same end in view—a well-designed, well-made pot, and one which, above all, affords satisfaction to the user. If it is a jug, it will pour without dripping and the handle, easy to grasp, will be correctly positioned. Very often the decorative element will be quite restrained; in fact, some of the finest pots have been almost devoid of decoration.

45 WILLIAM DEW WITH HIS CORACLE AT KERNE-
BRIDGE ON THE RIVER WYE   *Hereford City Museum*

"6. HARRY ROGERS AND HIS CORACLE ON THE SEVERN AT IRONBRIDGE.

47 NETTING SALMON FROM CORACLES ON THE RIVER TEIFI

Museum of English Rural Life

HEDGE WELL LAID FROM COARSE SHOOTS

49 WEAVING A BASKET   *Barlow-Jones*

50 SOME PRODUCTS OF THE BASKET WEAVER *Barlow-Jone*

51 BASKET-WORK. A POTTERY CRATE

Museum of English Rural Life

52 MAKING A SPALE-OAK BASKET. FURNESS
Museum of English Rural Life

20

Hedge-laying

Some form of division between fields has been the practice in agriculture, even in the early times of the Saxon open-fields and possibly long before then. It was, however, the advent of the enclosures and the long period leading the peak of these enclosures, that hedges, wallings, and earth baulks in the form that we now know them were constructed. Eventually, the farmers of Leicestershire, doubtless at the nod of the big hunts, developed the practice of trimming, laying, and training of thorn hedges. This practice prevented a hedge from exhausting itself by excessive and extended growth, and the Leicester type of hedge was eventually cultivated through the greater part of England and parts of Wales, wherever the soil was rich and deep enough to support the hawthorn, which formed the body of such hedging. Elsewhere, in those parts where the soil was too thin or too acid or the land at too great an altitude, alternate forms of division were resorted to, either by stone walls or by earth baulks.

With all the subsequent changes in farming, these related crafts have been generally unaffected, except that in certain areas the hedgerows have been grubbed up. In some parts landowners, often under economic stress, have tended to or been obliged to neglect their properties in this respect. Generally speaking, however, hedges continue to be laid every winter and dry-stone walls to be constructed.

The laying of hedges has always been a winter's task in the farm calendar, partly because there is more time and partly because the task is easier when there is no foliage. In the fields, then, shortly in the New Year, one is likely to come across a solitary man working along a hedge, though if there is any amount of heavy work involved there may be a second man. If a hedge has been previously laid, not more than a few years back, then the job will involve no more than 'maintenance', which will consist of trimming the mass of the hedge with a few upward strokes of the slasher, and taking out unwanted and recent growths. But a hedge run wild after many years will require some drastic attention and use of the axe and bille. A row of hawthorn or hazel shrubs will be trimmed of all branching stuff, to leave the main stems, which are cut half through near the base and then carefully bent over to a low angle. The method of making this cut is really the foundation of good hedging, and properly done ensures that the sap will rise unchecked through the uncut fibres. This work is begun at the left-hand end, with each stem being bent over to the left, so clearing the way for the next cut. Working gradually along, the result is a row of turned-over stems each often 10 ft or more in length and all overlapping.

At close intervals, of 2 ft of a little more, stakes of cleft ash or chestnut, or anything available, is driven into the ground, to form a rough 'weave' or pleach, depending on the flexibility of the stems. Everything is then knocked in and the whole mass is 'tightened' up with the mallet. The tops of the exposed stakes are usually bound with some slender stuff. Often this will be of 'runners' of bramble or briar sometimes taken out of the same hedge. Bramble is especially suitable, because if it is 'shredded' of its thorns, its runners are often of considerable length. A number of these runners are 'plaited' to form an unbroken and very flexible 'rope'. If there is insufficient bramble then maybe

Winter's work on a Herefordshire estate.

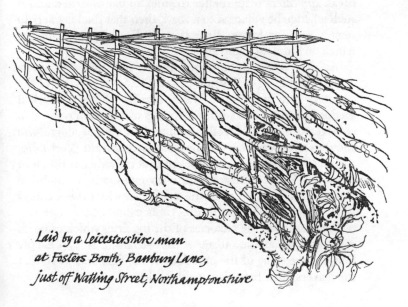

Laid by a Leicestershire man at Fosters Booth, Banbury Lane, just off Watling Street, Northamptonshire

there will be enough hazel. Truly a stitch in time can save a great deal more than a later nine.

As the men work their way slowly along the hedge they grub out the unwanted stuff and clean the hedge of anything tending to choke it. If there is a ditch to one side, that is cleared of accumulated rubbish. Any stuff that is of no use goes on to a steadily burning fire.

All this work contributes a great deal to the quality of the land, and the satisfactory containment of livestock. Both sheep and cattle, having all day in which to do nothing but grow fat, seem to go through life with a fixation about the other side of the hedge, and once any animal has succeeded in working itself through even a small gap, with a few more to follow, nothing will stop an attempted repetition of the experiment. Patchwork and stop-gap repairs are nearly always ineffectual and only reflect unfavourably on the farmer.

A loose, thin hedge, however high, is also a poor windbreak and offers little shelter to stock in bad weather, and if such a hedge be adjacent to a road, then that road is likely to remain wet for longer than if it be lined by trim hedges which do not hold damp air.

At first consideration, one might feel that one single design of hedging-bill would be satisfactory to all parts of the country, but in practice, each locality shows a marked inclination to be as traditional in this matter as in others. In consequence of this, an edge-tool tool-maker's catalogue will show a variety so great the the bills used in Kent, Yorkshire, and Radnor might well be thought to serve radically different purposes. With these tools as with many others, tradition means local practice over the centuries when these things were made locally, until the time came when edge-tool making passed to the factories of the big firms which came in, some at least, at the outset of industrialism. But so deeply founded are some of the practices of the field and wood that the makers must list this considerable variety.

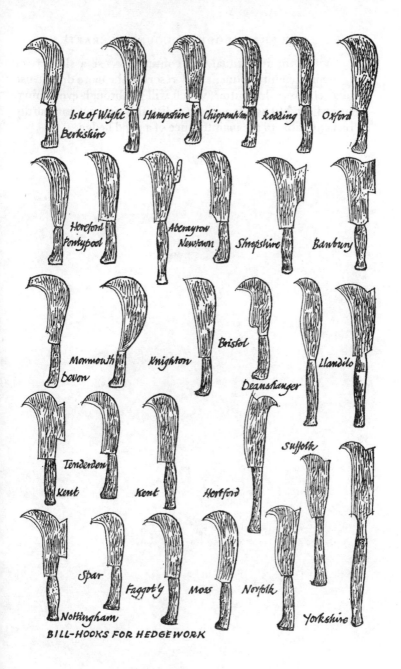

BILL-HOOKS FOR HEDGEWORK

Isle of Wight
Berkshire
Hampshire
Chippenham
Redding
Oxford

Hereford
Pontypool
Aberayron
Newtown
Shropshire
Banbury

Monmouth
Devon
Knighton
Bristol
Deanshanger
Llandilo

Tenterden
Kent
Kent
Hertford
Suffolk

Spar
Nottingham
Faggot'g
Moss
Norfolk
Yorkshire

Where the individual will continue to use a slasher for trimming, county councils now resort to the more drastic use of a self-propelled cutter, which will go through everything, regardless, but as a long-term policy this practice can hardly be favourable to the maintenance of a good hedge.

21

Dry-stone Walling

The use of stones, taken directly from the immediate neighbourhood, for the demarcation of fields, land, and properties may be dated from the settled farmers of the Bronze and Iron cultures. In some parts this was simply for demarcation alone, and in others to form wind-breaks. This latter, was then, and has been ever since, the practice wherever the land was subject to exposure to the elements. On the higher wind-swept lands, these walls became much more substantial and capable of withstanding years and years of buffeting. From this experience, there evolved, over the many centuries, a peculiar technique, whereby such walls, made of stones without cementation, could be made to endure the elements for a very long time indeed. By working without mortar, which tended to retain rainwater and by so arranging the stones as to permit a good circulation of drying air and ventilation, all the consequences of frost-action were eliminated.

In a masoner's wall, bricks or dressed stones are laid in and bound by mortar but in the dry wall, or dyke, the structure depends upon the adhesion between the touching rough surfaces of the stones and in this, the weight of the stones contributes to this adhesion. To this end, such a wall should not have too much weight low down. With local variations, determined by the nature and structure of the rock, from Scotland to the Pennine and the Peak and so to the Cotswolds, these principles appear to be universally observed.

On the High Peak and the great wandering back-bone of the Pennines, the nature of the limestone and the 'round-the year' weather prevailing at those altitudes cause the rock to break down naturally into irregular shapes and sizes. The Pennine walls, especially, run away for mile upon mile, all over the lonely fells, all amid a sublime quiet that is broken only by the cries of sheep, red grouse, and curlew. You will need a compass, up on those lonely heights, unless, like the dyker and the shepherd, you may know the hills like the back of your hand, and even then . . . You may follow one of those walls over the stumbling turf, grateful for the protection afforded, up and on, into the mists, encountering puzzled Blackfaced sheep, and if your luck is in, you may also meet a man working on a section of wall. A methodic man, able to think ahead in regard to the material to hand, making the best use all the time, sometimes throwing out certain stones for a particular part of the wall. If he must start from the bare ground, he is likely to progress at the rate of about six or seven yards a day.

It requires experience and time to build even 100 yards of wall, but given these the result will be a wall which will remain for generations and during that time will require no more than detail repair or maintenance, often less even than that. The points about ventilation and frost having been noted, one may see, on close examination, why a Pennine wall, and therefore why any drystone wall of irregular stones, will stay put. It depends on the careful placing and gradation and the provision of a slight 'batter', whereby the thickness of the wall decreases from the base to the top.

The permanence of a wall also depends upon good work on the foundation which is slightly greater than that of the wall itself. These Pennine walls, or dykes, call them how you will, are of single or double thickness according to their height. Dykes of the boundary type, dividing estates, are usually higher than 4 ft and are therefore of double thickness, having small stuff between the two, called 'hearting'. To call it 'filling' suggests that the space has simply been filled in, instead of which the small stones are just as carefully placed to ensure good ventilation. Walls of 4 ft and less are made to a single thickness, so that all the stones occupy the full width. The higher walls have stones, exceeding the general width, set at regular intervals to act as ties to the structure. The interval is usually 36 in., and if there are more than a single course of these 'throughs', then these courses overlap each other. Along the top copestones are placed in a row continuous for the length of the wall. These copestones are selected from large flat stones, comparatively thin in section and are placed on edge.

These Pennine walls, as those of the Peak and of Scotland, especially between the Clyde—Forth and the Romall Wall, must of necessity run up- and downhill, as contours determine, and this condition necessitates a technique which is peculiar to the high hills, in order to prevent any collapse of the wall on those slopes which are often quite steep. The high winds which occur at those altitudes must also be reckoned with, and the walls strengthened accordingly. The Blackface sheep, too, appear to have very sharp wits and will often 'inspect' a length of wall for any weak point, but the curious thing in this respect is that a wall which is apparently tottering and liable to collapse will not be attempted. If a sheep can see through a wall it will leave it alone. In many parts of Scotland they have therefore built for a very long time what has come to be known as a galloway-dyke. It is constructed 'double thickness' up to about 40 in., at which height the covering is laid on. The next 22 in. is laid as a single wall, with plenty of light showing through.

It is a testimony to the dyker's craft that these walls, some of which were built early in the eighteenth century, remain today in sound condition. Although the craft of dyking was well established by the Celtic times, and later, in the second to fourth centuries A.D., refuges known as 'brochs' were built against the continual invasion by Danish longship-men, it was actually during the eighteenth century when so many of the extensive dykes were built. Before that time much of the northern hill ranges of Scotland and England were without much division.

THE COTSWOLD WALLS

The dry-stone walling which is such a feature of the Cotswold landscape is essentially different from the types of wall previously described. Although some parts of these splendid hills do attain to 1,000 ft, they are mainly a lowland range, for all the bold front they present to the traveller from Wales or from the Midlands. From this escarpment they fall away in undulations to the Vales of Aylesbury and the White Horse. Approaching the Cotswolds from this side, one is aware of only a gradual transition.

Over all this range the soil is comparatively thin, except in some of the valleys, such as the Churn or the Cherwell, and if this be removed to a depth of no more than a few inches the subsoil rock on which the walls are built is revealed. It is the nature of this rock, its accessibility, the ease of extraction, the manner in which it weathers, especially in regard to frost action, and finally its response to the artistry of the Cotswold mason all down the centuries, that have contributed to the breath-taking splendour of the architecture of the Cotswold Hills, whether it be the multi-pinnacled grace of Chipping Campden or the little cottage by the wayside.

The stone at all levels naturally breaks down, without blasting, into flat rectangles; in fact, frost action near the surface is an agent in this process. Near the surface the layers are generally about 1–2 in. in thickness, which increases downward to about 15 in. Further fracturing will produce excellent roofing slates, which are laid from eave to ridge in graduating sizes.

On the Cotswolds, near the Fosse Way

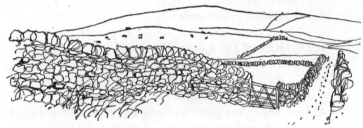

On the high Pennines, near Malham

Between Strumble Head and St Davids, Pembrokeshire.

These walls, intended to enclose stock of a more composed disposition than that of the Blackface sheep, are usually about 3 ft in height, although there are many estate boundary walls which are up to 6 ft in height, and correspondingly thicker at the base. It is usual practice to give the 3 ft walls a base thickness of some 20 in., which tapers to 16 in. The large slabs, of 2–3 in. thickness, are laid to incline very slightly downwards to the faces of the walls, in order that the rain water or melting snow shall drain away from the heart of the wall. Walls of this dimension are constructed to a single thickness. The tops of the walls are crowned with a continuous row of slats, laid vertically and called combers. Seen in profile this top appears irregular, but is designed to deter any attempt by animals at scaling. Wherever there is a break for field gates or where the wall makes an angled turn, then the walls are squared with a more robust construction.

Contrary to Pennine or Galloway practice, it is sometimes the practice of the Cotswold wallers to resort to mortaring of the combers as a further precaution against the wanderlust of farm stock. Provided the wall is on a good, hard foundation, they apparently have little trouble, but it seems to be a departure from the original principle. Many of the estate walls look extremely well with gate pillars composed of large blocks, dressed and laid 'dry' and with fine pinnacle and finials surmounting, the last being the work of the village mason; the whole structure strikes a quiet dignity which is befitting the way of life among these hills.

Cotswold stone varies appreciably in colour. In the middle hills, between Cirencester and Chipping Norton, the stone fresh from the 'Quarrs' is amber, which mellows to a duller sienna-grey. About Banbury the ironstone content produces a distinct sienna-brown. There are extensive ironstone quarries at Hornton, the ore from which is conveyed directly by rail to the main line. The stone of Wiltshire and Oxford appears a quieter greyer colour.

The men who construct walls and dykes use very few tools; a 4 lb. mason's hammer, a pick such as is used by road-men, or a crowbar, are about all. Generally, they work with leather palm-pads as a protection against the continuous abrasion which their hands would suffer. They set their course in convenient working lengths with a taut string, as bricklayers do, one end pegged in the already standing wall while the far end is attached to a wooden frame which conforms in outline to the transverse section of the wall.

PEMBROKESHIRE

In this westernmost part of Wales, where in the course of history the Irish, the Normans, the Flemings and, of course, the Welsh have made their various imprints in culture and cultivation, they have made a different kind of wall alto-gether, but by the absence of mortar it is still a dry one. The greater part of the many miles of walls is composed of small 'boulders' from the peneplain, which is mainly Cambrian with various intrusions. For the most part this material lies 'ready to hand'. In some parts, the rock is easily prepared as 'slates' which are dressed to a rectangular shape of not more than an inch of thickness, and in their tens of thousands they laid or stood side by side at about 30° from the vertical in two or three courses, all 'herring-bone' fashion. Thus laid, the courses are self-wedging, and when this structure is complete it is covered with a fair layer of earth and turf. These walls serve the same purpose as other kinds and stand for decade on decade, accumulating natural vegetable humus, which will in a short while throw up a fine grass. It is usual now to superimpose such walls with a fencing of fire. These walls stand 3–4 ft high and are some 2 ft thick. In the climate of the county which knows little snow or frost, but a lot of sun, wind, and rain of the Atlantic, it is but a short time before these baulks are transformed in spring and early summer into natural flower-beds all alight with sea-thrift, and campion.

22

Making Baskets and Traps

In the matter of tools the weaver of baskets is as lightly equipped as any workshop man, whether he be blind or sighted. He requires several bodkins for opening the weave when letting in rods, shears and a shop-knife for cutting and pointing them, and a small knife for trimming; a wooden cleaver for dividing rods and a driving-iron for closing the weave as work progresses. If dipped in a grease-horn now and again, the bodkin works easily. A yard-stick completes the range; if used by blind men, the inches are each marked with a brass stud, the 1 ft intervals with three studs and the 6 in. with two.

Basket-makers are to be found everywhere, producing for both the local market and the national, and tend, from preference, to use osier material from one area. While the bulk of English supplies comes from Somerset, the name of osier beds tell us of other sources, the 'hopes' of Essex, the 'garths' of the North, and the 'holts' of the Midlands. The Kennett valley also provides a considerable source. Most of the foreign matter comes from Poland and the Argentine.

The beds of osier, or withy-willow, are planted with cuttings from the previous season, about 16,000 to the acre. After three years, they are cut back annually to stimulate growth; this continues for the next thirty to fifty years, with an annual crop, until exhaustion, after which the plantation is cleared and reset. After each crop, the bark is stripped by pulling each rod, butt-end first, through a stripping brake, from which comes the folk-dance, 'Stripping the Willow'.

There are several grades of rod, according to quality. 'Green' rods are cut any time, for the cheaper baskets. 'Brown' rods are cut first, during winter and stored away from damp. 'White' rods are cut when the sap has begun to rise and are stacked in water to keep them supple for peeling. They are the best seasoned and are used for first-quality work. This grading also spreads the work over the season. When the rods are dry they are made up into bundles called 'bolts'.

Basket-makers sit very close to the floor, feet stretched out, and with a large board on the lap, on which their work is done. The variety of baskets they make and the weaving techniques employed are so varied that a whole book is necessary to deal with them. This has, in fact, been done excellently by Dorothy Wright in her book *Baskets and Basketry*. Here we must confine ourselves to the basic method.

All such weaving begins with the base. A round or oval one is started with the 'slath', an interlaced cross-work of rods of at least four each way, around which the weaving begins until the required dimension is reached. A frame-base, round or rectangular, is made by forming a cane frame on which the cross-weaving is made.

No matter what the technique, all weaving is made from left to right and each new rod 'let in' overlaps the previous, and periodically the driving-iron or beater is used to 'close' the weave—refer to the batten in a weaver's loom. Some makers use a lead weight to hold the basket down while working, but others seem to prefer a large bodkin, about which they can rotate the progressing basket. While industrial baskets are left 'bare', many domestic baskets are coloured and varnished, for the sake of appearance.

Handles are constructed by letting in a cane as a foundation and binding several rods according to size with an anchorage to the basket itself. They have been making baskets in this fashion since the days of Glastonbury, and with no fundamental change since those distant times, there is no prospect of serious competition either from alternative methods of manufacture or the use of materials other than willow or cane.

LOBSTER AND CRAB POTS

The making of these is confined locally to the fishing areas. Where in most basketry the maker 'starts at the base and works up', these simple pots are started at the inverted 'neck' through which the unsuspecting victim enters. This is begun by inserting ten or twelve willow rods into a wooden stand. Thus secured, weaving is made with fairly slender rods, and at a height of 9 in., about thirty additional rods are inserted and the domed turnover is made to form the bell-like cage. This is secured by three rows of plaited rods, set equidistantly, and at the third row all the verticals are turned over and in to the centre. Like all traps, these pots are designed to permit easy ingress, but to prevent escape.

EEL TRAPS

As used on Severn-side and in the Fenlands they provide an industry as local as other traps. They are made of either hazel or willow. The usual method of weaving is as that of the willow basket, forming a closely woven structure with the peculiar double waist. Some Fenland traps are made in the manner of a waste-paper basket, through which the trapped eel may espy the free world beyond.

SALMON TRAPS

Salmon traps, putchers or putcheons, are quite different in

Nailing in the centre-board of a Trug

Gardening Trug

Starting a crab-pot, 'neck-first' on the stand

Bushel sized Trug for farmers

Starting a Spaleoak basket, also called a Spelk, Wisket, Slop or Skip

structure and the manner of setting. They are about 5 ft in length and from an opening about 2 ft across they taper almost to a point. They are made of twelve or fourteen stout hazel rods, bound at each end and at two points between by withy rods. In rows, three deep, the putcheons are arranged in a stout, permanent framework, forming a 'barrage' extending for scores of yards across the Severn grounds below Frampton on the Gloucestershire side, and the Monmouthshire below Chepstow to the confluence with the Usk. The rise and fall of the Severn is one of the greatest in the world, and as the tide runs down these traps are exposed.

SPALE-OAK BASKETS

The potato baskets of Furness, Wyre Forest, Monmouth, Cardigan, and Yorkshire are superficially similar in construction, since each is woven on a hazel frame, but while most are woven with willow in rod or strip, the Furness 'spelk' is made with rent oak strips or band, rendered pliable by a period of boiling in a water-tank. The bands are arranged like the warp and weft of textile weaving, with the ends of the bands turning over the rim. As in many other 'coppice industries', the shaving is done on a 'horse', that universal steed which will be encountered in various forms according to the industry. Although the variants of spale-oak basket are to be found as described, the word does appear to have Norse origins. The manufacture of all these traps and spelks and similarly 'local' articles is a cottage industry, one-man affairs or family concerns all employing the simplest of equipment.

SUSSEX TRUGS

In comparison with the 'cottage' industries so far dealt with, the two firms which make trugs, at East Hoathly and Hurstmonceaux, are fair-sized 'shops', each employing a

small number of people. Even so, the equipment is comparatively simple. There is a steam-chest, a number of
setting-frames of various sizes, special hammers and a
swage saw for cutting the 'veneers' of willow. This is a
power-driven circular saw, thin in section and with fine-set
teeth, to ensure a minimum waste in the kerf.

The somewhat boat-like shape of the trug has seven or
nine boards, according to size, arranged clinker' fashion,
but upside down, that is overlapping from the bottom up-
wards. The boards are cut and sawn from fifteen-year white
willow, and after sawing with the swage are about $\frac{1}{8}$ in. in
thickness. Some of this thickness will be lost during the
process of shaving with the draw-knife, some of which have
their blades quite slender from generations of use, and may
be used only for the finest work.

As these boards respond better to shaving 'in the wet',
they are soaked in rain-water beforehand. Later they are all
placed in the steam-chest, and then in a very pliable condition they are curved to the required shapes in a brake.
In a still damp state, they are nailed to the frame from the
inside, with a broad-headed hammer, the nail-points being
clenched on a mandrel.

The hooped frames, handles, and braces are made preferably of cleft ash, though chestnut is a second choice.
Either is from coppiced underwood, grown locally. After
cleavage, all the material is steamed and then set. They use
double-sided setting-frames, each of which enables two
hoops to be set. There is a frame for each size and therefore
a large number of frames is required. When 'cold', the
hoops, etc., are ready for assembly.

According to the size of trug, the number of boards varies
and some have handles, some not, and are variously braced.
The middle board is called a centre and on each side there
are two or three 'seconds', while the outermost is known as
a 'side'. The two smallest sizes have seven boards, a pair of
stands, and a hooped handle. Next, the market-gardening

size has seven boards, no stands, and a braced handle. The largest, of bushel capacity for agricultural use, has nine boards, no central handle, five braces, and end-openings below the frame by which it can be carried.

In common with many wood-using industries, all the resultant shavings are used as fuel, in this case for the steam-chest boiler, additionally to other fuels. The word trug is uncertain in origin, but it has a Saxon ring which is to be expected in this very Saxon county. This type of basket is of practical design and its strength and simplicity enable it to withstand many years of hard and constant use.

23

Saddlery and Harness-making

Once a wild horse was tamed and found to provide an excellent mount men realized that some method of control had to be devised and also some support for the rider. The subsequent evolution of saddlery and harness is a story in itself, involving many changes in the design of equipage. In regard to harness-work, it was the horse which so slowly displaced the ox in draught. Two factors determined the nature of changes henceforth. Firstly, the differing anatomies of ox and horse and their way of working in draught. Secondly, the sweat of the ox is greasy and kept the metal work bright, while that of the horse is acid and conducive to rust.

Although some photos show draught-oxen harnessed similarly to that of the horse, it had always been usual to harness with the yoke, which was attached to the centre-pole of the wagon. While medium-draught road vehicles can be satisfactorily drawn by pole-harness—and all stage-coaches were so drawn—heavy-draught wagons, intended more often than not for use in the field or at best over farm roads, were always drawn by horses harnessed in shaft. Some wagons had double shafts, but it was usual to attach additional horses by trace-harness. Here it may be noted that the ox yoke took the weight of the pole, while that of the shafts was taken by a large pad, resting on the horse's back. With the advent of horse-draught, management of animal and wagon or plough became much easier; as horses were capable of a more sustained draught than oxen. The ox was retained in some parts partly from possible sentiment and partly because it was cheaper.

The trend through history, in the design of saddles and bridlery, has been toward simplicity and lightness, so that today, only the Army and the Police use equipage of a ceremonial pattern. Saddles, today, comprise no more material than is necessary. A general-purpose saddle will weigh about 8 lb without irons and leathers, while the finest flat-racing saddles scale no more than 8 oz and provide little more than a point of suspension for the irons, because the rider hardly uses a saddle except to and from the paddock. On the other hand, with a general-purpose pattern, the rider can 'spend the day in the saddle'. In fact, this pattern is usually fitted with two metal loops on the off-side, to which a 'sandwich-case' can be attached.

The general-purpose saddle is built on a saddle-tree, which is carved from beech and is fitted with two steel plate-springs and a pair of forged steel brackets to which the stirrup-leathers are attached. This bracket is designed to release the leathers should the rider fall with feet engaged in in the irons. All trees are made at Walsall and their manu-facture is indeed a separate craft followed nowhere else. Underneath the tree the pad is fitted and this rests directly on the horse, unless an additional cloth is used. The best-quality pads are of calf-skin; the cheapest are of serge and the intermediate of linen. On top of the tree the first layer, again of calf, is the flap and then atop comes the seat with its extension, the skirt which covers the stirrup-bracket. The seat, alone, is of pigskin, grained side uppermost. Both seat and pad are stuffed with flock, which process entails as much skill as the rest of saddlery. The leather pads are secured to the tree by four 'nails', or steel rivets, two at the

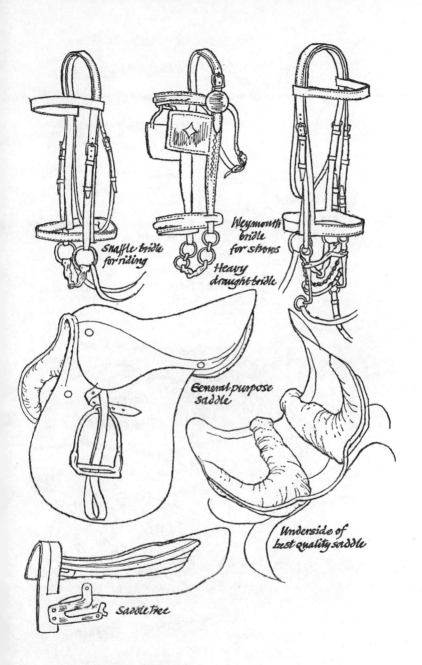

Snaffle bridle for riding

Weymouth bridle for shows

Heavy draught bridle

General purpose saddle

Underside of best quality saddle

Saddle Tree

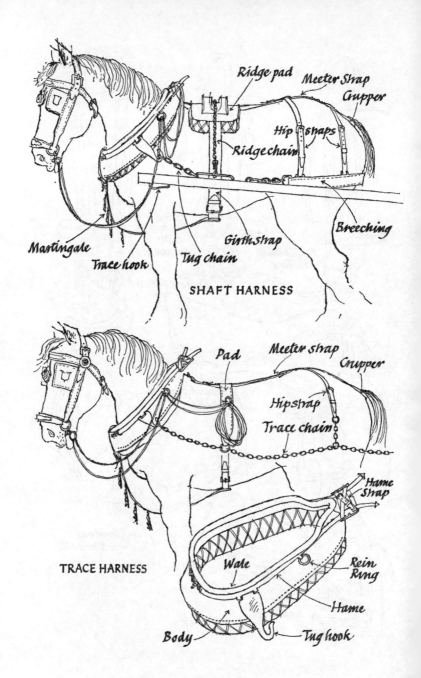

Ridge pad Meeter Strap Crupper

Hip straps

Ridge chain

Martingale Girth strap Breeching

Trace hook Tug chain

SHAFT HARNESS

Pad Meeter strap Crupper

Hipstrap

Trace chain

Hame Strap

TRACE HARNESS

Wale Rein Ring

Hame

Body Tug hook

front and two at the rear. The best-quality saddles have a
'kneel roll', made in the fore-part, and all qualities are
secured to the horse by three girth straps.

DRAUGHT-HARNESS AND BRIDLERY

Sadly, perhaps, this is becoming a memory, but this work
has formed an important part of a saddler's craft. The bridle
is heavier than that for riding, and the blinkers are an
addition. The harness is in three parts; the collar, against
which the horse works; the pads, which take the weight of
the shafts; and the strap-work which includes the breeching
and joins the whole together. The breeching comes into
use when the horse is backed or when descending a hill.
When a harnessed horse is in the shafts, it is said to be 'shut
in' and when taken out is 'shut out', so they speak of 'shutting in' and 'out', which is described in detail in the chapter
on The Wheelwright.

The pad, like the saddle, is built on a tree, but is stuffed
with straw. It is secured to the horse with a broad webbing
strap. The collar is likewise stuffed, with straw, and is fitted
to a frame known as the hames. Formerly of wood, but latterly
of brass or wrought-iron, the two parts are hinged at the
base, or joined by a chain. The leather part of the collar
consists of a 'tube' shaped to the horse's neck and stuffed,
that part next the horse being faced with serge; this is the wale
and body. The hames fit in a groove formed by the wale
and body and are closed at the top by straps, though some
were permanently closed. Attached to the hames are tug-
hooks and rein-rings.

Since a horse is broader across the eyes than the nose, a
collar must be slipped on upside down and then reversed
to its normal position. As satisfactory working must depend
on a good fit, everything rests on the saddler's ability.
Inferior work will shortly be revealed by chafing and bad
pulling. All draught-harness work is dye-black, for regular

greasing without spoiling the colour. Our best opportunities for observing the use of draught-gear are at the various shows and ploughing matches.

Since the introduction of the collar by the Romans, draught-harness appears to have developed differently from the Continent, where the draught-pad and collar are hardly known. In the considered opinion of scholars, the collar originated in China during the third century B.C., and for further information the reader is referred to *Agricultural Transport in Wales*, by Geraint Jenkins, and published by the National Museum of Wales (Welsh Folk Museum, St Fagans).

SADDLERS' EQUIPMENT

The tools and appliances used are extensive. For making straight cuts in leather, such as straps or rolls up to a width of 6 in., a plough-gauge is pushed with the right hand while the increasing cut-off is held with the left hand. Not all saddlers, however, use this interesting tool, for some prefer the more familiar knife. For cutting out irregular shapes, some use a curious knife called a half moon, but here again, others keep to the conventional knife. Whichever tool is used, the steel must be of the best and a perfect edge maintained.

When two pieces of leather are to be sewn together they are held in position in a curious wooden vice which has quick-acting jaws. Before stitching is commenced, the line must be marked out with the holes for the needle to enter. This is done by means of a stitch-wheel, which rotates in a holder, or carrier, running with a 'castor' action. There is a range of wheels, nine to a set, marking the holes from six to fourteen to the inch. Here again, some saddlers use punches, each of which has a number of points, similarly graded. For degrees and situations of stitching there is a variety of needles, from the $2\frac{1}{2}$ in. sail needle to the 8 in.

waling needle, some straight, some crescent, all diamond in section. Where the needle woman uses a thimble, the saddler uses a hand-iron. It is gripped in the palm of the hand, and has a skew-hole by which the needle is pulled and a recess in the tip by which it is pushed.

For stuffing saddles, collars, and pads there are stuffing rods, variously shaped, according to the task, but all quite long and with pronged tips. During this process the shape is preserved by careful pummelling with a mallet of lignum vitae. For making buckle-holes in straps, a series of punches is used, designed to produce round or oblong holes. Some straps are made with an indentation along the edges. These are produced by a creaser which is heated over an open flame. The hammer has various uses, such as securing brass-work and rivets.

Some saddlers prepare their own thread of linen by taking a number of strands at a time and rubbing in beeswax. Others use thread already waxed: 3 cord No. 18 is used for most work, but No. 35 is for the finer.

WALSALL

Reference to the craft of making saddle- and pad-trees has been made and here it is noted that the entire equipment of saddlery and harness and all tools are likewise made by several firms in Walsall, whence, too, come the horse-brasses. In their day they formed an essential decoration of all draught-harness, whether for the farm, the road, or the canal, for the waterways, too, had their own traditions. These brasses had pre-Roman origins and came to this country by the routes of trade. They were used originally as amulets against the evil forces of Darkness, against which Light was the antidote. After their introduction here, the motifs gradually changed from the original to become commemorative of any and every event. The Hull Municipal Museum has a collection of nearly 1,000 brasses, terrets, and

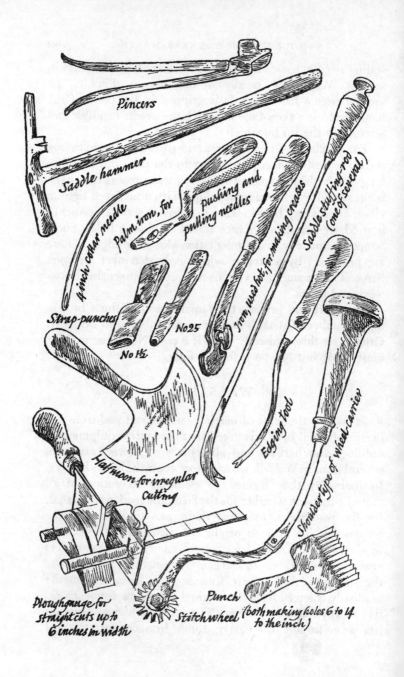

Pincers

Saddle hammer

4 inch collar needle

Palm iron, for pushing and pulling needles

Saddle stuffing-rod (one of several)

Strap-punches

No 1½

No 25

Iron, used hot, for making creases

Edging tool

Shoulder type of wheel-carrier

Half moon for irregular cutting

Ploughgauge for straight cuts up to 6 inches in width

Punch

Stitchwheel

(both making holes 6 to 14 to the inch)

swingers. The finest display was to be found on the martingale.

If the splendid days of the Shire, the Clydesdale, and the Suffolk Punch are over, it can be said that as long as hunters, cobs, and thoroughbreds are ridden for recreation and sport, so the saddler's craft will continue in its long-established form, since there is no prospect of this work being made by machine of other material than leather. A man *might* be persuaded to wear a badly fitting suit, but the horse can be surprisingly uncooperative.

24

Horn-work

Where the old cattle drovers' routes crossed or terminated, often in the vicinity of navigable rivers, there were usually a number of industries to be followed. Most activities concerned with the processing of by-products from cattle were situated downstream from the towns, but as little effluent came from horn-working, such establishments could be located elsewhere about the town. The rivers afforded the facility of transport in considerable bulk downstream to the sea for transfer to coastal craft. The student may wish to follow up these clues, for Llanthony Abbey, in the Black Mountains, is mentioned in old documents.

In those far-off times the horns of British breeds of cattle were used. This horn contained more moisture and was softer. Today, however, most of this material is ox-horn of Nigerian origin. For a variety of reasons the better material from other parts of the world cannot be imported. It is in the nature of horn that it can be cut and sawn, moulded to required shape under gentle heat, it is unaffected by mild acid, will not discolour or affect flavour on the palate and it readily washes quite clean. For the sake of appearance it can be made to produce a high gloss by buffing.

The raw material, as received, is sorted for division into that suitable for manufacture and that which will be ground down for nitrogenous fertilizer. The first category is critically examined for any kind of flaw, such as cracks and spots.

Some faults may not be detected until the polishing stage, when much labour will have been wasted. The greatest scrutiny can, however, reduce this to a minimum. The passed, satisfactory material is graded for size, grain, and colour and stored in hoppers for subsequent working.

It is one matter to put the band-saw through a piece of horn, and quite another to do so without wasting potential material, but to use every piece to the best advantage. Only the tip of a horn is solid, the rest of it is hollow. Each piece therefore presents its own problem. The man at the band-saw, like certain other types of craftsman, must be able to see the potential, the finished products, in a whole horn, to realize that this part will make a shoe-horn, and that a handle. The choice of cuts, the 'plane of entry', the weight, age, origin, and colour, all must be understood and exercised. An inexperienced sawyer could easily waste a cut-off in order to produce something from an otherwise inaccessible part. Every part is, in fact, made use of, for rings, spoons, ladles, shoehorns, brooches, and necklaces, etc. Only years and years of experience will enable a man to know what he can do or not do, and just where that dividing line occurs. A man with fifty years behind him has an invaluable asset in craftsmanship which may be meaningless elsewhere.

By subjection to gentle heat from a gas flame, it is possible to mould and change the shape of a piece taken from the hollow part. There is a degree of heat below which no permanent change can be made, as the horn will return to its original shape, but above which the material will be damaged and permanently lose its quality. A surface burning, or 'burring', occurs and a distinctive and not unpleasant smell is produced. This 'burring' has to be removed by the use of a band-saw.

The next process is to remove all the unwanted material and to refine the shape of the product. This was, at one time, done with 'scivers' or knives, but nowadays it is all done by using abrasive discs. The abrasive has a silicon carbide base, the resulting dust from which process is extracted to produce a meal-fertiliser. At Kendal, they have an old disc, of Portland Stone, which is over 150 years old. The shaft of this disc runs in a bearing of lignum vitae and every twelve months or so they give it 'a drop of oil' and renew the horn-meal packing! It does make one wonder. The rotation of this disc must be controlled to avoid what they call 'schoring', or burning. This process is followed with the use of two grades of abrasive tape, the second, which is finer, removes any scoring from the first, which is a little coarser.

This brings the piece of horn to the final process of polishing, by buffers. This again, is a two-stage process. Firstly, the horn is buffed against a mop of heavy calico which has been impregnated with a wax-based compound. The diameter of the buffer and the speed at its periphery are of great importance, since the polishing takes effect at a certain temperature—it will be noted that temperature is a vital factor. In this last process a microscopic slurring of the surface takes place and fills any cracks and seals the surface of the material. The second buffing is done on a mop of swansdown, impregnated with a mixture which produces the final high gloss.

Some processes entail the horn being held to the tool; while others require the tool being applied to the horn. Only a craftsman's two hands can exercise skilful manipulation. Tongs, somewhat like those used by a blacksmith, are used during the process of moulding. Salad-forks, for example, are cut without previous marking by a hand jig-saw. This, like everything else depends on the ability to make symmetrical cuts, by 'glint of th' eye, ant skew of t' gob'. It all requires time and experience.

Products made of horn are obtainable in four colours:— a mottled horn called 'Jaspé', a dark green or black, called 'Schwartz', a 'Blonde', which may be white or cream, and

53 MAKING EEL-TRAPS   *Museum of English Rural Life*

54 HARVESTING NEAR LEWES, SUSSEX. LATE NINETEENTH CENTURY

Museum of English Rural Life

55 MAN WITH YOKE, WILLERSLEY, WORCS. LATE
NINETEENTH CENTURY   *Museum of English Rural Life*

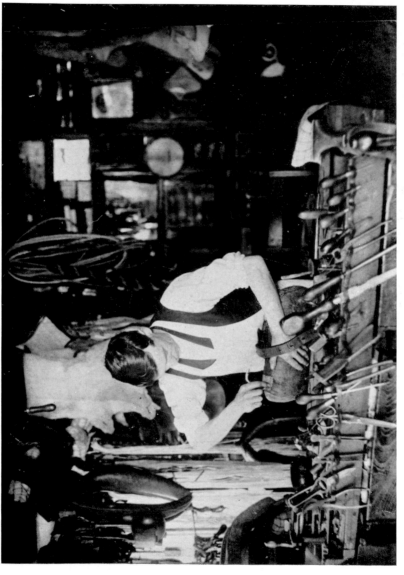

THE SADDLER AT WORK. TOOLS IN USE READY TO HAND

57 HORN-WORKER POLISHING SPOONS

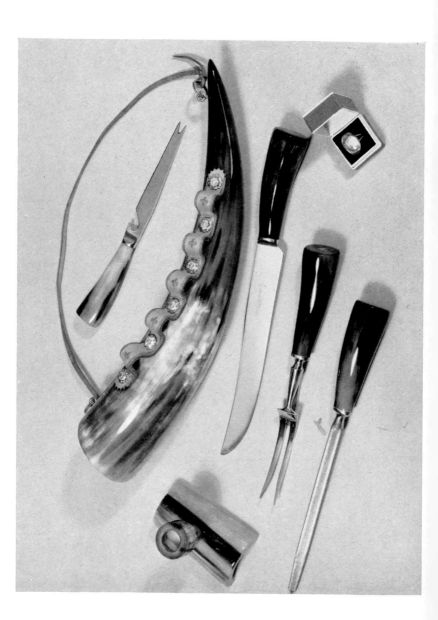

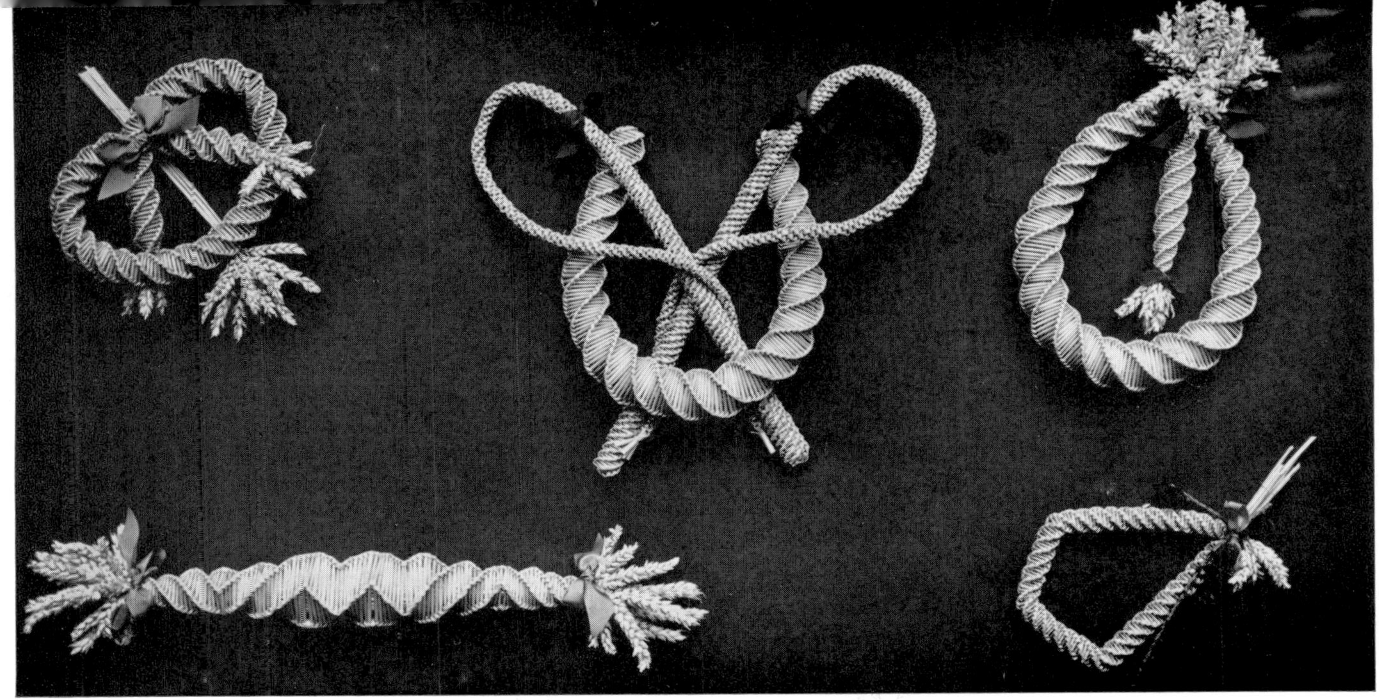

Percy Hennell

59 CORN DOLLIES

1 STAFFORDSHIRE KNOT   4 DOUBLE TWIST
2 SUFFOLK HORSE-SHOE   5 MODERN TRIANGLE
3 ESSEX TERRET

60 CORN DOLLIES
1 CROSSED KEYS
2 SUFFOLK HORSESHOES
3 DEVONSHIRE CROSS

Percy Hennell

finally a red, known as 'Fush', which last name may be derived from the fushsia. To anyone outside the craft or the trade the original names of varieties of horn sound confusing, to say the least. 'Irish' horn comes from Australia; 'Brazil' can be either from Central America or the South African Cape; 'Moon' signifies horn from either Egypt or Siam; while 'Zambeze' indicates a mottled form of the colour of 'Irish'. Finally, 'Buffalo' is the horn of ox.

It is significant that the products of this one craft shop in Kendal are not only widely used in this country but are exported to thirteen countries.

25

Making Corn Dollies

When our distant ancestors had no longer to seek food daily, but obtained it by tilling the soil in stages and in tending their livestock, they also found that in between these activities they were beginning to ponder, and had time to wonder upon deeper things and perhaps to fear something quite different from the raids by men from other tribes. That primeval fear, for all our advances in other directions, seems never to have left us.

The twin customs of expressing hope, by propitation and offering thanks by gifts, have been practised by all civilizations ever since the land was first tilled, sown, and harvested. The primitive peoples were no less hopeful and thankful than those of more advanced cultures, though at root the manners of such expression show remarkable similarity; some are simply more elaborate than others. Whatever the god, whatever the ritual, however the assembly proceeded and whatever form the procession took and whatever the decorations and symbols used, the motives and purpose were the same. Demeter, Ceres, the Corn Mother, the Goddess of Fertility was worshipped as the Awakener of Life. In Cornucopia, the Horn of Plenty, lay the symbol of all hopes, and in the physical form of it lay also the beginning of a creative art which we, today, know collectively as Corn Dollies. This art is so distant in its origin that we are forced to resort to conjecture as to the meaning of the word 'Dolly'.

Certainly, it has no affinity with any resemblance to a child's doll, but may be closer to idol, and since fertility was the vital feature of existence, it was natural that one of the figures to be worshipped should have a female form.

Both after sowing and after harvest symbolic figures, made of straw, were carried around the fields in procession; the first in propitiation and to awaken the seeds of life, the second, in celebration, was in accompaniment to 'The Last Load (of Corn)'. Since it was a celebration, there was joy and exuberance in the form of decoration, to be followed by a still greater celebration of giving thanks in the churches. This journey of triumph was a survival of the pleasure of ancient people in the gifts of Mother Earth. In Britain, at least, the Corn Dolly was never in itself an idol, a thing to be 'worshipped', but simply a focal point in the decoration, a symbol of expression. With the passing of century after century the harvest became also a time of feast and merriment, much as Christmas was. This was so as long as the agricultural calendar was dependent entirely on the good fortunes of the seasons. The modern combine has become the centre-piece of farming. As slowly as it may move, it can still clear a field with such expediency as to make farmers less apprehensive of the weather, once harvesting has begun, though the original fear may be replaced by a fear of mechanical failure.

In the days before the combine and the tractor, and right back to the beginning, everyone engaged in farming, watched the sky overhead and the soil at their feet and the ultimate celebrations were all the more jubilant. The details of ritual varied from region to region, but they all had the same end. A 'Lord of the Harvest' was elected by the farm-labourers from among themselves. The elected Lord set the pace with the sickle and saw that the men were fairly and promptly paid when the harvest was completed. He was first to be served at meals and was addressed by his fellow men and seniors according to his temporary status. Any shortcomings in work done were subject to a system of fines, payable to his Lady, not always in money, nor even serious in nature. There was indeed a deal of merriment, not inconsiderable horseplay and doubtless some fun between the sexes.

The Last Load was a formal procession of all the wagons, all gaily decorated and crowned with floral ornament, the horses all groomed and decked out and belled, their harness polished. The men and women themselves were gaily dressed for the occasion. So the procession moved to the accompaniment of much ringing of bells and rattling and the calling of ancient rhymes, 'Well cut, well bound, well shocked, well saved from the ground', all repeated and shouted, to ensure that not only they but neighbouring farms might know that one more harvest was home. The prettiest girl was chosen to ride the leading horse. It required little ingenuity to introduce various pretexts for kissing, with few holds barred. The feast that followed all this jollification was a vast, communal, uproarious affair 'on the house'. It would have been an ill omen to destroy the Horn of Plenty, so it was kept till next harvest, as were similar straw figures. There were variations in procedure and decoration from region to region and a study of the very many Dollies can best be made by reference to Mrs Lambeth's book *A New Golden Dolly*. It is a positive mine of information, written by one who lives in the midst of this craft and who has made a life-study of every aspect of the Dolly and is an accomplished maker and exhibitor. The ceremony itself, but not the Dolly, was virtually killed by the entry of the tractor and the combine, whose alien coughs and groans are hardly a fitting continuo to:

> Harvest home, Harvest home,
> We have ploughed, we have sowed,
> We have reaped, we have mowed,
> We have brought home every load.
> Hip! hip! hip! Harvest home.

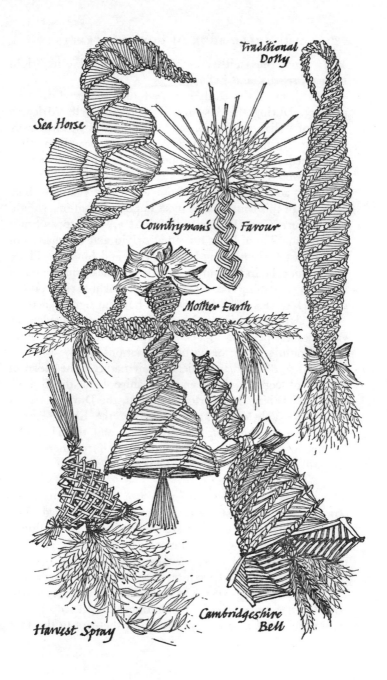

Sea Horse

Traditional Dolly

Countryman's Favour

Mother Earth

Harvest Spray

Cambridgeshire Bell

You cannot dress either a tractor or a combine in bright harness, regalia, and bells.

The theme of the Dolly is to be found in every European country. During the last war I met, in North Africa, a group of Italian prisoners, one of whom was whiling away boredom by making Dollies. As I remember them, they conformed, both in general appearance and in construction, to our own. Since he had not visited this country, he could not have acquired the art from elsewhere than his own country. In this context it is most important that one should not confuse Corn Dollies with what are known as Stack Ornaments. These have no ritual origin and are made not by the customary plaiting but by tying and binding. There may be an echo in the imitation in some stack ornaments, an idea that something like a Dolly would look just right on top of a stack or rick. The figures used have no significance.

The figures represented by Dollies cover a considerable variety, some peculiar to a country, some common to a number of counties, with or without variations locally. We may name a few of them to indicate their nature. The Horn of Plenty, of course, the Cambridgeshire Bell, the Suffolk Horn and Whip, the Norfolk Lantern, the Durham Chandelier, the Vale of Pickering Chalice, the Essex Terret, Mother Earth, the Staffordshire Knot, and the Horns of Northamptonshire. For decoration in the church there were, and still are, innumerable floral sprays.

The makers of Dollies prefer to use winter-sown wheat straw, although the straw of rye or oats can be used. The tough pliable straw which is required cannot be produced on land which has been heavily treated with artificial manures. Nor are the more recent varieties suitable, because the straw is too short. Winter-sown wheat is longer and tougher than spring-sown and it is the older varieties which have the necessary length. In plaiting, only the top length from each straw is used, that is, from the ears to the first joint, and it is necessary to grade such straws into coarse, medium, and fine. The coarse are for the larger work, the medium for the smaller, while the fine straws provide good material for details and for button-hole favours.

The selected straw is dampened—tempering, they call it —in water for an hour or so, no more than enough for two days' work. Every stage of the art, from the tempering, requires a considerable amount of practice and, of course, some knowledge of the qualities of various straws. Just how Dollies are made and the principles of plaiting and braiding would be difficult to explain concisely; it is the work of an instructor, nor does the present writer wish to intrude upon Mrs Lambeth's charming book. It can be obtained for 16s. post paid, from the Cornucopia Press, 22 Stonebridge Lane, Fulbourn, Cambs. To this lady I am indebted for all the information contained in this chapter, enough to wet the creative appetite. It is remarkable that the products of a craft now some thousands of years old are of a character to fit harmoniously into the contemporary living-room.

26

Flint-knapping

Among a small number of crafts which, in the courses of their histories, have not essentially changed, or advanced in technology, that of the knapper of flints offers an interesting study. Its course nearly run, it is on the point of closure, since there are now only one or two men still following the oldest of all the crafts. The day of the knappers is almost finished. Soon it will recede in history as a lost craft with only the artifacts and the tools, to be seen in museums, to recall this link with the first tool-makers.

It was an industry which came into being during the Paleo-Neolithic times, and although there is every evidence of a primitive industry, we need not, in the present context, concern ourselves with it. Several millenniums before Stonehenge tools were being made from several materials; antlers and shoulder-blades of ungulate animals; hard kinds of stone, such as limestone, which could be fractured, ground to shape and drilled; and nodules of flint which occur in bands in some parts of the chalk. These nodules are to be found in every irregular shape and size, varying somewhat in quality. The best, for knapping, is very hard and black, while the less suitable is more brittle and greyer in colour. Contact with soils in the course of millions of years has caused the surfaces to become stained and impregnated, so to produce the white coaling, which is familiar to the wonderer and too familiar to the farmer who has to plough the chalk-land fields.

Doubtless by some accident, such as dropping a nodule, or giving it a particularly hard knock, men found that flakes could be struck off from the mass. Then, by systematic striking, something like predetermined shapes could be produced and the remnant core could be worked to a shape, tapering or otherwise. All these products were pointed or edged and, in fact, far more sharply edged than was possible with stone. The first of these axes made in Paleolithic times were intended to be held in the hand. With an increasing understanding of fragmentation the most skilful manufacture was accomplished. When the communities or tribes became settled rather than nomadic, industry was able to develop and 'factories' to become established, together with well-used routes of distribution. The possibilities and limitations of the material were becoming realized.

While flint was and still is to be found spread over large areas of chalk-land—the stone-curlew country—the greatest quantity was to be obtained by sinking shafts to a depth of as much as 40 ft, and usually between 20 and 30 ft in diameter at the surface, though the smaller pits were not more than 14 ft in depth and of a proportionate diameter. As in any form of mining, the depth was determined by the seam. Once the working level of the floorstone was reached, a number of small galleries were cut, radiating in all directions from each shaft. Some galleries penetrated to link up with those from adjacent shafts. Sinking those shafts must have entailed enormous labour, with the tools then available.

Until a systematic study and excavation was made onward from 1870, the large cluster of shafts situated on a part of the great heath we know as Breckland, between Brandon and Thetford, were attributed in succession to Woden, to the Romans, and to the Vikings. Grime's Graves have finally been accredited to the Neolithic people. This cluster of 700

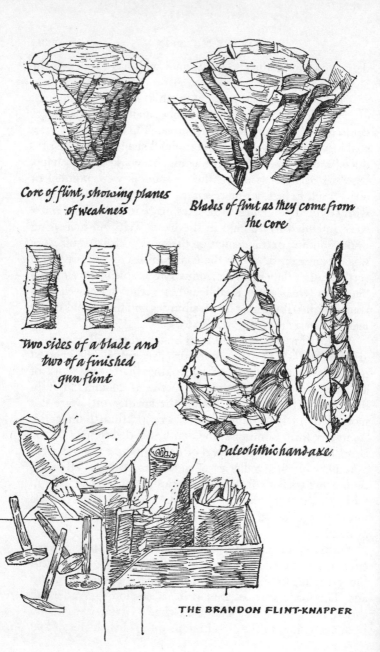

Core of flint, showing planes of weakness

Blades of flint as they come from the core

Two sides of a blade and two of a finished gun flint

Paleolithic hand-axe

THE BRANDON FLINT-KNAPPER

or 800 shafts, covering some thirty-four acres, now in the care of the Ministry of Public Building and Works, is continuously open to the public.

The efficacy of these edge-tools in flint was such that by about 2000 B.C. the manufacture and distribution of the earlier stone axes appears to have slowed down to an insignificant output. The stone factories of North Wales, of Cornwall, and the Lake District ceased to make tool-heads and implements and the flow of trade along the former routes either died away or the direction was reversed. There were a number of sources of the new material, but Thetford Heath was the main centre of the industry.

From the beginning knapping was carried out on 'the site', and continued so, with fluctuating activity to the present time. When bronze and iron displaced flint as material for tools and weapons, the craft of the knapper had to adapt or succumb. As old shafts were exhausted new ones were sunk in lesser number.

A new life came with the advent of flint-lock firearms. A vast number of flints had to be provided for the British Army from the seventeenth century to the early nineteenth. This was, in fact, the period of greatest activity. The industry, today, provides solely for export to the native peoples of West Africa and to the U.S.A., where the use of the flint-lock gun appears to be favoured as a pastime. For this, the few men still working at Brandon have been producing 15,000 flints a month.

The Neolithic, pre-metal-age men had to rely upon 'hammer-stone' and 'percussion-table' for manufacture. The Brandon knappers use a variety of hammers and a small steel anvil which is set in a block of heavy wood, on the same principle as the blacksmith's anvil. The five stages in production are excavation, drying, quartering, flaking and the final one of knapping. Commencing with a nodule of black dry flint which may weigh as much as 30 lb, the knapper places this between his knees and strikes it with a steel-faced hammer, weighing some 5 lb. The experienced man has an infinite knowledge of the 'planes of weakness' which exist in most rocks and can tell by the 'ring' made by the hammer, where such weaknesses are and how they lie. The inexpert person could attempt to strike off pieces from the core and only succeed in producing a pile of irregular chips, flakes, and grains, knowing nothing of the use of the hammers.

The core is now left with a number of faces or striking-platforms. Using a lighter hammer, the knapper can now strike off a number of long, parallel blades which leave the original core a fluted cone. This process is continued so that each blade includes a pair of ridges left by the previous round of flaking. Each blade produced may be compared very roughly to a carpenter's paring-chisel in having a bevel along its two sides. With a special, light, chisel-headed hammer, the gun-flints are made. These are not quite square, and measure in the 'horse-pistol' size, about 1 in. one way and a little less the other. This process is done on the anvil and the sizes of flint were made as follows: Musket, Carbine, Horse-pistol, Large gun, Small gun, and Pocket-pistol. Reference to the drawing will show how the 'breakdown' from the nodule to the gun-flint takes place. The precision of such work depends entirely on the skill and experience of the knapper and his dexterity with the right hammer.

The nature of flaking in the primitive tool-heads varied according to whether this process was done by direct or indirect percussion, that is striking with or without an intermediate tool, or whether done by applying pressure on a 'line of weakness'. The Aztecs of Mexico had their methods, the Aborigines of Australia still have theirs, and so it has been in many parts of the world, wherever the material was accessible to men.

The writer is indebted to the Keeper of Paleontology, the Natural History Museum, British Museum, for permission to make use of certain material.

27

Coopering

It may be said that the craft of the cooper is more 'wrapt in mysteries' than most. Certainly, it entails full seven years of apprenticeship and the accumulated experience of a lifetime of journeying. Coopers have worked 'on their own' or as employees at breweries. Overall, coopers have been responsible, not only for the various sizes of beer and wine cask, but also for 'dry casks'—those intended for butter, tallow, apples, etc., and for various types of measure and sieve. As employees there have been regulations concerned with time 'away from the block'—or off the premises, stipulations as to the employers' provision of certain tools and materials and which tasks shall not be performed by the cooper.

There have, too, been 'travelling' coopers, who were journeymen in the added sense that they moved about the country from brewery to brewery, last week in Stratford, this week in Birmingham, and the week after in Shrewsbury. They were 'on the road', as were the travelling blacksmiths, enjoying, perhaps, a certain independence which was worth the risks involved. Usually, they had a reputation for first-class workmanship and could put just that bit extra into a cask.

They have always made beer casks of oak because of the 'sympathy' between that wood and the old-fashioned beer. It left a 'crust' on the interior because it consisted almost wholly of malt and hops. The increasing use of chemicals in present-day beers has had a corrosive effect, it is said to 'eat away', quite different from the deposited crust. This factor, together with a phenomenal rise in the price of Baltic and American supplies, has resulted in the increasing use of metal casks. Economics and beer apart, there have been other changes, especially in regard to sizes or capacities of the casks. There is little or no call for butts and hogshead.

The sequence of operations in coopering may be grouped as Dressing, Raising, Heading, and Gathering.

Dressing, is the preparation and shaping of the staves from the butt.

Raising is the initial assembling of the staves in the truss hoops.

Heading is the making of the heads which fit into the ends of a cask, and

Gathering is the completion of the hooping to produce the finished cask.

Each cask, when finished, is liquid-tight. The capacity of each size of cask is made one or two pints over, to allow for wastage.

Making casks is 'heavy' work from start to finish; with all the precision involved there is no light-weight work, so that all the cooper's tools are robust. There is a considerable range and almost every one of the tools is peculiar to the trade, though some have a 'family' likeness to those of other trades. One may cast one's eyes around the exciting array in the shop and learn of some which have had 100 years and more of continuous use, and be told that 'my grandfather bought that one when he finished his prentice years'. One is conscious of the craftsman's affection for these tools.

DRESSING

Both the staves and the heads are made from butt oak.

Formerly, this was quartered by cleavage, but latterly it has become increasingly the practice to use the saw instead of the fromard.

According to the size of cask, the staves are cut and dressed, the outer face with a backing-knife and the inner with a hollowing-knife. The segmental or radial meeting edges are first roughly formed with a side-axe to effect a quick removal and then planed to the finished state on the jointer. Work on the staves, previous to the use of the jointer, is done on a shaving-horse, which 'animal' is to be found in the equipment of a number of woodcrafts.

We may digress for attention to the jointer. Firstly, we note that it is 'upside down' and supported at one end on two legs. Secondly, one is struck by its remarkable length, as much as 6 ft. Where the ordinary plane is held in the hands, face down on the work, the jointer is stationary, and as we have noted, upside down with the fore-end supported by legs and the hind-end on the floor. The stave to be dressed is held edge down and moved against the iron, so that in effect, the planing motion is transferred to the stave, the reverse of normal action.

The best jointers have always been made of beech—the plane-maker's wood—for the experienced workmen always say 'wood to wood'. Steel jointers are obtainable and listed, as many other types of plane, but coopers say that the stave does not respond as readily as on wood. If, for some reason, steel jointers have to be used, some coopers will effect a partial remedy by applying a film of vegetable oil or by, roughening the face of the jointer. If such a tool has this innate defect, then it would surely be advantageous for the makers to provide a different face. In continuous planing, wood and steel tend to 'stick'.

One may say that in the making of staves there lies the root of the cooper's skill, for the edge produced by the jointer must be *absolutely* radial and exact to either side of

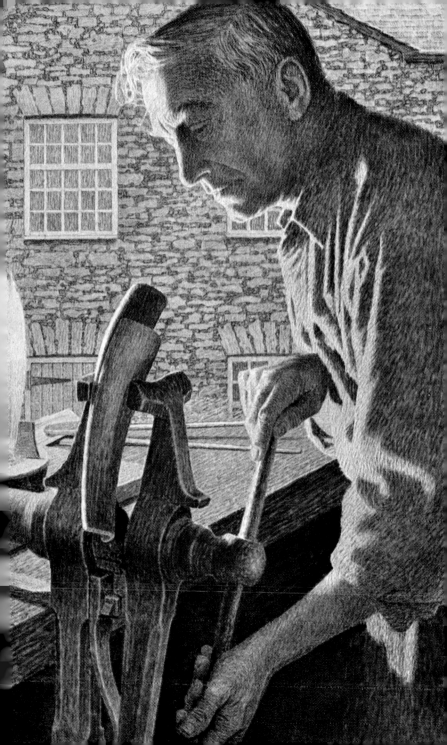

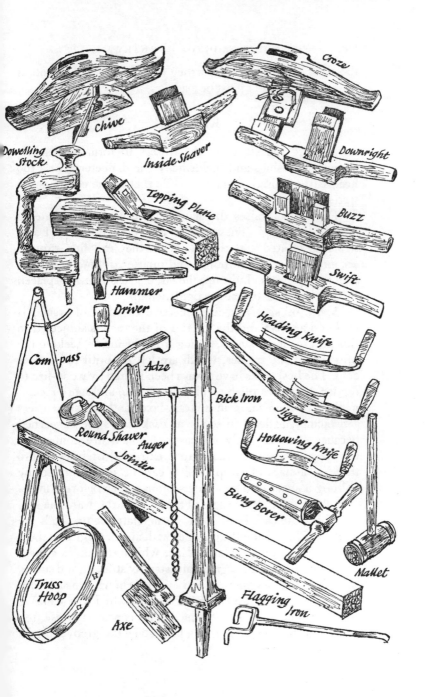

Chive

Croze

Dowelling Stock

Inside Shaver

Downright

Topping Plane

Buzz

Hammer
Driver

Swift

Com-pass

Adze

Heading Knife

Bick Iron

Jigger

Round Shaver

Auger

Hollowing Knife

Jointer

Bung Borer

Truss
Hoop

Mallet

Axe

Flagging Iron

the centre-line. One stave wrong or askew and the whole is useless and another must be made.

RAISING

Assembling the staves in the trusses to form the cask is known as raising, and incidentally the diameter across the head is the 'raised' diameter, while that at the centre is the 'pitch'.

The cooper raises the staves and calls for his mate to help in 'trussing'. These trusses are robustly made of ash, which is cleated and riveted. What they call first runner, second runner, pitch, bulge, and quarter, follow in succession as the cask is built up, the larger truss being displaced by the smaller as the cask is tightened up.

A fire of shavings, and effective disposal of waste, is made on a trivet and the interior of the cask is subjected to this heat until the staves, drying from the inside, yield to the pressure of the trusses, which are left on until the cask is cold. The best casks have always been heated by wood-fire to render the staves pliable. The alternative, and more recent, method of immersion in a steam-box has been shown less satisfactory, at least in so far as cask-staves are concerned because steaming only increases the moisture content of the staves. When the moisture is extracted by internal fire there is a natural warp, which can be demonstrated by holding a sheet of damp water-colour paper before a fire— very shortly the outer edges of the sheet curl toward the fire.

Whilst the cask is still in a 'warm' state the two ends are worked. They shape the outsides with an adze and level them off with a topping- or sun-plane, which resembles a jack-plane, except that it is segmental instead of straight, and curves 'away from the cooper'. The bevel or chime is made with an adze, to be followed with chive with which the concave surface below the chive is formed. This concave part is often known as the 'howel' and at a later stage the groove to take

the head will be made in the howel, which groove is made
with a croze. A glance at the diagram of a stave will show
these parts and the page of cooper's tools will, in turn, show
the remarkable shape of the chive and croze which have a
convex surface which conforms exactly to inside circumference of the cask. For this reason, each size of cask must
have its respective size of chive and croze, i.e. pin, firkin, kil-
derkin, barrel, and hogshead, as shown in the tool-maker's
lists. This applies also to the inside-shave, which is used
during the finishing stages. All this work, with plane, shave,
chive, and croze, is done 'at the block'. This block is simply
a section of a large butt of elm or ash, let into the ground,
and similar to that on which the blacksmith's anvil rests,
but of a height convenient to the cooper.

When the cask is cold, the steel hoops—best Staffordshire—are put on, splayed so that they can be driven tight.
These hoops by their position on the cask, are known as
indicated on the drawing and they are always put on with
the riveted laps facing opposite ways at each end. In this
process the 'preceding' hoops are eased on with a drift, or
cooper's driver, which is struck with a hammer, in the
manner of a cold chisel. The edge of a drift has a groove
which engages with the edge of the hoop.

HEADING

The heads are made in four or five sections, of oak, according to the size of the cask. These sections are joined by
means of dowelling. The outer are called the cants, then
come the quarters, and in the larger heads the middle piece,
called the centre. The holes for the dowels are made with
the familiar stock and bit, a tool much favoured by a number
of craftsmen in wood. The surfaces of the dowelled-up
sections are finished off with a heading swift which appears
to be something of a hybrid between a plane and a spokeshave, in having an inclined, iron, wedged in a box, which

Making staves on the jointer

Chime Hoop

Middle

Cant

Quarter

Quarter Hoop

Bulge Hoop

Raising staves in truss hoops

has handles each side. The downright and the buzz are shaped similarly to the swift. These various shavers are used for cleaning up the joints in both the heads and the casks. For the internal work it will be noted that they use an inside shaver and a hollowing-knife. For this inside work a jigger is used additionally to the forementioned tools. It bears a superficial resemblance to a draw-knife, but has a much shorter blade which is hollowed. The right-hand handle is more or less 'in line' with the right side of the blade, whereas the left hand is of normal draw-knife shape. This handle is held more or less in one position, while the right-hand 'does all the work' in a kind of lever action.

When the heads have been prepared, with bevels on top and underside to engage with the cask grooves, they are put in the casks. For this, the chime edges of the staves must be eased—the chime-hoops, so far, having been left off and worked into the groove. We should notice that the perimeter of the heads, described with suitable dividers, are not, in fact trimmed to a true circle. They are made very slightly ovate, the greater dimension being across the cants. This is done so that after fitting in or 'heading up', as they call it, the staves, when enclosed by the chime hoops, compress the heads across the grain of the wood, to further tighten the joints between cants and quarters. In addition to this measure, the heads at each end go in at right-angles to each other—if the grain at one end is north and south', that at the opposite end is 'east and west'. This, together with the hoops at each end being put on facing opposite ways, all helps to keep the cask in good shape during its lifetime.

There is one more useful tool for internal cleaning-up, and that is the round shaver, which has a more or less semi-circular blade with draw-knife handles close together. Some round shavers have a ring-shaped blade fixed to a single handle. This tool is made in a 'wide' size for coopering and a 'narrow' for casework.

The stave containing the bung-hole is made a little wider

than the others and the hole is started with a twist auger, which is followed by a special borer. This tool has a tapering, malleable cast body fitted with a blade, detachable for periodic resharpening.

GATHERING

Hoops are made of three gauges of iron, the heavier for the larger casks. They are riveted with mild steel rivets on a bick iron, which is a special kind of anvil, standing high, to support the two ends of the hoop.

When the hoops have been driven right home the cask is said to have been gathered, and the hoops are secured by a number of tenter-hooks. It is part of a cooper's skill that each pair of hoops, chime, quarter, and bulge are equidistant from the end. No cooper would accept a quarter of an inch difference between the two of any pair.

Sometimes the staves of an old cask have sustained damage. So the cooper will mark off any which need replacement and especially will he look under the chime hoops, because if a cask has been dropped on its chime, then the stave at that point will be broken. All hoops, with the exception of the other chime are removed, as well as one head. The damaged stave is eased out and replaced with a 'case stave'. The cask is then trussed up and the other end is worked. The head is replaced with the aid of a flagging-iron and rushes inserted and caulked. When the joints have been shaved the cask is re-hooped. The flagging-iron has a long handle which is held against the right hip, leaving the hands free. The rushes are purchased by the bolt.

The cases referred to above are made the same as a cask, but worked at one end only. They are 'knocked down' and the staves are used as required, in place of the damaged ones.

An older name for the bung or large 'stopper' was the shive, and the air-vent for regulating the air when the cask has been tapped is stopped with a spile. Both shive and spile have old derivations, from Frisian and Middle Dutch. The bung-hole is fitted with a metal bush.

The names of the casks are to be found on many an old pub, or wayside inn. 'The One Pin', at Hedgerley, near Beaconsfield, and 'The Three Tuns' at Southall, Middlesex.

Certain types of casks were not made round but oval. Such were those with which ship's boats were equipped; they went under the seats and didn't roll out. In the far-off days of horse-drawn stage-wagons and carriers, these great vehicles were often or usually equipped with a carrier's flask, which was a cask in miniature, usually suspended from a hook at the near-side fore-end of the wagon. Many a country inn had them, hanging among the curing hams, and some still have a few, hanging ornamentally from the ceiling beams.

Travellers to Wales, from Craven Arms and beyond, who leave Clun by the grand little road through Newcastle, will eventually pass or halt by a fine old inn, 'The Anchor', whose present owners are restoring it to its former glory, when the old shepherd kept it. I always had the impression that if he was away on the hills, tending his sheep, the regulars drew their own cooling draughts and left the money on the counter. I don't think 'The Anchor' had any hours. From the ceiling there hung an inverted forest of casks and what have you, all quite genuine and gloriously unsophisticated. I'm glad I made a drawing. It was a long haul, on a bicycle (and still is), up that beautiful road that one just had to stop.

The following table indicates the size and capacity of casks. Also the number of hoops.

Butt		8 hoops
Hogshead	54 gal.	6 hoops
Barrel	36 gal.	6 hoops
Kilderkin	18 gal.	6 hoops
Firkin	9 gal.	4 hoops
Pin	$4\frac{1}{2}$ gal.	4 hoops

28

Pillow-lace Making

The making of lace in this country had its beginnings during the sixteenth century, when it became an occupation by women and children. To a great extent it was certainly a cottage industry, pursued to augment the meagre wages received by the 'breadwinner' of the household. It also provided employment in village schools and 'the institutions' wherein were housed the 'children of the poor'. Generally, this system continued until the latter part of the nineteenth century. The frequency with which one encounters the word 'workhouse' in connection with a craft is somewhat depressing. This establishment was a product of the nineteenth century. During the early part of the same century, 'lace-schools' were established, where a number of children of any age, from five on, worked under supervision.

During the 1840s there entered a decline in productivity and the numbers employed, which gave no cause to depress thinking people. Neither from the point of working accommodation and amenities, nor by the hours worked or the posture in which the work was done, could the health of those employed derive any benefit. An Act, passed in 1867, and concerned with the running of workshops, was at that time difficult to enforce. Eventually, the craft, as such, still further declined near to vanishing-point when alternative and better forms of employment were found and the compulsion of school attendance gathered momentum. An industry which began and grew interwoven with poverty could never have become a healthy one. It is unfortunate that this aspect is inseparable from the study of this craft.

Hand-made lace was of two kinds—needlepoint and pillow lace. Needlepoint evolved from drawn-thread and open embroidery, and by gradual changes the base fabric was discarded early in the sixteenth century and thence forth the needle-thread alone was used. This final technique later produced the Venetian lace and the French of Alençon and Argentan, in which form it became known in this country as 'Holie-point'.

Pillow lace was made by twisting and plaiting the threads, which had previously to be wound on bobbins. Manufacture in this country developed in two different parts; in and about Honiton and Beer, in Devonshire; and in the large area defined by Banbury, St Neots, Wellingborough, and near to Dunstable, with an 'outlier' to the south, about High Wycombe and Marlow. While the Honiton makers worked the pattern first and then 'grounded' it with meshing, as in Italy and Brussels, in the East Midlands pattern and ground were made in a single process, in conformity with Flemish practice as in Antwerp, Mechlin, etc. Thus the making of needlepoint never became an industry here.

The East Midland form of the craft received a considerable impetus when refugees came from the Continent to escape persecution, and though the industry, through its history, was a province of women and girls, there were a small number of men at work. A study of the map will show that the maximum activity was in the cluster of villages centred all about Bedford, Olney, and Newport Pagnell, and it was from this centre that further activity spread.

By the eighteenth century the industry enjoyed some prosperity. This was based on the sale of a cheap product in the popular market, since Continental lace was judged to be of a superior quality. English lace had not only to contend with Continental lace in the open market, but also through the supplies obtained from smuggling—laces for a lady. In the whole trade, in Devon and the East Midlands, there were by 1770 some 100,000 people engaged, and in spite of a decline which began during the last quarter, the total increased.

The conventional image we have of the pillow-lace maker is usually of a gracious elderly lady, sitting before the rather conspicuous cushion or 'pillow', over which are suspended a considerable number of bobbins. Closer examination reveals a pattern laid across this pillow, together with a great number of pins, set in a dense cluster on a portion of the pattern. By means of plaiting and weaving white thread —or sometimes black—in and about each of the pins, the band of lace is slowly produced by the repetition of a pre-scribed order. One soon appreciates this is work for quick and nimble fingers.

The pattern is made of parchment or vellum, which has been 'pricked' according to the lace-design. The basis of this work is composed of 'twisting' and 'crossing' the threads of four bobbins, in two pairs. Twisting consists of laying the right-hand thread of each pair over the left-hand. Crossing consists of laying the left-hand inner thread over the right-hand inner. A half-stitch consists of a single twist and cross, and a whole-stitch is completed by a repetition of these movements and it is from these elements that all the sub-sequent variations in the movements of the bobbins are derived. (To a mere man, this, together with the art of knitting, remains one of the esoteric mysteries beside which such everyday exercises as nuclear-fission are indeed trivial.)

As worked on the pillow, the straight edge of a lace border is always to the right of the lace-maker, and therefore the outer edge irrespective of its shape lies to the left. When wide lace is worked in a continuous strip it is called a flounce and is intended to be 'gathered' or pleated. Narrow laces are called borders or edges and are likewise gathered. Insertions are straight-edged strips. Each part of a design had a name by which it was known throughout the craft.

The design and preparation of the drafts or prototypes of the pattern was the responsibility of the lace buyers from the seventeenth century onward. Some skill and invention in their design was called for, although the elements of these designs and their arrangement was traditional. They were drawn on vellum or card and contained one complete unit of the design, the whole surface being pricked with holes for the later insertion of the lace-maker's pins. From each draft the whole pattern could be obtained by movement. The working-pattern was reproduced by repetition on a strip of vellum about 14 in. long. In later years pasteboard or linen which had been stiffened with shellac was used as a substitute. The transparent vellum placed over the draft, enabled the worker to transfer by pricking off the design-unit and repeating along the length of the strip. The working-pattern was kept taut over the pillow by the attachment of linen tabs. Many of the earlier designs were Flemish, French, or Italian in origin.

The peculiar pillows which focus one's interest are of two types. The less familiar one is 'squarish' in shape, but the more familiar is like a very short bolster, being round in section, and oblong, with 'open' ends. They are, or were, made of hessian or canvas and lightly stuffed with straw, much in the manner in which a saddler stuffs a horse's collar', even to the stuffing-rod and the mallet, both of which are used in the same way. It was the pillow which was used throughout the East Midlands, while the Honiton makers used a cushion shaped more like a flattish mushroom. In other countries, cushions different from either are used.

The pillow rested on a wooden cradle, of one design or another, called a horse, which was kept steady by the feet

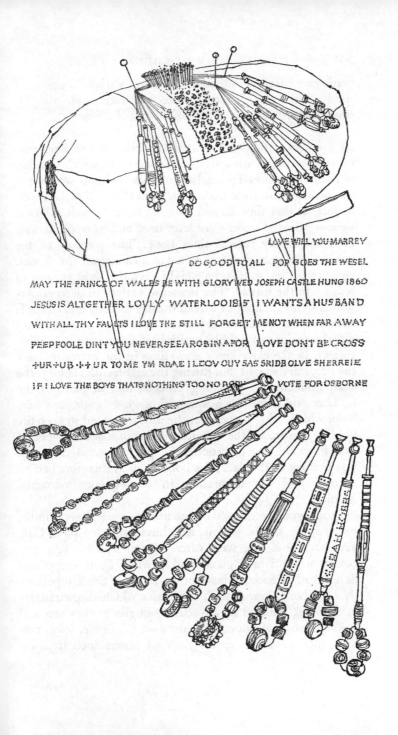

resting on a transom situated low down. Various covers were used to aid the work and to protect the lace and by the side was a pin cushion, usually in the shape of a heart.

In common with many other industries, lace-making contained within its own activity a second craft, which was that of bobbin-making. The earliest of these bobbins were made by turning them from bone and, from this, pillow lace was, in fact, at that time known as bone lace. As well as bone, various kinds of wood were later used and so wood became more commonly turned than bone. The purpose of the bobbin was, as in weaving, to act as a carrier for the thread, and in addition to this, its weight gave the right amount of tension to the thread. The immense variety of designs permitted quick identity of thread during the process, and it is now a matter of historical interest that in no other country did the designs of bobbin multiply into such an incredible variety. In the early kinds a swelling in the extremity gave the necessary weight, but during the eighteenth century, the shaft underwent a slimming process, and in place of the bulbous end there was a 'spangle' of glass beads on a wire loop, which, lying flat against the pillow, helped to keep the bobbin steady. In the Honiton technique such shapes of bobbin would have obstructed the 'passing-through', which was peculiar to that lace; the bobbins used therefore had no spangle and the decoration in consequence remained simple.

Among the words used by the turners were plum, spindle, hazel, apple, maple, willow, ash, birch, and dogwood. Oak, yew, and box, too, were often turned. Occasionally one comes across ivory, glass, and pewter. Each shape and design had its name or inscription. Many of them, especially those of bone, bore inscribed phrases which ring strangely in our ears, dimmed by advertising jingles as they are, and are suggestive of hope, anguish, and, of course, love. Perhaps they were less casual than we about such things—

'peep foole peep dint you never see a bobbin afor'—'love is a sharp thorn'. A large collection of these bobbins affords one more interest than the lace itself. The Museum at Luton has such a collection, together with examples of lace and all the fascinating impedimenta of pillows, stools, and bobbin-winders.

When pillow lace was made at the cottage-door in the fine weather of summer the question of adequate light did not arise, but as long as work had to be done indoors, whether during the day, near a window, or after dark by artificial light—invariably candles—then some device for concentrating this poor source was necessary. This was obtained by means of a glass globe or flash, which was filled with water; such a device is also employed for concentrating a point of light from electricity by many engravers in wood. The girls sat around the candle in a circle and the ideal was one flash per worker, since more workers than flashes defeated the idea, and that unfortunately too often occurred in the schools. A high 'stool' with holes in the seat for the flashes, enabled the candle to perform its feeble task. By the nineteenth century lighting in country cottages had progressed as far as candles, while a little higher up the social scale one found oil lamps—now much sought after.

The linen thread was originally imported, but by the nineteenth century this was being produced in Britain. It came to the lace-maker in skeins, which were graded according to fineness, ranging from 14 slip, the finest, to 3 slip, which was the coarsest. The skeins were placed on winders from which the thread was transferred on to the bobbins. Though the winders did vary in design they functioned to the same end.

'Buckingham Point' or 'Point-ground' lace was that lace containing Lille or Mechlin elements. Though ascribed to Buckingham, it was produced in all parts of the East

Midlands, likewise 'Bedford Maltese', which was derived from the craft of Malta and which eventually displaced point-ground, and from Maltese origins it developed along its own course, losing the original elements. Other styles were Plaited Lace, Cluny, Torchon, Blonde, and Yak.

61   THE COOPER. RAISING THE STAVES WITH TRUSSES

62 THE COOPER: CUTTING THE GROOVE WITH A
CROZE   *Museum of English Rural Life*

63 PILLOW-LACE MAKING

64　DURHAM QUILT-MAKER　　　　　*Miss K. R. Drummond*

29

Quilting

The craft of Quilting has long been practised in many parts of the world. In China, as material for clothing protection against the cold, and likewise in parts of India. It also had its place in the many regions of Mohammedan Asia and Africa. Nearer home, it was to be found in most of the European countries. In Britain, the use of quilting for bedding and clothing came into being during the fourteenth and fifteenth centuries.

The word 'quilt' has contrived to pass through history by way of many spellings—twilt, cowlte, qwhite—the Latin 'culcita' and the old French 'cuilte' indicate the derivation and intermediate course. Culcita—a stuffed mattress or cushion—indicates its original use. The *O.E.D.* definition— 'An article of bed-furniture, consisting essentially of two large pieces of woven material, having a layer of wool flock, down or the like placed between them . . . in later use, a coverlet of similar make, especially one in which the lining is kept in place . . . by lines of stitching. . . .' We are familiar now with a quilt as a covering, but originally it was used for lying on, doubtless a great deal better than straw. The craft is thus a functional needlework which produces a textile sandwich between an upper and lower layer, and the many designs which we associate with quilting indicate a way of doing the job beautifully.

In the era in which we are privileged to play our parts

quilts have largely been relegated to the bygones of museums, along with warming-pans and brass candlesticks, though the latter at least are in some demand against power failure. The original warming-pan, designed to contain red-hot coke or coal, has reappeared in a modified form in which electric elements have taken the place of solid fuel. The original forms, if not in museums, provide a pleasing visual background in our homes and a tangible link with our great-grandparents.

The craft, in the country as a whole, reached a peak during the seventeenth and eighteenth centuries. By then quilting had been used not only as bed-furniture but as part of male and female clothing, as breeches, doublets, petticoats, and waistcoats. Not only was it a means of providing bodily warmth in domestic life, but as a part of military armour, to be worn usually under the armour, but in some cases outside. For the more lightly armed troops, intended for quicker movement, the equivalent of our present-day light infantry, as a light armour in place of metal.

Fashion had dictated the incorporation of quilting in dress, and fashion again its demise, so that by the end of the eighteenth century quilting had no place in either male or female dress. The development of textile printing was a major factor in this process, in providing an entirely new range of materials, especially cotton, which was receptive to the new technique. For furnishing, too, taste turned to the new chintzes in flowered patterns, so that the designs which were a feature of quilting would have been lost amid these patterns, since they naturally required a plain ground to set them off. A new method of providing warmth was at the same time coming in, in the woollen blanketing. The changes and declines were, of course, anything but uniform, as local standards of living and some conservatism meant that the cottage homes still used the older and cheaper forms. The new trends in this, as in other things, were mainly for the wealthy. In the South-East, where standards, even then, were higher, the changes were quicker and ran deeper.

In the northern counties and in Wales the quilters' craft continued to satisfy a demand. In Northern Ireland, too, it maintained its place, though with less elaboration, surviving into what we call 'living memory'. In these three areas it is now largely a hobby, but in the standard attained in the North, often referred to as Durham quilting, the craft is actually supplying a luxury market, which suggests that we may be in the process of turning a full circle.

This renewed life is to the credit of hard-working officers of the Rural Industries Bureau and the Women's Institutes. who in their respective fields are co-ordinating quilters and directing a channel of supply. Both the Bowes Museum and the Victoria and Albert Museum contain many examples.

The outer material may be wool, poplin, silk, or fine linen, while the interior can be wool, cotton, flock, or downy material. A quilt has an upper side of some finer material than the under side, in the way that an eiderdown has. In so far as the art and the traditional designs have generally been passed from mother to daughter through the generations, quilting may certainly be regarded as a folk art. It is on this continuity that the Women's Institutes are working.

In the matter of a livelihood, quilting was part of a cottage economy, though the financial return for the labours of one to three weeks assiduous and painstaking care could have been but slender. Today, the craft is established on a different basis. During the nineteenth century there was a considerable influence from the contemporary activity of making patchwork covers, so that many quilts, in consequence, incorporated patchwork in the stitching design.

In America, the craft was perpetuated by the early settlers from England and Holland, and during the westward expansion in the nineteenth century the craft became practised in Kentucky, Tennessee, Virginia, and Carolina, in the remoter parts of which it is being followed today. Once established in America, the craft aesthetic diverged in some degree from the 'parent' stems. Henceforth, patchwork became dominant, while at home, in the North, in Wales, and Ulster, the original quilt element retained its position.

There is a curious similarity between quilting and lace-making in that the work was produced from designs prepared and supplied by professional 'markers', in the form of templates, units of which could be arranged at the will of the quilters. It is also curious that, as in lace-making, the quilting markers were men, and it was particularly during the nineteenth century that this procedure developed, from a small beginning in Allendale, in that lovely part of Northumberland.

The process of quilting was carried out with the materials held evenly together on a frame, which for a bed-spread, would measure as much as 8 or 9 ft—one wonders how so large a frame, demountable or not, could be accommodated in some of the cottage living-rooms. When such a work was set on its frame it was nevertheless possible for as many as six people, in the larger rooms, to be sewing at the same time. Such gatherings became known as quilting parties or feasts, at which the company present might exchange items of news over tea and cakes, or, as formerly, a cold posset. This was very much the way of doing things in Durham and Northumberland, and this charming convention had its counterpart in the quilting bees of America.

Standards of living, high, low or medium, do not bear solely on the presence of such a craft. In what is called the 'Black' Country and the 'Industrial' North there has been a long-lived vitality in 'popular' or folk-art forms, which have been the products of a vigorous and forthright people. The art of the canal has its roots entwined in those of the potteries. If the North, externally, does appear hard and often severe, there is a warm interior awaiting one's seeking.

Generally, the designs incorporated fall into two groups. There are those which consist of a large set or arrangement of motifs grouped in the centre and enclosed by various kinds of border. The second group includes the infinite variety of 'all-over' designs, placed together in blocks or strips. The one is often characterized by a certain amount of 'movement' in the design; that is, it is often pictorial, or sometimes an arrangement of some plant form. The 'all-over' designs contain unit-motifs each repeated or alternated in strip. These are often more abstract and usually more static in design. Many pillows were made in which an 'embossed' pattern, floral or otherwise, was obtained on a silk or cotton ground. Such pillows—or pillow-cases—were a product of the eighteenth century. Whether quilting, as a craft, continues as a trade or a hobby, it remains likely, in terms of aesthetics, that the high standards of the past will be maintained.

As well as the Bowes Museum, near Barnard Castle, Co. Durham, which has the finest collection of relevant exhibits, there are museums at Gloucester, Hereford, St Fagans, and Bristol, which can show local examples. The collection at the Victoria and Albert is, of course, both national and international. They have there a part of a Sicilian covener of about 1400, depicting scenes in the life of Tristan. One must go to the Bargello in Florence to see the remaining part.

30
Making Highland Bagpipes

In the three groups of musical instruments, the flutes and recorders, the reeded family, and the trumpets, the second group contains the clarinet, which has a single reed, the oboe, cor anglais and the bassoons, which all have double reeds, and finally the vast range and variety of bagpipes—including hornpipes, with which latter the dances of that name have no connection.

Those bagpipes which have always had a single reed are generally the more primitive—the clarinet, with its single reed, was invented by Denner, of Nuremberg, at the beginning of the eighteenth century, but those fitted with the double reed have some affinity with the oboes.

Some bagpipes have the air supplied by a mouthpiece or blowpipe, while others are equipped with bellows, strapped to the left-side and operated by that arm. The musical sounds are created by pressure on the bag by the left arm. In almost every kind of pipes—one uses the plural in the singular sense, since each instrument has a number of pipes —the air in the bag is held there by a non-return valve, usually of leather. The greatest skill is demanded of the player in maintaining a 'balance' between the supply and the exhaustion of air, to ensure an even pressure on the reeds, for any variation would adversely affect the tonal quality of the music. Most pipes are played in a standing position; some like the Irish, are played whilst sitting, and some whilst

marching in military formation, or standing like the Highland.

It is the chanter which produces the melody in any pipe
music, and this part is pierced along its length with a
number of finger-holes, which in the case of the Highland
pipes are seven in number, with an additional hole above the
first, with two unfingered vents in addition. The reed is
fitted to the inner extremity—of both the chanter and the
drones—and is thus concealed by the stock into which the
pipes fit. Within the context of the present chapter it would
be irrelevant and would offer too much digression to discuss
the whole range of technical variations in chanters and
drones. Suffice it to say that the great pipe of the Highlands
has a chanter with a wide mouth and a conical bore—the
nature of both affect the tonal character.

The drone, or drones, provides a continuous 'background' note in accompaniment to the melody of the chanter.
The sound is not only continuous but remains on one note,
because the drone has no finger-holes. The number of drones
on any one type of instrument vary from one to four, and in
the case of the great pipe there are three, one bass and two
tenor. They are tuned below the octave of the chanter, the
bass being two octaves below. The bass is made in three joints,
and is longer than the tenors, which are in two joints. Drone
bores, unlike those of chanters, are uniform throughout, and
cylindrical. Tuning is done by means of slides, which are
adjusted whilst a tuning-note is sustained on the chanter,
the equivalent of the A of the orchestra, sometimes the most
thrilling of sounds.

THE PIPES OF THE OLD WORLD

The origin and development of reed instruments in so many
countries of Europe, Africa, and Asia, is a subject in itself
for study, and to this end the reader is directed to a book
published by the Pitt-Rivers Museum, Oxford University,

Bagpipes, by Anthony Baines. In addition, there is also *The History of the Bagpipes*, by Dr Fraser, whose collection is to be seen in the Royal Scottish Museum, Edinburgh. The Pitt-Rivers Museum contains the Balfour Collection.

Bagpipes of the various peoples of the three continents have always been pastoral instruments, played by the shepherds whilst tending their flocks. Not until the pipes reached this country did they attain a sophisticated status, nor was there such a high level in technology employed in the manufacture nor a cultivation in the playing. The pipes of the Highland regiments provide a greatly different musical form from that of the shepherds of the Abruzzi, or the Balkan mountains. Curiously, the great pipe of the Scottish hillsides was once quite obscure or comparatively so. Perhaps the regimental music of Scotland established the instrument in the estimation of other countries; certainly that was so in India.

The pipes played in various parts of the world may be grouped as follows:

1. The primitives, with single reeds and with or without a bag.

Morocco	Zāmar	Malta	Zampogna
Balearics	Zampona Xeremia	Crete	
Tunisia	Zūkra	Greek Islands Cyprus	Tsambouna
Tripoli	Zūkra	Macedonia	Gaida
Egypt	Zummara	Armenia	Parakapzuk
Arabia	Zummara	Turkestan	Tulim?
Palestine	—	India	Pungi, Mashak
Syria	Zummara	Assam	Pepa

2. Eastern Europe
   (*a*) Double chanter, no bass drone and with blowpipe to bag.

| Dalmatia | Mih | Montenegro | Mih |
| Istria | Mih | Bosnia-Hercegovina | Mih |

(b) Double chanter with bass drone. Blowpipe to bag.

Carpathia	Dudy	North Serbia	Gaida
Danube	Dudy	South Poland	Dudy
Slavonia	Gaida	Ukraine	Volynka
			Duda

3. Single chanter with bass drone. Blowpipe to bag.

(a) Western types

Bohemia	Dudy	Poland	Koza
Moravia	Dudy	White Russia	Dudy
	Gajda		Koza

(b) Southern types

| Macedonia | Gaida | Rumania | Cimpoi |
| Bulgaria | Gaida | | |

(c) Northern types

| Sweden | Dudey? | Estonia | Torupill |

4. Southern Italy. Two chanters, two drones, double reeds. The Zampogna. The drones are fitted with double reeds, which are made of willow-bark.

5. Western Europe.

(a) French peasant. Narrow chanter. Small drones on separate or common stock.

The Cornemuse, with blowpipe Normandy Landes
The Cabrette, with bellows Anvergne

(b) Western. Wide chanter. One to three drones in separate stocks. Blowpipe to bag.

| Spain | Gaita | Scotland | Piob mhor |
| Brittany | Biniou | | |

(c) Pipes with regulators in common stock. Bellows to bag.

Ireland Union pipes

(d) Derived from the Musette of France. Bellows to bag.

Northumberland Small pipes

The Pibcorn, of Wales, dating from the eighteenth century, was a pastoral hornpipe. In quality, its music came between the flute and the clarinet.

THE PIPES OF SCOTLAND, IRELAND AND NORTHUMBERLAND

In consequence of bans on the playing of pipes after the '45 and Culloden and also on the wearing of the Clan tartans, very few records of the history of the Scottish pipes have survived. At this juncture it is convenient to define the features which distinguish the various pipes to be heard in Britain. They are the Great Pipes, or Piob Mhor; the Reel Pipes; the Lowland Pipes; the Northumbrian Small Pipes; the Union or Uillean Pipes.

The Great Pipes (the reel pipes is a smaller version)

The bag is blown by a mouthpiece. The chanter has a tapering bore and seven finger-holes, plus an additional hole above the first hole with two additional vents. There are three drones, one bass and two tenors. The chanter is tuned to the major scale of A plus one note below. The tenor drones are tuned to one octave below the low A on the chanter and the bass drone one octave below the tenor.

The makers also produce a practice chanter, for soft fingering, without bag or drones. This chanter has a longer-bladed reed than in bagpipes, which is enclosed in the blowpipe. The notes are softer and deeper pitched.

Scottish Lowland Pipes

The bag is blown by small bellows, not dissimilar from the one-time household kind. One half is secured to the players right waist, while pressure on the other half is applied by the right arm, the bag being held under the left arm as in all bagpipes. The drones, one bass and two tenor, are fitted into a common stock. The chanter has the same fingering and scale as the great pipe and was possibly introduced about the beginning of the eighteenth century. By the latter part of the nineteenth century it was played but rarely.

The Northumbrian Small Pipes

The bag is blown by bellows as with the Lowland pipes and the Uillean pipes. The chanter has keys and is tuned to the major scale of G. There are four drones in a common stock, of which three only are used at one time. They are tuned tenor, baritone, and bass. The chanter is closed at its extremity and every shade of articulation from smooth legato to sharp staccato may be produced. These pipes first appeared in Northumberland toward the end of the seventeenth century.

Irish 'Union' Pipes or Uillean Pipes (elbow pipe)

The bag is bellows-blown, and is made of goatskin and covered with a tartan cloth. The instrument is played while the performer is seated. There are three drones fitting into a common stock, which are tuned treble, tenor, and bass. In addition to the chanter and drones, there are two 'regulators', tuned treble and tenor, operated by keys. The Union pipes became popular early in the eighteenth century. At that time there were one chanter, two drones, and no regulators. This instrument is more popular in Eire. The subtle beauty of its music is best appreciated when unaccompanied. It is pitched lower than the Highland pipes, approximate to the oboe, and has the melodic range of that instrument.

THE MAKING OF HIGHLAND BAGPIPES

The first pipes were made from laburnum or rosewood, and embellished with deerhorn or bone. The mountings were made from German silver and beautifully worked. With the development of trade with Africa and India, the potentialities of new woods was exploited, and such woods as ebony, cocus, brazil and blackwood came into use, largely to displace materials formerly used. Similarly, deerhorn gave way to ivory and silver to nickel.

Most of the wood now comes from Tanzania, in log form up to a few years ago, but more recently the wood has come in the form of billets of a suitable dimension. This conversion is done in the forest, so that easy transport is thenceforth permissible. At the maker's shops the billets are worked on and cut and trimmed for tuning and boring. This process is done on a lathe, motor-driven and of modern design, and the chisels and gouges are all of the normal end-edge kinds. Altogether, there are fourteen different parts to be prepared; the chanter and blowpipe, the three drones, in seven parts, and the five stocks into which they fit.

The bag is made from the skin of a sheep. The cured skin is cut to a pattern, and with the five stock-holes made, it is stitched and dressed to render it air-tight. This stitching is made with ten-strand Irish linen, waxed, and is done on a saddler's vice, that familiar kind which is on a stand held in position by the feet and closed by knee-pressure. Sets of pipes exported to countries in tropical climates have cowhides substituted for sheepskin. The five stocks are permanently secured in the bag from the interior and are enclosed by a decorative frill. All pipes are removable and, as already indicated, the drones are jointed. The finished bag is enclosed in a woven tartan cloth, which is either laced or buttoned along one side to facilitate removal. The three drones are held in position by an ornamental, tasselled cord, which matches the tartan. In playing, the bass drone rests on the player's left shoulder.

The music of bagpipes ranges from the 'rougher' wild music of south-eastern Europe, through the wistful nostalgia of the Appenine mountains, which attracted both Händel and Bach. In 'Harold in Italy' there occurs a distinct little air which Berlioz must have heard, to give him, and us, his own

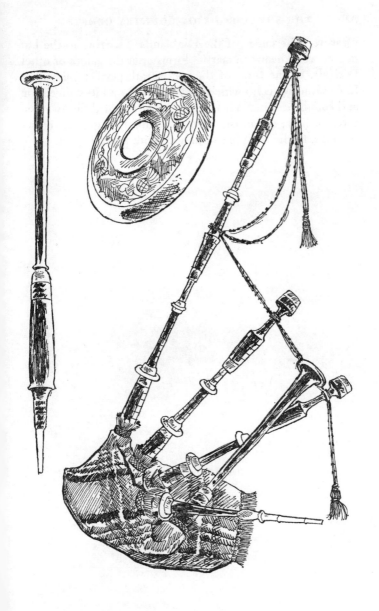

pleasure. The music of the Highlands is stirring to the last degree when heard in martial forms or at the games or other festivals. In the form of the reel, strathspey, or pibroch it has a primitive echo which is evocative for all its convention and sophistication. When a solo piper is heard far away on the brae-side, the music acquires a different quality, closer perhaps, to the truly pastoral and more primitive art.

31

Timber

In this section each of the principal timber-producing trees of Britain, both the native and the introduced, is described, each accompanied by reference to some of the uses to which the timber is put. This is not exhaustive, but indicative.

Especially in the crafts of wood-carving and turning, often collectively known as treen, a number of woods are used. They include apple, rosewood, mahogany, cherry, and white beam, and are only omitted because they are not cultivated in forestry or coppice, or because they are imported from abroad.

HARDWOOD AND SOFTWOOD

One may well be surprised to learn that balsa, the lightest of commercial woods, is classified as a hardwood, although it will grow up to 80 ft in five years and a piece of it may be compressed by the fingers. Equally, one may be surprised that yew, though as hard and heavy as oak, is classified as a softwood. Various alternatives have been considered and all have some drawback. Scientific terms, such as deciduous and coniferous, though most appropriate to the botanist, are unsuitable for the trades. All hardwoods are not slow-growing—poplar and birch come to mind—nor are all softwoods fast-growing, for yew is even slower than oak. Generally, however, denseness, hardness, and heaviness are attributes of slow-growing trees, while fast-growing trees are generally less dense, and are softer and lighter in weight.

ASH

Gracing many hills up to the 1,000 ft contour, the ash is a thriving tree, and one that shows a partiality for the older limestones. It is found intermediately between the empty moorland above, and the dense woods and farm lands below. It is abundant, too, on the Cotswolds, where it intermingles with beech, which tree is generally more chalk-loving. Where little can live in the deep shade of the beech, the thinner foliage of the ash, penetrated better by light, will permit of the presence of flora and therefore fauna. Above those hill-draping cloaks of ash one will usually find the soaring, sailing buzzard.

The best timber, however, is to be obtained from the lower slopes of this somewhat 'mountain' type of country, where the tree is likely to be grown best in plantations of standard trees, or at still lower levels, especially in the South, as coppice or stooled ash. One may notice, incidentally, that not a few plantations of coppice hazel have a protective 'umbrella' of standard ash.

As timber, ash has tremendous value and diverse usage, by reason of its strength, resilience, and very clear grain. These qualities provide an important wood for those industries using cleft-timber, and together with oak and elm it is one of basic trio of the hardest of hard woods in general use. Hornbeam is even harder, but has only a very limited application. The resilience of ash lends it to use where sudden or continuous shocks must be sustained and for this reason it has for a very long time been the traditional wood for the shafts of wagons and parts of the undercarriage, for the helves of many kinds of tool and implement. Likewise the framework of motor-van bodies. Ladder-poles may be of ash, too, though it is more customary to use Scots pine or spruce. Ash is used for making heavy crates—see Hazel— and for gate hurdles, and because it responds well to steaming it is used for the snaiths, or curved handles, of scythes.

ALDER

The alder is a tree which requires some shelter and alluvial, fertile soil. It favours the watersides of glens and valleys. Each seed has a pair of 'floats' which keep it on the surface of the water, until they should drift to the bank. Because of this, the spread of the tree upstream is naturally uncertain, for the only agency which can help is the wind. It is not often that one will find a maiden alder of 60 ft, and the presence of the alder in groves of coppice is the result of generation of cutting, having transformed these trees from the naturally bushy growth into more upright forms resembling coppice timber.

At one time alders were deliberately planted along streams and river banks so that the interweaving roots would reinforce the banks against erosion. The timber to be obtained is soft and perishable, and because of its high water-content requires a longer period of seasoning than other timber. Before present-day methods of gunpowder manufacture came in, alder as a fuel was the mainstay in the factories of Surrey and Hampshire. The Scottish furniture-makers used alder, which in the log had acquired a mahogany-like colour from immersion in peat bogs. The presence of so much alder along the Lea, the Brent, and other London rivers is due to the alder providing easy turnery-wood by the London turners, who were still going until the later half of the nineteenth century.

The best use to which this wood has been put has been for hat-block making, this because it retains its shape when exposed to steam. Clogs, whether hand- or machine-made, are invariably made of alder.

BEECH

In its wild state, as a standard tree, the beech will attain a cathedral dignity with which few other trees, if any, may be compared. As timber, beech is not durable in outdoor usage, but as a material for various pieces of furniture, both 'traditional' and according to the contemporary trend, it has the admirable qualities of ease of working and a fine presentation in the finished state. In the matter of traditional styles, that group of chairs we know of collectively as Windsors is an example of the cottage furniture of the eighteenth century.

Timber for such chairs is not derived from the tree in its natural state, but from a plantation of close-set trees of straight growth with high crowns. Such plantations are cultivated on the 'selection' system, whereby trees of all ages are growing intermingled in the one plantation. By this system, the mature established trees provide shelter, by their height and to the younger, which, in turn, shelter the seedlings. Thus, no one plantation is subject at any time to total felling, but instead, to a continuous process of 'thinning', as each tree attains the required age and dimensions. This type of woodland has for long dominated the Chiltern country for many miles around High Wycombe.

Among other uses, beech is favoured for woodworking planes and other tools. A great deal of timber was thus used to supply the trade for home consumption and export.

A tree so splendid and stately as the beech, whether in the full growth of the Hampshire Highlands, or those glorious clumps that grace the Cotswolds, or the more slender trees of the Chilterns, and if one may go further afield, to Holland, between The Hague and Amsterdam, such a tree is too fine to be termed a weed, as they did in High Wycombe.

BIRCH

The slender, dainty grace of the birch, well belies its hardy constitution and its ability to thrive in the wild state. It is regarded as a pioneer, on new ground, rough common, and heath, and this innate hardness in such circumstances fits it well for this role. Its wind-borne seeds will readily take root wherever they fall, but it can be retarded, where necessary, by stock-grazing. In this environment it is found commonly in irregular scatterings throughout the southern half of Britain, though it is best seen on various types of heathland. In the mountain and moorland it occurs frequently in the valleys, where, however, it has to compete with the dominant mountain ash or rowan.

For a variety of reasons, many birches in their wild state, are considered poor timber by woodmen and foresters, who prefer trees of straighter growth and greater volume. Nevertheless, the birch, from the base of its trunk to the tips of its slender twigs, is put to a variety of uses. Makers of brooms and brushes use wood from the trunk, while the twig cuttings are bound into carefully formed besom-heads. We may look to the far-away rivers of Canada and the United States and remember the birchbark canoes so skilfully constructed by the Indian tribesmen.

BOX

Turners and cabinet-makers have always highly valued box, and, of course, wood engravers use it exclusively, working with their gravers on the end grain, whilst wood-cutters, working on the face, use apple or pear. And for draughtsmen's instruments, such as scales and rulers, it is unequalled.

The box is not at all commonly met with, but it certainly favours the North and South Downs. There are groves of it in the vicinity of Box Hill, in Surrey, where too one may find juniper and spindle, quite numerous. The timber is pale yellow, very dense, hard and heavy, and is one of the few timbers which are sold by weight and not by volume.

In the Wallace Collection, in London, there is one of the finest collections of carving in box wood.

SWEET CHESTNUT

'Tradition has it' that the Romans introduced the sweet chestnut, but as a result of archaeological field-work, remains of this tree, in the form of charcoal, have been found on pre-Roman sites. With certain favourable exceptions, the tree is confined to the most southern part of England. One will find quite extensive plantations of coppice in the Weald of Kent, Surrey, and Sussex, and also in similar regions of Hampshire. As coppice timber, the sweet chestnut is grown mainly for cleft-wood products, and estate work such as fencing-pales for boundary work. At ten years' growth it will make excellent gate hurdles, and 'in the round', that is, as uncleft poles, cut at sixteen years' growth, it is used in large quantities for hop-poles.

ELM

The exiled Englishman, on some distant foreign-service, with every 'amenity' to hand, and tennis and cricket weather all day and every day for monotonous weeks on end, may recollect a vision of a scene that is essentially English and to be found nowhere else in the world. And all that that scene is composed of will be fields, hedgerows, and trees, and while those trees will in any case be deciduous, it is most likely that they will be elms, tall and stately even when one limb has been shed in a past gale.

Some authorities have regarded the elm as an alien, introduced with the sweet chestnut by the Romans, but others, expert in arboriculture, tell us that certain forms or species of the tree do occur exclusively in Britain. While the elm is quite absent from heathland and thin soils and likewise the chalk and limestone, it is common enough on the heavy clay of the Thames basin and Oxford. It was once the dominant feature of the quiet Middlesex countryside when it was all orchards and market-gardens, that is pre-London Airport.

It is also still a characteristic of Lamb's Hertfordshire, much of Essex, and many other parts of southern England.

Its liking for the vicinity of water gives it qualities that make it excellent timber, especially where conditions of varied and continuous exposure to damp and wet have to be considered. So we find the lock-gates of canals and harbour-works built of sawn elm, generous in bulk and dimension. The clapboards or weatherboards of houses in Essex especially, and Hertfordshire, and the remaining counties near to London, and south of the Thames, have nearly always been made of sawn elm—for this wood will not respond to cleavage. It was this ability to withstand indefinite immersion in water that fitted elm for use as water-piping, before it was possible to produce piping in either cast-iron or stoneware.

Elm, having a twisting grain, has the very great merit of not being prone to splinter. This makes it suitable on the one hand for 'rough usage', such as partitioning and boarding for stables, and this same resistance makes it eminently suitable for the bare seats of chairs and tables, and also the treads of staircases, where other woods are prone to splinter both in the process of manufacture and in the intended usage. If an old house should have timber flooring, its age may be judged by the width of the boards, for the oldest were also the widest. Again, this characteristic of elm made it the only wood for the naves or hubs of the old wagon. No other wood, mortised for as many as fourteen spokes and with a large tapering hole through the centre, would have stood up to the process, let alone a generation and more of use. They used elm for the keels of wooden ships, for chocks and wedges, capstan blocks, bakers' dough troughs, and Indian clubs.

A Note on Elm Disease

What is known as elm disease was discovered to be present

as recently as 1928, in Hertfordshire. Doubtless certain tendencies in the elm had been noticed for a very long time, but investigation of infected trees showed that the cause was a fungus, which could exist in the vessels of the wood. The effect on the tree is a combination of poisoning and the restriction of water. Transmission of the disease is by the agency of two species of elm bark beetle, which can breed freely in the bark of elms weakened by one cause or another. Readers wishing to follow up this subject are referred to *The Status and Development of Elm Disease in Britain*, a Forestry Commission Bulletin, No. 33, obtainable from H.M.S.O. bookshops or any bookseller.

HAZEL

In its wild state the hazel grows into a fine, large shrub and appears to flourish in nearly every part of Britain, except the exposed, weather-swept hills and fells. The Kentish Cob, as a symbol or motif of decoration, gives the key to its habitat. It is the cultivated form which concerns the craftsman and user and in this it is a coppice plant each of which throws up a considerable number of slender, straight shoots. Many of these copses are very old and date, in some cases, from the days when sheep were still the wealth of the nation. The method of enclosing a flock of sheep, called 'folding', was developed by many lowland farmers and not a few downland, except in Sussex where the one-time flocks of the Southdowns ranged on the open grassland under the care of shepherd and dog.

For this folding, a temporary partitioning of land is made, by means of wattle-hurdles, placed end-to-end. Such a plot of land within a large field, containing roots is cropped clean by a flock, which at the same time manures and treads the soil, so to enrich it naturally. For this, hurdles are made in their thousands.

Josiah Wedgwood, tired of his lovely wares being broken

in transit looked around, and with the co-operation of basket-makers devised a crate made of hazel which would carry pottery unharmed. Hazel rods have many other uses, such as for salmon-traps on the Severn, lobster-pots, eel-traps and, of course, as spars, runners, and pegs for roof-thatching.

HOLLY

The Holly is a native evergreen that is locally abundant in the Weald, in the Valley of the Spey, the Dee, and other Scottish rivers. It is also a roadside plant in parts of Here-fordshire, and in the Punchbowl, at Hindhead, in Surrey, you will find what this tree looks like in full, wild growth, a substantial densely foliaged tree of some 50 ft in height. Very occasionally one may come across a tree having everyone of its leaves clear of spines. Very often the topmost leaves of an otherwise densely spined tree will be clear. The holly is a slow-growing tree producing a dense and very close-grained wood suitable for turnery and tree inlay work and engravers' blocks. The shuttles for hand-weaving looms are also made of this wood, as was at one time the 'swinger' of a flail. Incidentally, a couple of holly logs on the Christmas fire will give a hotter fire than is possible with any other fuel.

HORNBEAM

This tree is generally uncommon. It is the most conspicuous memory to many people of Epping Forest. Among all the variety of hardwood trees, this hardest of all is not to be overlooked. It has a very dark, fair, smooth trunk which has gentle serpentine flutings or ribs. While the intractable nature of the timber renders it unsuitable for craftsmen, its very hardness has been an asset. It was largely used for the cogs in water and windmill machinery. Carpenter's plane-blocks, ships' pulley-blocks, and large wooden screws, such as are sometimes found on the old carpenters' benches.

When threshing was done with flails, the floors were made of hornbeam planks, and until lignum vitae came to this country hornbeam was used for bowls and still is for butchers' blocks.

LARCH

In the sixteenth century, the European larch, was introduced from its native habitat, the Alps, though the uses to which the Swiss put this timber, such as pails and churns, was not adopted here. It was, however, recognized for other potentialities, by the Scots, who used it extensively for estate work, carpentry, and shipbuilding. It was valued by shipwrights who, noting that larch will often grow with a pronounced curve at the base, made great use of it for the ribs and planks of boats, since the grain followed the curves of these parts of their craft. Field gates are often made from the timber of large trees.

LIME

The majority of our limes have been trees planted as part of the tremendous activity of landscape gardening, so that the traveller today will observe these splendid parklands, each still reflecting much of the inventions of their creators. Frequently, the 'avenues' from the gate or gates will be lined with lime trees, a favourite for this purpose, presumably on account of the stature of the mature tree.

In its application as timber it has for a very long time been a favourite with wood-carvers, for its comparative ease of working, its permissive response to the carver's chisels and gouges. Gibbon's work remains as a high-water mark of the Renaissance.

OAK

At Winforton, on the road between Hereford and Brecon,

where the last English county brushes with Wales, there stands a black and white house, set well back from the road. The facing gable-end bears the date 1400, so this old house has witnessed over half a millennium of history. Because of its distance from the road and because hewn oak, over the centuries, acquires an iron-hardness, it would not be an economic proposition to demolish it. Oak is like that, hewn or sawn. The *Victory*, launched in 1755, is a young structure, by comparison, even though fifty years old, at Trafalgar. From all the *Victory*'s contemporaries came timber for the building of half-timbered houses, even though the mode of construction was out of date for large houses. Many stand today and have every reason to continue standing.

Such timber framework was built more or less prefabricated in sections, all mortise-and-tenoned and pegged with oak. Earlier still than the house at Winforton, were the 'Cruck' houses, which in the earliest examples consisted of two gently curving timbers at each end of the house forming an apex, with the stout roof-tree making the ridge which joined them. On this primary structure the rest of the house could be added.

In the days before power failures they relied upon wind and water for power. The windmiller must have put in phenomenal hours when the wind was fair, against the few days of calm. In both water- and wind-mill oak was essential for the structures of the early mills and for the machinery of all of them.

When Alan of Walsingham was working on the Octagon of Ely Cathedral, after the collapse of the central tower in 1399, he searched far and wide for timber for this octagon, daring in its concept, even for the fourteenth century. The eight vertical beams, 63 ft tall, and their supporting framework together require dimensions of oak which probably would be unobtainable now.

Given its freedom, the oak tree can attain a height of as much as 130 ft, but the majority fall appreciably short of this. But it is in the vast, rugged 'spread' of its boughs and branches that the tree is best known. It is a slow grower, that does not produce acorns until about the sixtieth year and timber suitable for use until it is 200 years old. When one considers the extent to which the timber has been used, and the variety, it is not surprising that it became symbolic of strength. Nearly all oak was grown for heavy construction and the timber for furniture and panelling was largely imported even as far back as the beginning of the fifteenth century. After the seventeenth century, as shipbuilding absorbed most of our oak, the foresters set their trees more widely spaced so as to obtain low-branching trees which would provide the natural curves required by shipwrights. Such timber being no longer in demand, we must look elsewhere for present-day requirements.

SCOTS PINE

For purely industrial purposes, the cone-bearing softwoods are of greater importance than the slow-growing hardwoods. By the million the Scots pine, is planted cultivated and felled by the Forestry Commission for the primary purpose of providing pit-props and telephone poles, railway sleepers, and at one time for paving-blocks. It has also been used for the masts and yards of sailing-ships and boats. The village carpenter has for long used it to make ladder-poles, alternatively to using ash.

SPRUCE

Norway spruce or Christiana pine, long used in Continental countries, is a comparatively 'recent' introduction to this country, but is now one of the most important of the Forestry Commission plantations. When 'clean-grown', spruce will readily yield to cleavage and for this reason has been used in the mountain districts of Europe for those uses for which we in this country have always used oak, beech, or willow. Among this variety have been, shingles for roofing, barrel staves, hoops, and baskets of interwoven strips. Because spruce, even when thinly cleft, was unlikely to warp, it was always used for the slats of Venetian blinds. In addition, it has the merit of strength and lightness. Of all the uses, the most remarkable is that for the belly of instruments of the violin family, the violia, viola, cello, and double-bass. Spruce grown at high altitude provides the sounding-boards of pianos. In regard to the further use, by division into nearly threadlike pieces and the making of baskets and matting and even fishing lines, the peoples of other countries have exploited the potentialities of spruce far more than we.

SYCAMORE

Considered by some as a 'doubtful' native, there are no definite records of its introduction. The name is derived from a fig tree while the name maple is of Saxon origin. The scientific name is *Acer pseudo platanus L.* The genus Acer indicates its sharpness, since it was used for lances and pikes. The species indicates that it is a false plane, because of a similarity between the leaves of sycamore and London plane. There is some substance for the opinion that it was native to Wales, for the Welsh have known the sycamore as *masarnewydd mwyaf* and used it for turnery and kitchen ware for a very long time, long enough that they had no need to resort to the importation of an English term.

The sycamore is less commonly encountered in the southern counties, but it thrives well in Wales and Northern England. On good soil, it will withstand exposure, but its seeds, though winged, like 'keys', are heavy and cannot travel far from the parent tree.

When the sycamore is felled in winter it provides a stain-free wood eminently suitable for every kind of kitchenware where freedom from taste is necessary. So bread and cheese

boards, platters and rollers for pastry-making are all turned
or made from this wood. The old-fashioned mangle, not yet
surpassed for its efficiency, had sycamore rollers. Likewise
the 'old-fashioned' table-top, which one could scrub as
'clean as a new pin'.

WALNUT

The walnut, a tree of the parklands and big estates, was
introduced from south-eastern Europe and Asia Minor
during the fifteenth century, partly for the nuts, but also
for its timber, although furniture-makers and joiners prefer
the native timber but have needed a supply greater than can
be provided in this country.

Timber for the craftsmen carries a built figuring and it
is customary to apply veneered facings of walnut to a hardwood base. The early two-man veneer saws were similar to
the frame saw, but used horizontally instead of vertically. In
1806 Marc Brunel, engineer of the Thames Tunnel and
father of Isambard, patented a powered, multiple circular
saw capable of cutting fifteen to twenty veneers per inch
against the laborious six to twelve by hand.

What they call burr-walnut is a growth or burr of incipient twigs on the trunk. If this burr is removed and sliced
through, the resultant faces shown exquisite figurings, and
provide excellent material for the wood-carver's skill. Owing
to the shock-absorbent quality of walnut, the stocks of
sporting-guns have nearly always been made of this wood,
which requires 100 years to obtain maturity.

WILLOW

A gay lace-like tree in summer, responding to the slightest
air, the willow quickly sheds its leaves in an amber shower.
It is a characteristic tree of lowland valleys which have a
water-table near the surface. Our confusion over the different

willows is surely permissible, for there are supposed to be over eighty species, varieties, and hybrids. Here we are concerned with the white or crack. In the familiar pollard willow we have a useful source of willow 'poles', the product of a seven-year rotation. This crop is used mainly for gate hurdles.

The blades of cracket-bats are made from a variety of the white-willow. The timber of these two trees is not very easy to distinguish, but the cricket-bat willow is lighter in weight and quicker in growth. It is native to the Anglia counties and Essex. Very great care and attention are required in the cultivation for bats. In the nursery, shoots grow to about 8 ft in two or three years. The plants are then transplanted to stream side position and at twelve-year growth roughly are cut for preparation. The aim is to get knot-free wood. Other uses, one of them of the greatest importance, are the manufacture of artificial limbs, the second of these is polo balls.

Willow grown in intensely cultivated coppices provides, in the term osier, a large supply of rods for basket-making. There are a number of osier-growing centres, Sedgmoor, in Somerset, of course and the Kennett Valley in Berkshire.

YEW

The yew is native throughout Britain and the greater part of the Temperate Zone. While being found on many soils, the ancient groves and woods appear confined to the chalk and limestone. The reputedly oldest yew 'forest' in Europe is in Kingly Vale, north-west of Chichester, in country where one may encounter wild fallow deer, following their immemorial paths, and during the same day that strange bird the stone-curlew.

The seed of the yew-berry is poisonous, but not the flesh. As to whether the leaves are or not, sheep on the Sussex Downs and horses and cattle in the New Forest graze

unharmed all around the trees. But the same leaves, if cut
and left to wither, will become dangerously poisonous.

In both history and prehistory the yew held a significant
place in religion and war. To the priestly castes of pre-
Christian beliefs the tree was a symbol of veneration, im-
mortality, and sanctity. And although the early missionaries
of the Christian belief regard nature as the Kingdom of the
Devil, the veneration of the yew did not die out. It was a
point of worship until churches were built, usually upon
previously sacred sites. So the village church and the yew
have come to be familiar to us as occupying the same holy
ground. While one naturally thinks of the remarkable ninety-
nine of Painswick there are in fact, hundreds of churchyards
in England, Wales, Scotland, and Ireland, some of them
truly 'venerable', but in many cases they have 'acquired age'
somewhat exceeding possibility. None the less they grace
very well many a churchyard.

The earliest known use, apart from bows, was by the
Vikings, who made nails of it, with which to secure the
timber of their clinker-built longships. In more recent times
it has been used for barrel hoops. Today the furniture-
makers and turners, when they can get it, appreciate the
qualities of its grain. For the bows of the backs and arms of
Windsor chairs it has been indispensable.

Although the yew is classified as a 'softwood', it is, in
fact even slower in growth than the hardwood oak and its
timber is as hard as the oak.

32

Making Briar-pipes

The man who enjoys a good pipe, knows that his favourite pipe came not from the *Rosa eglanteria*, the Sweet Briar of our hedgerows, but from the *Erica arborea*, a White Heath, or Tree Heath, a relative of the heathers, which grows in certain Mediterranean countries. It is from the root of this slow growing tree that pipes are made.

The roots are extracted, collected and cut up by circular saws into 'ebauchons', the rough shapes from which each pipe is made. At this stage root-flaws are revealed, and considerable wastage is unavoidable. From the grading centres, the ebauchons are exported all over the world, but it is to London that the best are sent and from London that the best finished products are sent. Several of the craftsmen, however. do not work in London.

At one time, pipes were turned by hand and this method is still used for pipes of special shape. The increasing use of machines—all French—has made it economically possible to market pipes at a reasonable price. Although machinery is used, the dexterity and intelligence of the operators are indispensable and amount to craftsmanship. The rough ebauchon is cut to overall size by a circular saw and then, held by a kind of rotating mandrel, the interior of the bowl is turned, in four stages, against stationary cutters. In stage two, the exterior of the stem is cut by tangential knives on a rotating disc. Then the exterior of the bowl is turned, the parts inaccessible being removed by hand or another machine. The last shaping process is that of drilling the stepped bore of the stem for the mouthpiece.

We now have a batch of pipes finished and ready for polishing, but at this stage, it is usual to grade them as 'clean' or 'flawed'. Those with large holes are rejected, but the majority have only slight imperfections which can be filled. The best are without any flaws. There is a sequence of stages in polishing, all of which require sensitive handling. It follows that a top-grade pipe receives the greatest attention. These principles are no less applied to the making of the vulcanite stems, which, in the cheaper pipes are moulded to shape, but in the best are hand-cut from sheet vulcanite. This substance expands when hot, from the cutting and turning and this must be allowed for so that the cold mouthpiece conforms exactly to the bowl. It must be a dead fit when inserted.

The popularity of a particular shape is not determined solely by fashion, for while many shapes 'come and go', the Billiard seems to go on the universal favourite. Whether one prefers a straight to a bent depends upon where one smokes. Some really old armchairs just ask for a bent.

33

Further Reading

This bibliography is provided to enable readers to follow up their especial interests. The titles are given irrespective of their being in or out of print. Of the latter, many are, of course, obtainable through second-hand sources, whilst others are usually available for reference in museum libraries. Some titles are not directly concerned with crafts but provide social, historical, technical, or topographical backgrounds, often with indirect reference either to a craft or the usage of its products. The *English Dialect Dictionary* provides a vast source of definition of crafts, tools, and terms.

Sociological, Historical, Technical
Travel in England. Burke. Batsford.
Stonehenge of the Kings. Crampton. Baker, 1967.
Trinity of Craftsmen. Derrick. Chapman & Hall, 1945.
Country Craftsmen. Derrick. Chapman & Hall, 1945.
A Short History of Technology. Derry & Williams. Oxford, 1960.
The Horse in the Furrow. Evans. Faber, 1960.
Fifteen Craftsmen and Their Crafts. Farleigh. Sylvan Press, 1945.
Folk Life. Welsh Folk Museum, St Fagans, Cardiff. Journal of the Society for Folk Life Studies.
The English Tradition in Design. Gloag. Penguin, 1946.

* Museum Libraries.

A History of Woodworking Tools. Goodman. Bell, 1964.
Countryman's England. Hartley. Batsford, 1935.
Life and Work of the People of England. Hartley & Elliot. Batsford, 1925.
William Morris. Henderson. Thames & Hudson, 1967.
Change in the Farm. Hennell. Cambridge.
Artifacts: Early Materials and Technology. Hodges. Baker, 1966.
The Making of the English Landscape. Hoskins. Hodder & Stoughton, 1965.
Handbook of Crafts. Hulton. Lewis, 1960.
The Story of the Saw. Jones and Simons. Neame, 1960.
The Roof Tree. Kenward. Oxford, 1941.
Observations in Husbandry. Lisle. 1757.
Rural Economy of the Southern Counties. Marshall. 1798.
The Secret People. Martin. Phoenix House, 1954.
Ancient Carpentry Tools. Mercer (U.S.A.), 1929.
A History of Technology. 5 vols. Oxford, 1954–8.
A History of Everyday Things in England. 5 vols. The Quennells. Batsford, 1950, 1959.
The Social History of England. Trevelyan. Longman, 1944.
500 Points of Good Husbandry. Tusser. 1573 (1931 ed., Hartley).
The Country Craftsmen. Williams, Routledge, 1947.
The Old Farmhouse. Williams. Harrap, 1961.
The English Dialect Dictionary. Wright. Oxford.
Story of the Countryside. Wymer. Oxford, 1952.
Six weeks Tour through the Southern Counties. Young, 1768.

Crafts, General, or the Products

The Countryman's Workshop. Arnold. Phoenix, 1952.
Woodland Crafts in Britain. Edlin. Batsford, 1949.
Folk Life, as above.

* Museum Libraries.

Made in England. Hartley. Methuen, 1939.
The Countryman at Work. Hennell. Architectural Press, 1947.
Country Crafts and Craftsmen. Hogg. Hutchinson, 1959.
Traditional Country Craftsmen. Jenkins. Routledge and Kegan Paul, 1965.
Country Relics. Massingham. Cambridge, 1939.
The Rural Industries of England and Wales. Oxford, 1926–7.
Crafts of the Countryside. Stowe. Longmans, 1948.
The Country Craftsman. Williams. Routledge and Kegan Paul, 1958.
Rural Crafts of England. Wood. Harrap, 1949.
English Country Crafts. Wymer. Batsford, 1946.

Crafts, Individual or the Products
Bagpipes. Baynes. Pitt-Rivers Museum, Oxford.
Nineteenth Century English Pottery. Bemrose. Faber, 1953.
Modern Archery. Bilson. Paternoster Press (Exeter), 1956.
Cotswold Stone. Derrick. Oxford University Press, 1952.
The Gentle Art of Smoking. Dunhill. Reinhardt, 1954.
Saddlery. Edwards. Country Life, 1960.
Traditional Quilting. Fitzrandolph. Batsford, 1954.
Pillow-lace in the East Midlands. Freeman. Luton Corporation, 1958.
Windmills and Millwrighting. Freese. Cambridge, 1957.
English Country Pottery. Haggar. Phoenix, 1950.
Staffordshire Chimney Ornaments. Haggar. Phoenix, 1955.
Horse Brasses. Harfield. Abelard-Schumann, 1965.
Hammer and Tongs. Hogg. Hutchinson, 1965.
Living Crafts. Hughes. Lutterworth, 1953.
The English Farm Wagon. Jenkins. Oakwood Press, 1961.
Agricultural Transport in Wales. Jenkins. Welsh Folk Museum, 1966.
English Furniture. Joy. Country Life, 1964.

English Furniture. Joy. Batsford, 1962.

Tools and Devices for Coppice Crafts. Lambert. Evans, 1957.

The New Golden Dolly. Lambeth. Cornucopia Press, Fulbourn, Cambs.

Country Baskets. Legg. Mills and Boon, 1960.

Decorative Wrought-iron Work. Lister. Bell, 1957.

Hand Weaving Today. Mairet. Faber, 1939.

The History of Chair-making in High Wycombe. Mayes. Routledge and Kegan Paul, 1960.

Country Blacksmith. Niall. Heinemann, 1966.

The Windsor Chair. Ormsbee. Deerfield (U.S.A.).

Craftsman in Wood. Pinto. Bell, 1962.

Treen. Pinto. Batsford, 1949.

Medieval English Pottery. Rackham. Faber, 1948.

Dry-stone Walling. Rainsford-Hannay. Faber, 1967.

The Village Carpenter. Rose. Cambridge, 1937.

English Cottage Furniture. Roe. Phoenix, 1961.

The Thatcher's Craft. Rural Industries Bureau, 1961.

The Din of a Smithy. Stevenson. Chapman and Hall, 1932.

The Wheelwright's Shop. Sturt. Cambridge, 1963.

British Watermills. Syson. Batsford, 1965.

Wrought-iron Work. Victoria and Albert Museum.

The English Windmill. Wailes. Routledge and Kegan Paul, 1954.

Esgair Moel Woollen Mill. Welsh Folk Museum.

Baskets and Basketry. Wright. Batsford, 1964.

34

Museums

Aberdeen. Provost Skene's House.
Alton, Hants. Curtiss Folk Museum.
Athwell, Herts. Herts. Museum.
Aylesbury. Buckinghamshire County Museum.
Ayr. Carnegie Museum.
Barnard Castle, Co. Durham. Bowes Museum.
Barnet, Herts. Museum.
Bath. Claverton Manor.
Bedford. Bedford Museum.
Belfast. Ulster Museum.
Bolton, Lancs. Hall i' the Woods.
Bradford. Bolling Hall.
Bridlington, Yorks. Bayle Gate Museum.
Bristol. Blaise Castle Museum.
Bury St Edmunds, Suff. Moyses Hall Museum.
Cambridge. Fitzwilliam Museum.
         Folk Museum.
Cardiff. National Museum of Wales.
        St Fagan's Folk Museum.
Cheltenham, Glos. Art Gallery and Museum.
Colchester, Essex. Castle Museum.
Coventry. Jordan Well Museum.
Dartford, Kent. Museum.
Devizes, Wilts. Museum.
Doncaster, Yorks. Museum.

Dorchester. Dorset County Museum.
Douglas, I.o.M. Manx Museum.
Dublin. National Museum of Ireland.
Edinburgh National Museum of Antiquities of Scotland.
          Royal Scottish Museum.
Filkins, Lechlade, Glos. Museum.
Glasgow. Old Glasgow Museum.
Glastonbury, Som. Lake Village Museum.
Gloucester. Folk Museum.
Guildford. Museum.
Halifax, Yorks. Bankfield Museum.
               Shibden Hall.
Haslemere, Hants. Educational Museum.
Hereford. City Museum.
Hertford. Museum.
Huddersfield. Tolson Memorial Museum.
Hull. Municipal Museum.
     The Horse Brass Museum.
King's Lynn, Norf. Museum.
Kingussie Inverness, Highland Folk Museum.
Leeds. City Museum.
       Abbey House Museum.
Leicester. City Museum.
          The Newarke Houses.
Lincoln. Museum of Lincolnshire Life.
London. Bethnal Green Museum.
        British Museum.
        Geoffrye Museum.
        Horniman Museum.
        London Museum.
        Science Museum.
        Victoria and Albert Museum.
Luton, Beds. Bagshawe Collection (at the Library).
Maidstone, Kent. Museum.
Manchester. Wythenshawe Hall.

Manchester. Museum of Arts and Crafts.
          Queens Park Gallery.
Middlesbrough. Doman Museum.
Northampton. Abington Museum.
Northwood, Mddx. Pinto Collection of Wooden Bygones.
Norwich. Bridewell Museum.
          Castle Museum.
          Strangers Hall.
Orford, Suff. Museum of East Anglian Rural Life.
Oxford. City and County Museum (Woodstock).
          Pitt-Rivers Museum.
Plymouth. Buckland Abbey Museum.
Portsmouth. Cumberland House.
Reading University. Museum of English Rural Life.
          Silchester Collection.
St Albans. City Museum. (Finest collection in Britain of
          craftsmen's tools.)
          Verulamium Museum.
Saffron Walden, Essex. Museum.
Salisbury. Museum.
Scarborough. Museum.
Scunthorpe, Lincs. Museum.
Sheffield. City Museum.
Snowshill, Broadway, Worcs. Manor.
Southend-on-Sea. Prittlewell Priory.
Stoke Bruerne, Towcester, N'hants. Waterways Museum.
Stratford on Avon. Mary Arden Agricultural Museum.
Stroud, Glos. Museum.
Swindon, Wilts. Museum.
Truro. Museum.
Wakefield. City Museum.
Whitby, Yorks. Pannett Park Museum.
Winchester. Westgate Museum.
York. Castle Museum.

35

Note on Tools

One may examine some of the primitive tool-heads and consider the care which was exercised in their making, and be struck as much by their intrinsic beauty as by their utility. Were their makers quite satisfied with a rough finish as long as the tool did its job, or did they, like their descendants thousands of years later, put a little more into the work for the satisfaction of doing a job well.

In those flint and stone industries there was some centralization, according to the geology, with distribution along well-used routes. Likewise, the later bronze and iron industries had their sources and distribution. From the smith's forge came every kind of device, tool, and appliance. This activity developed all through the ensuing periods of Roman, Saxon, and medieval life and into the seventeenth and eighteenth centuries. The blacksmith was the traditional maker of edge-tools, supplying the requirements in iron of nearly all the other crafts. Developments during the eighteenth century and after required a new range of tools. A new centralization of the tool industry came into being, so that very soon nearly every craftsman henceforth obtained his tools from the new sources.

In spite of this, village blacksmiths continued to meet special demands, particularly where there were concentrations of people in one craft or another. In the villages about High Wycombe there were smith's who seemed able to 'put an edge' on tools that could not be bettered. In northern Hampshire, the Moss family, who had their forges at Bramshott, Bucks Horn Oak, and Canford, held their reputation through the nineteenth century, so that even today a Moss tool is very much sought after. Tempering, it seems, was the secret. We may note, in passing, that until Whitworth devised standard threads every blacksmith had his own taps and dies. In this context, reference has been made to the Filkins Museum, in the chapter on the wheelwright. This village tool-craft was the last echo of something which began a long time ago.

Index